Financial and Monetary Policy Studies

Volume 41

Series Editor

Ansgar Belke, Essen, Germany

More information about this series at
http://www.springer.com/series/5982

Philipp Bagus

In Defense of Deflation

Springer

Philipp Bagus
Economia Aplicada I
Universidad Rey Juan Carlos
Madrid
Spain

ISSN 0921-8580 ISSN 2197-1889 (electronic)
ISBN 978-3-319-13427-7 ISBN 978-3-319-13428-4 (eBook)
DOI 10.1007/978-3-319-13428-4
Springer Cham Heidelberg New York Dordrecht London

Library of Congress Control Number: 2014959100

Printed on acid-free paper

Springer is part of Springer Science+Business Media (www.springer.com)

To my parents

Preface

I am very pleased to see my Ph.D. thesis finally published as a book. There are only small changes, actualizations, and adaptions from the version that I defended in December 2007 to obtain my Ph.D. degree from the Universidad Rey Juan Carlos in Madrid.

I had decided to write on deflation because I regarded the fear of deflation as a decisive barrier towards the installment of a better monetary system. The fear of falling prices has again and again been misused to justify monetary inflation with all its detrimental consequences. Especially, in times of crises the specter of deflation is invoked to inflate the money supply with the aim to prop up failed elites. Indeed, in December 2007 a storm was in the making that a few months later brought the international financial system to the verge of collapse. In autumn 2008 after the default of Lehman Brothers, a deflationary spiral was on its way to wipe away the international banking system and with it highly indebted governments, companies, and individuals. It was a unique opportunity to have a system liquidated that through institutional inflation continually redistributes wealth, generates business cycles, hampers savings and growth, and protects the political and economic elites from competition.

However, this option was not chosen. For 6 years now, the system has been stabilized thanks to an enormous inflation of the money supply via unprecedented instruments. The consequences have been a delay of the necessary restructuring of the economy, redistributions in favor of failed investors, a deterioration of central banks' balance sheets, and a surge in government debts among others. The recovery has been severely disturbed. A sustainable improvement of the situation and a solution to the general overindebtedness is not insight. Furthermore, the inflation meant to stop the deflationary spiral may well finally require some sort of monetary reform, if it does not cause an outright breakdown of the monetary system.

It cannot be a surprise that political and economic elites did anything in their power to prevent a deflationary meltdown. What is surprising is that they got away with it so easily. It is astonishing that even most of the people that were losing due to the inflation accepted the measures, because they thought something worse would be prevented, namely a deflationary meltdown. It is understandable that economic and political elites fear deflation, but it is not so clear why almost all economists have developed a deflation phobia. It was this fear of deflation that has ensured that we are still stuck in the monetary system which was about to melt down in 2008. Unfortunately, at the time *In Defense of Deflation* was not out there to help combat the myths about price deflation.

There are all kinds of myths about price deflation that inhibit the surge of free market institutions, because these myths are used to justify interventions. The fear of a deflationary spiral is only one, albeit probably the most important of them. An almost equally harmful myth is that the rate of the growth of the money supply must be at least as high as the rate of economic growth, because otherwise there would be a harmful price deflation. This is an argument that even well-trained economists bring forward against the introduction of a gold standard or against the chances of bitcoins to become money.

Another myth that has become very relevant recently is that policies aiming at lowering costs, especially wages, and reducing public budget deficits would drive an economy into recession. Indeed, in the European sovereign debt crisis, austerity is branded as a harmful deflationary policy. Commentators recall the supposedly fateful deflationary policies of German Chancellor Heinrich Brüning in the early 1930s as a deterrent example of austerity. Moreover, the "rolling deflation" of 1931 is even used to argue in favor of an international lender of last resort, a step close to the introduction of a world currency.[1] In this book all these myths are rebutted. There is even an historical analysis of Brüning's policies, showing that they helped to speed up recovery.

For the future of liberty and capitalism, it will be essential to eradicate the myths about deflation. Otherwise, no thorough changes in our monetary setup will be possible. Indeed, the fear of deflation feeds the advocates of inflation with powerful arguments. And inflation in turn feeds governments. Governments would have never reached the size they hold today without the financing of an inflationary monetary system. And as the government grows, liberty dies. Thus, it is essential for the future of liberty that the myths on deflation are rebutted. This book is an attempt to contribute to this endeavor.

Majadahonda, Spain
May 18, 2014

Philipp Bagus

[1] See Kindleberger and Aliber (2005, p. 258).

Acknowledgments

Let me first thank the Ludwig von Mises Institute for the fellowships granted to me in 2003, 2006, and 2009. I especially thank the staff and donors of the Ludwig von Mises Institute who made my research there possible. With regard to the Mises Institute, I am especially grateful for the guidance of my friend and mentor Guido Hülsmann. In fact, Guido Hülsmann had suggested the analysis of deflation as a possible study for my first fellowship at the institute. My gratitude also goes to those at the Juan de Mariana Institute, especially to my friend and colleague, Gabriel Calzada. Thanks also go to my friends Juan Ramón Rallo, José Ignacio de Castillo, and Antonio Zanella who have read previous versions of my dissertation. To my friend Barbara A. Hinze, my debts, put quite simply, are immeasurable. She sacrificed much of her time to edit my dissertation. I am also immensely indebted to the director of my dissertation, Jesús Huerta de Soto. He has always assisted me where possible, and his confidence in me has always been a special source of encouragement. Finally, I want to thank my family and friends who made this project possible.

Acknowledgments

[illegible]

Contents

List of Charts

List of Tables

Chapter 1
Introduction

Traditionally, inflation has been the focus of economics. A myriad of articles, books, and papers have been written about the costs, benefits, consequences, and causes of inflation. In contrast to inflation, which constitutes an important part of nearly every monetary theory textbook, deflation is still neglected. At times, deflation is not even mentioned in monetary theory textbooks, and at other times, it is merely defined as the reverse of inflation in a chapter about inflation.[2]

A main reason for this, historically speaking, is probably that inflation or price increases have been more common than deflation, at least in the second half of the twentieth century (Stiglitz 1993, p. 652; Svensson 2000, p. 1). As David Laidler writes in *The New Palgrave Dictionary of Money and Finance* concerning deflation: "Since World War II, inflation at various rates has been endemic throughout the world economy, and it is tempting to regard deflation as being of merely theoretical interest."[3]

However, theoreticians have recently returned their focus to deflation again (Borio and Filardo 2004). Declining prices in Japan, China, and other emerging economies have alarmed economists who fear deflation. Because of a long period of inflation, as Bradford DeLong notes, almost "no one had seen actual falls in the price level as even a remote possibility. Now people do" (1999, p. 225). Because of this, economists have begun to discuss the possibility of a deflation in Europe and the United States, and how such a threat might be prevented.[4] Economists also have raised their concerns at a May 2003 meeting of the Federal Open Market Committee (FOMC),[5] and in the same year the International Monetary Fund (IMF)

[2] One example of this can be found in Miller and Upton's textbook (1986, p. 363).

[3] (Laidler 1992, p. 607); This neglect of deflation can be seen also in *The New Palgrave: A Dictionary of Economics*. This reference work includes an entry on inflation, but not on deflation (Eatwell et al. 1987).

[4] For instance, Ahearne and colleagues (2002) and Bernanke (2002) have addressed these concerns.

[5] Bordo et al. (2004, p. 1).

P. Bagus, *In Defense of Deflation*, Financial and Monetary Policy Studies 41,
DOI 10.1007/978-3-319-13428-4_1

published a study assessing the risks of deflation.[6] Otmar Issing, of the European Central Bank (ECB), has also addressed the issue in a speech—although he did not consider deflation an imminent danger (2002). Amazingly, we find many studies and articles spending energy and resources to find ways which might prevent price deflation—something that seems to be quite easy if one is in possession of a printing press and prints fiat money in order to bid up prices. In contrast, however, detailed analyses of the causes and effects of price deflation are still quite rare.

Thus, Ludwig von Mises' words are still as true today as they were in 1933:

> Unfortunately, economic theory is weakest precisely where help is most needed—in analyzing the effects of declining prices. A general decline in prices has always been considered unfortunate. Yet today, even more than ever before, the rigidity of wage rates and the costs of many other factors of production hamper an unbiased consideration of the problem. Therefore, it would certainly be timely now to investigate thoroughly the effects of declining money prices and to analyze the widely held idea that declining money prices are incompatible with the increased production of goods and services and an improvement in general welfare. The investigation should include a discussion of whether it is true that only inflationistic steps permit the progressive accumulation of capital and productive facilities.[7]

Friedrich A. von Hayek points to a similar direction ([1931] 1966, p. 7). He regards the opinion as erroneous that price deflation always causes a decrease in production. Unfortunately, even to this day, a majority of economists continue to hold this mistaken view to a greater or lesser degree.

The significance of deflation theory to political economy is rooted in this fact: fear of deflation is offered as a reason for inflating the money supply.[8] When price inflation rates slow down, economists recommend precautionary easing of monetary policy.[9] This ensures that inflation remains at a high rate. The inflationary policies, installed to prevent price deflation, lead to tragic consequences, such as an artificial boom bust cycle, asset price bubbles, financial instability, and severe redistributions. To justify these inflationary policy, economists must show, of course, that deflation must be prevented at almost all costs. Deflation must be shown to be harmful for economic activity. Many economists, indeed, have taken

---

[6] Kumar et al. (2003).

[7] The English quotation is taken from Mises (1978, p. 218), which stems from Mises' essay "Der Stand und die nächste Zukunft der Konjunkturforschung," published in a Festschrift in honor of Arthur Spiethoff (Mises 1933, pp. 175–180).

[8] As Hülsmann (2003a, p. 55) states: "It [deflation] is the *prima facie* justification of inflationist monetary policy and of the institutions designed to apply it—in particular, monopolistic paper money producers." (Italics in the original).

[9] For example, see Ben Bernanke's reasoning, He also states, as an advantage of fiat paper money that in contrast to a commodity standard, deflation could be prevented by increasing nominal spending through monetary and fiscal policies in all cases (2002, pp. 4–5). Lars Svensson recommends an inflation targeting of 2 % instead of 0 %, and justifies this because of the allegedly negative effects of price deflation (2000, p. 30). Paul Krugman even argues that when an economy is in a liquidity trap, it is stuck there because the "economy needs inflation." (1998, p. 161). He suggests a price inflation rate of 4 % for 15 years for Japan (p. 181).

on this task. My intention here is to do the opposite—to show that deflation per se is not harmful to the economy and therefore, that inflationary monetary policies to counteract deflation cannot be justified on this account. This might be the most important practical implication and contribution of this work.

The neglect of a scholarly analysis of deflation is also apparent in the all-too-common failure to provide a precise definition of deflation in such discussions. As Issing remarks, "the term 'deflation' is often misused as a catch-all phrase describing all kinds of negative future developments" (2002, p. 5). However, scientific definitions of deflation do exist. For instance, Laidler provides a common definition (1992, p. 607): "Deflation is a process of falling prices, of a rising value of money. It is the opposite of inflation." Nowadays, this is the most common definition found in textbooks.[10]

Mises defines deflation as follows:

> Again, deflation (or restriction, or contraction) signifies a diminution of the quantity of money (in the broader sense) which is not offset by a corresponding diminution of the demand for money (in the broader sense), so that an increase in the objective exchange value of money must occur (1981).[11]

According to Mises, deflation occurs when the purchasing power of money increases, because the quantity of money (in its broader sense) decreases while no corresponding decrease in the demand for money (in its broader sense) takes place.

Definitions are not so much to be considered right or wrong, but rather useful or not useful for a particular investigation. In the following chapters, I consider the fear of increases in the purchasing power of money, a widespread concern of both economists and non-economists alike. Therefore, I define this dreaded increase in the purchasing power of money, i.e., a situation where prices in terms of monetary units generally fall, as price deflation, or more succinctly, as deflation. One cause for price deflation is, as will be shown, a decrease in the amount of money, which I will distinguish as monetary deflation. Other advantages of these definitions are their simplicity and etymological correspondence to the original Latin meanings. Thus, the root for the term "deflation" is drawn from the Latin verb "flare" which means "to puff." The prefix "de" indicates the opposite. Therefore, "deflate" means to go down and "deflation" means a fall. A monetary deflation is, therefore, a fall in the money supply, and a price deflation a general fall in prices. A monetary inflation is, analogically, an increase in the money supply, and a price inflation a general increase in prices.[12]

---

[10] Kumar and colleagues state: "Deflation is defined as a sustained decline in an aggregate measure of prices such as the consumer price index or the GDP deflator" (2003, p. 6).

[11] Mises (1981, p. 240); The original text is as follows: "*Deflation (Restruktion, Kontraktion) wieder bedeutet: Eine Verminderung der Geldmenge (im weiteren Sinne), der kein entsprechender Rückgang des Geldbedarfs (im weiteren Sinne) gegenübersteht, so daß ein Steigen des inneren objektiven Tauschwertes des Geldes eintreten muß.*" (1924, p. 224).

[12] On the evolution of the meaning of the term "inflation"see Bryan (1997).

As the analysis of price deflation has been neglected, I will follow Mises's inspiring words and analyze the effects of declining prices. In particular, I want to answer the following question: Is deflation or are falling prices harmful to an economy? Some often argue that due to market imperfections, price deflation is very harmful, even more harmful than price inflation.[13] I challenge this view by "thinking the unthinkable."[14] I argue that a value-free economist cannot claim that price deflation per se poses an economic problem or is bad. Some people gain, while others lose, as happens with every change in the economy. Scientifically speaking, one simply cannot say that these expected gains and losses, in and of themselves, would inhibit or disturb economic development.

In developing the argument, I will proceed as follows: In Chap. 2, I analyze major economic theories of deflation, and point to anti-deflationary bias where present. Because many thinkers have considered deflation as something disturbing for the economy, the thesis of this investigation is rather unusual. As one might call a deflation harmful to the economy with respect to its cause, I examine several causes of price deflation in Chap. 3. In Chap. 4, I analyze the consequences of price deflation to determine if its effects are really so harmful as is widely assumed. In this context, I discuss some common errors made concerning the consequences of deflation and the origin of anti-deflationary bias. This study ends in Chap. 5 with the analysis of two historical cases of deflation: the American growth deflation from 1865 to 1896, and the German bank credit deflation from 1929 to 1933. They will serve as an illustration of the theoretical analysis made in the previous chapters.

[13] See for instance, Warren and Pearson (1933, p. 180) or Kumar et al. (2003, p. 14).

[14] Rothbard (1976, p. 35).

Chapter 2
Economic Theories of Deflation

2.1 Introduction

Many economists have written about deflation or touched upon the subject in passing while focusing on their development of related monetary theories. My aim in this chapter is not to comment on every reference concerning the subject of falling prices. This endeavor would be virtually impossible. Rather, I provide an overview of the main currents and changes in economic theories of deflation. This overview aids in explaining how and when theories of deflation in economic thought were formed and why views on deflation have changed. To explain why certain theories of deflation and deflation phobia have emerged, I place special emphasis on the circumstances and backgrounds of these deflation theorists. My exposition of the theories of deflation proceeds mainly in chronological order; however, at times I will group theorists with similar views together, though they may not be contemporaries of each other.

2.2 Mercantilists and Deflation

In the Middle Ages, prior to the sixteenth century, hoarding, sticky prices, the fear of falling prices, and the need to stabilize the price level were not discussed and, thus, seem not to have been regarded as an urgent problem.[15] Possible reasons for this disregard of deflation in the Middle Ages are that a money economy and credit money were not widespread. Instead, self-sufficient granges dominated the economy.

[15] For example, John Locke argued that the money supply was irrelevant as any amount of money would be sufficient for the needs of trade (Locke [1691] 1824, p. 48).

P. Bagus, *In Defense of Deflation*, Financial and Monetary Policy Studies 41,
DOI 10.1007/978-3-319-13428-4_2

Keeping their focus on monetary inflation, mercantilists are among the first to implicitly address the subject of deflation. According to mercantilist doctrine, a favorable balance of trade, i.e., an excess of exports over imports, would be beneficial for a country in terms of increasing its stock of precious metals.[16] Mercantilists championed the accumulation of money as the best store of wealth and correspondingly feared the circumstances in which a country would be bereft of its money. Thus, they implicitly feared a monetary deflation. Mercantilists also touched upon the subject of hoarding. However, these theorists differed on the question of hoarding, forming two groups with regard to this particular manner.

One group, which included William Potter and John Law (1671–1721),[17] argued that more money in "circulation" meant more trade. For them it was important that money was not sitting "idle" in a hoard but "circulating" and stimulating trade. Hoarding money could counteract the supposed benefits of inflation, as the new money would not be spent. Hoarding might hurt that at which inflation aims, namely, greater spending. Similarly Thomas Manley condemns the miser, because "money locked up in the misers's coffers is like dung in a heap, it does no good, but being dispersed, and orderly disposed abroad, enricheth the land."[18] Accordingly, these authors condemned private hoards and anything that would keep bullion from circulating as harmful.[19] Therefore, we have here one of the first incidents in which hoarding is considered ruinous.

The second group, included the likes of Sir Francis Bacon (1561–1626), Gerrard de Malynes (1586–1641), Thomas Mun (1571–1641), and John Briscoe,[20] who regarded the hoarding of precious metals be it as state treasure or as private stores of wealth as something very beneficial. Likewise, they considered money the best store of wealth. Hence, the increase of money in the economy meant an increase in the accumulated wealth of society and was regarded as something good. For this group, savings in the form of accumulation of precious metals was the primary aim

---

[16] Viner ([1937] 1975, p. 6).

[17] See Viner ([1937] 1975, pp. 36–37). These two authors, not surprisingly, were also advocates of paper money. Concerning two strands of mercantilists, see p. 40; See Rothbard concerning Law (2006a, p. 330) and concerning Potter's opposition to hoarding and of Potter as proposing one of the most odd theories of price deflation (p. 328). In one of the most curious lines of reasoning in the history of economic thought, Potter claimed that an increase in the amount of money could stimulate production to an extent that prices would fall. He obviously, did not see any problems in a price deflation stemming from monetary inflation.

[18] Manley (1669, p. 53).

[19] (Viner [1937] 1975, pp. 45–46); Later, when mercantilism was already in retreat, David Hume would still condemn state hoarding as "a practice which we should all exclaim against as destructive, namely, the gathering of large sums into a public treasure, locking them up, and absolutely preventing their circulation" ([1752] 1826b, p. 361).

[20] (Viner [1937] 1975, pp. 8–9, 23–24, 26, 49); Even though neither were mercantilists, both Richard Cantillon and Jacob Vanderlint advised the king to hoard money in order to keep prices low and competitive. See Rothbard (2006a, pp. 333–334).

of economic activity. The doctrine of thrift was inspired by Puritan moral and religious principles.[21]

2.3 Classical Theories of Deflation

2.3.1 Deflation and Early Classical Economists

Early classical economists generally do not approach deflation as a problem, nor do they discuss it in great detail, if it is considered at all. For example, Adam Smith discusses the effects that division of labor has on output without ever discussing the fall of prices. Therefore, we are faced with two possibilities concerning early classical economists: Either these authors did not foresee any problems caused by price deflation worth discussing, or they were not aware of the fact that economic growth can cause prices to fall, this last scenario being highly unlikely. However, some of these economists do touch upon deflationary processes.

One incident where a price deflation occurs is the specie-flow-price mechanism of the classical gold standard first described by Richard Cantillon (1680–1734).[22] Cantillon concentrates on the increases in the amount of money. He points out that changes in the money supply affect prices differently over a prolonged period of time, leading to a redistribution in favor of those economic agents that receive the new money first and a reallocation of resources in society. This effect is now called the "Cantillon effect." Without explicitly describing the process of monetary deflation, his analysis seems to imply that decreases in the quantity of money have symmetrical effects. Though his analysis is quite detailed, he does not notice—or at least does not discuss—any problems concerning the flow of money into another country or problems concerning price deflation.

David Hume (1711–1776) is another famous exponent of the specie-flow-price mechanism. His treatment of the specie-flow-price mechanism, which we will consider shortly, is not as detailed as Cantillon's analysis and is sometimes flawed, as he assumes that all prices rise in proportion to increases in the money supply. Yet, in contrast to Cantillon, Hume considers various kinds of deflation. More specifically, he describes price deflation caused by economic growth, price deflation caused by an extended use of money, and price deflation caused by a reduction in the supply of money.

[21] "The doctrine of thrift also led to emphasis on the importance of a favorable balance of trade through another chain of reasoning" (Viner 1975, p. 30) Viner explains that "[t]he disparagement of consumption and the exaltation of frugality and thrift were common doctrines of the period, not wholly dependent upon economic reasoning but deriving much of their vitality from moral and religious principles and class prejudices. The Puritans disapproved of luxury..." (p. 26).

[22] (Cantillon [1755] 1959, pp. 159–199); Cantillon wrote his treatise around 1730, but it was not published until 1755.

First, Hume does not devote much analysis to price deflation caused by economic growth, but he does mention this: "It seems a maxim almost self-evident, that the prices of every thing depend on the proportion between commodities and money. . .. Increase the commodities, they become cheaper."[23] In this brief mention of growth deflation, Hume fails to mention any reservations or fear concerning a price deflation. Second, Hume discusses a second kind of price deflation caused by an extended use of money or the emergence of money substituting barter:

> . . . [T]he sphere of circulation is enlarged; it is the same case as if that individual sum were to serve a larger kingdom; and therefore, the proportion being here lessened on the side of money, every thing must become cheaper, and the prices gradually fall.[24]

Again, we must note the absence of a problematization of price deflation.

Third, Hume discusses price deflation caused by a reduction in the supply of money, considering both one-time reductions and continuous reductions in the money supply. The consideration of a one-time reduction in the money supply is found in his analysis of the specie-flow-price mechanism in "Of the Balance of Trade." In this case, he does not note any adverse effects of price deflation. This is particularly curious considering an example Hume provides, wherein he supposes that four-fifths of all money in Great Britain disappears over night. He claims that in such a case all prices would fall proportionately, inducing exports and thus replenishing the money stock.[25] However, he does not see this severe four-fifths price deflation to be problematic, or if he does, he does not discuss it.

Considering the evidence, we might note that classical economist David Hume does not see price deflation as problematic per se. Yet, and this comes somewhat as a surprise after the comments above, he does see continuous monetary deflation as problematic. While he argues that every quantity of money is optimal for the proper functioning of a monetary economy, changes in the quantity of money would have short-term effects. Thus, he states that increasing the quantity of money would lift the "spirit of industry in the nation."[26] A decrease in the quantity of money would have the opposite effect.

> A nation, whose money decreases, is actually at that time weaker and more miserable than another nation which possesses no more money, but is on the increasing hand. This will be easily accounted for, if we consider that the alterations in the quantity of money, either on one side or the other, are not immediately attended with proportionable alterations in the price of commodities. There is always an interval before matters be adjusted to their new situation; and this interval is as pernicious to industry, when gold and silver are

[23] Hume ([1752] 1826a, pp. 326–327).

[24] Hume ([1752] 1826a, p. 329).

[25] (Hume [1752] 1826b, p. 351); Hume's reasoning that prices would fall proportionately must be criticized. Even though all individuals would lose nominal money proportionately they might react quite differently to that incident. He does not concentrate on the dynamic processes that are caused by reductions or injections of money in the real world but only on the long run price equilibria.

[26] Hume ([1752] 1826a, p. 324).

> diminishing, as it is advantageous when these metals are increasing. The workmen has not [sic!] the employment from the manufacturer and merchant; though he pays the same price for every thing in the market.[27]

Thus, in a certain way, Hume introduces a new assessment of deflation into economic thought. He sees it as being more problematic and employs the sticky price argument (i.e., deflation is harmful because some prices are rigid in that it is difficult for the prices to fall). Even though in the long run, a monetary deflation would be neutral, i.e., have no effect on real economic factors, in the short run there would be adjustment problems. More specifically, the process of monetary deflation would not be neutral in the short run. Hume's statement might be considered the first strong attack on monetary deflation in the history of economic thought. Yet, Hume does not understand that when all prices fall, both buying (monetary) costs and selling proceeds fall as well. This might be either pernicious or stimulating to industry, depending on how quickly buying and selling proceeds fall. In other words, there is no clear reason why buying costs should not fall faster than selling proceeds when the quantity of money diminishes. In sum, Hume's fateful assessment was to be the source of future arguments against monetary deflation, especially those arguments concerning the "spirit of industry" or rather, the motivational effects of deflationary policies on the actions of entrepreneurs.

One of the first classical economists to make an in-depth analysis of arguments concerning monetary deflation was Swedish economist Pehr Niclas Christiernin (1725–1799). Christiernin wrote during a period of monetary expansionism initiated by the Bank of Sweden in order to finance a government budget deficit, due mainly in part to the Seven Years' War (1756–1763).[28] Forming the Hat Party, privileged manufacturers and merchants, especially iron exporters, benefited from the inflation of money and credit. Their opposition, the Cap Party opposed these privileges and the monetary inflation. In 1765, the Cap Party rose to power and initiated a sharp monetary deflation accompanied by a price deflation. Favoring their deflationary course, the Caps stressed the redistribution argument,[29] claiming that deflation would reward those who had suffered losses during the previous inflationary period. In turn, those who had profited during the inflationary period, the wealthy merchants of the Hat Party, would suffer losses.[30]

Curiously, Christiernin was one of the few Cap opponents of deflation. Reminiscent of one of Hume's analysis, Christiernin writes that

> [i]t is easy for prices to adjust upward when the money supply increases, but to get prices to fall has always been more difficult. No one reduces the price of his commodities or his labor until the lack of sales necessitates him to do so. Because of this the workers must suffer

[27] Hume ([1752] 1826a, pp. 324–325).

[28] See Rothbard (2006b, p. 218).

[29] See Rothbard (2006b, p. 219).

[30] This is, of course, not necessarily so, but might be valid as a historical judgment for many individual cases.

want and the industriousness of wage earners must stop before the established market price can be reduced. ([1761] 1971, p. 90)

Christiernin's assessment that workers must first suffer hunger before they are willing to reduce their nominal wages appears to be extreme. Further, he does not explain why workers only demand excessively high wages in periods of price deflation but not during price inflation. Christiernin provides further arguments against monetary deflation. He argues that the consequent price deflation would have undesirable effects: unwelcomed inventory augmentations, increased real debts and bankruptcies, increased burden of taxes, credit crunches, a dampening of exports due to currency appreciation, and the idle hoarding of cash due to deflationary expectations. All this would lead to real spending that is short of its capacity.[31] Christiernin ([1761] 1971, p. 91) also points out that as a result of price deflation, the Crown's debt would increase. He also states that debtors suffer losses in a price deflation. Drawing a connection between debtorship and the economic establishment, he seems to be aware that the economic establishment suffers losses in a price deflation, and would have profited from a monetary expansion, otherwise. He writes, "[a]lmost all landlords, merchants, iron masters, and manufacturers are debtors" ([1761] 1971, p. 92). As a consequence of his views, Christiernin favors stabilizing the value of the monetary unit, the Swedish daler, and in doing so, anticipates the views of the zero inflationists or price level stabilizers which will be analyzed shortly. Obviously, confronted with the choice of inflation or deflation, Christiernin would opt for the first.

Yet, we should remember that in his treatment of deflation, Christiernin is an exception, the odd man out, among early classical economists. Prominent classical economists like Adam Smith (1723–1790), David Ricardo (1772–1823), and Jean-Baptiste Say (1767–1832) do not discuss deflation as a problem even though they discuss deflationary processes. Thus, in *Wealth of Nations* Adam Smith describes reasons for economic growth but does not state that an increase in the money supply would be necessary to accompany this economic growth. Smith analyzes the advantages of an increase in the division of labor[32] or of increased capital accumulation without making comments on negative effects of a possible price deflation.[33] Smith also points out that with an increase in the quantity of commodities and a constant money supply, the value of money increases. However, he does not address any problems with this process. On the contrary, he argues that the demand for labor increases due to this process.[34]

Like Smith, David Ricardo is interested in the long run equilibrium price, and consequently, is not concerned with short term price deflation. In *The High Price of Bullion*, for instance, he points out that any level of money supply is optimal and a shortage of money simply does not exist:

[31] See Humpfrey (2004, p. 17).

[32] Smith ([1776] 1976), Book I Ch. I.

[33] Smith ([1776] 1976), Book II, Introduction.

[34] Smith ([1776] 1976, p. 356).

> If the quantity of gold and silver in the world employed as money were exceedingly small, or abundantly great. . .the variation in their quantity would have produced no other effect than to make the commodities for which they were exchanges comparatively dear or cheap. ([1810] 2004, p. 53)

To the same extent he writes:

> When the number of transactions increase in any country from its increasing opulence and industry—bullion remaining at the same value, and the economy in the use of money also continuing unaltered—the value of money will rise on account of the increased use which will be made of it, and will continue permanently above the value of bullion, unless the quantity is increased, either by the addition of paper, or by procuring bullion to be coined into money. There will be more commodities bought and sold, but at lower prices; so that the same money will still be adequate to the increased number of transactions, by passing in each transaction at a higher value. ([1816] 2004, p. 56)

Here, Ricardo concentrates on the long-term effects and sees no adverse effects in either a monetary deflation or in a price deflation. For him, the classicist, money is neutral. Moreover, similar to Smith, Ricardo discusses processes with deflationary effects without regarding it necessary to discuss them in detail. For instance, Ricardo writes about the increases in wealth caused by increases in the division of labor due to international trade. In his example of international trade between two countries, the prices of the internationally traded goods fall in both countries.[35] However, Ricardo does not discuss this as problematic. Furthermore, Ricardo discusses the case where more abundant capital[36] and the introduction of machinery[37] lead to economic growth. Ricardo argues that costs of production determine prices and that machinery reduces the costs of production and thus indirectly the prices of commodities.[38] Thus, he speaks of causes of price deflation, namely economic growth, without being concerned about the phenomenon. However, because of his experiences, he would later come out against monetary deflation in certain circumstances, as we will see shortly. This indicates that in his later years he opposed, at least, this potential cause of price deflation.

French classical economist Jean-Baptist Say also writes about deflationary processes, following Adam Smith and David Ricardo that the division of labor results in an increase of production (1845, p. 91). He indicates its deflationary effects : "The division of labour cheapens products, by raising a greater quantity at the same or less charge of production. Competition soon obliges the producer to lower the price to the whole amount of the saving effected"(1845, p. 93). Say apparently does not see growth deflation as a problem.

In sum, Smith, Ricardo, and Say discuss processes (mainly economic growth processes) that could lead to price deflation without analyzing the question whether this would pose a problem to economic development. There are two possible

---

[35] Ricardo ([1817] 1973), Chap. VII.

[36] Ricardo [1817] 1973), Chap. XXI.

[37] Ricardo ([1817] 1973), Chap. XXXI.

[38] Ricardo ([1817] 1973), Chap. XXX, XXXI.

reasons for this. First, either they do not see any problems with deflationary processes or consider such problems not worth discussing. Or second, Smith, Ricardo, and Say are more concerned with the long-term "natural" equilibrium analysis. They analyze different long-term equilibrium states and are not concerned about the dynamic market process leading towards these states. The possible "intermediate" adverse effects of decreases in the quantity of money, consequently, are not discussed.

2.3.2 Theories of Deflation After the Napoleonic Wars

The theories of deflation and arguments against deflation spring from and surge in times of discontent as those suffering losses in a price deflation wish to profit by a credit expansion, i.e. monetary inflation. Thus, in the wake of a credit contraction in Great Britain new theories concerning deflation flourished. In 1798, in reaction to a threat of a French invasion, Great Britain went off the gold standard. Banks substantially expanded credit and increased the quantity of notes of the new fiat money. An artificial war-time boom ensued. After the war it became obvious that malinvestments had been undertaken and had to be liquidated. The corresponding credit contraction was accompanied by economic growth, and the expectation of a return to the old parity, leading to a strong price deflation.[39] During this period, many economists who had favored resumption of specie payment changed their position and argued against deflation. In these years fell the birth of a widespread deflation phobia that prevails in the profession until today. Not surprisingly, this was to the benefit of the establishment—mainly the companies with political connections that had made malinvestments during the inflationary war years. These companies favored easy money and inflation.[40] Thus, agriculturists who had indebted themselves by over-expanding production during the time of war strongly opposed the price deflation and agitated for monetary inflation. For instance, representing the Tory party and powerful aristocratic landlords, the Quarterly Review changed its initial position in favor of resumption of specie payments towards bitter attacks on price deflation.[41]

Concerning the new arguments against price deflation arising in this period, Jacob Viner ([1937] 1975, pp. 185–186) writes:

> There was general agreement at the time that changes in price levels resulted in arbitrary and inequitable redistribution of wealth and income. There appeared, however, during this period some new arguments in support of the doctrine that falling prices had adverse effects on the *volume* of wealth and production which made them particularly undesirable, and that rising prices might bring advantages for production and wealth-accumulation to

[39] See Rothbard (2006b, pp. 203–205).

[40] See Rothbard (2006b, p. 204).

[41] See Rothbard (2006b, p. 205).

compensate for their inequitable influence on distribution. The general trend of these arguments was such as to constitute at least a partial defense of the wartime inflation and to strengthen the opposition to resumption at the old par. (Italics in original)

Important for this period, therefore, are the new arguments against price deflation and their new quality. The emergence of bias in these arguments is related to the occurrence of a price deflation in this period that was to the detriment of many individuals. One of the first enemies of deflation is Thomas Attwood (1783–1859), as well as his brother Matthias. The Attwoods were both Birmingham bankers, and as such were inclined to be against deflation.[42] Moreover, both of them "served as the spokesmen for the iron and brass industry"[43] of their home city Birmingham. Their father, the elder Matthias Attwood, was a steel manufacturer.[44] Birmingham had been a main beneficiary of the war years due to its steel and armaments industry. Those industries entered into crises at the end of the war, at which time an adaptation of the structure of production to peace time conditions began.

Thus, it is not surprising that Thomas Attwood denounced falling prices as a serious evil[45] that could only be prevented by installation of an inconvertible paper currency and the continuous increase of its supply. In *Prosperity Restored* (1817, pp. 78–79), he argues that falling prices when they do not affect all prices at the same time (obligations included), would be depressing on business because of problems for debtors[46] and adverse psychological effects in the form of failing confidence in property:

If prices were to fall suddenly, and generally, and equally, in all things, *and if it was well understood, that the amount of debts and obligations were to fall in the same proportion, at the same time*, it is possible that such a fall might take place without arresting consumption and production, and in that case it would neither be injurious or beneficial in any great degree, but when a fall of this kind takes place in an obscure and unknown way, first upon

[42] Bankers fear price deflation because it may lead to defaults of their clients on loans and, thereby, losses.

[43] See Rothbard (2006b, p. 205).

[44] See Fetter (1964, p. Viii).

[45] David Laidler (2000, p. 17) comes to a similar conclusion and explains the deflation aversion by Thomas Attwood and interest groups with ties to steel and agriculture as follows: "Agriculture was faced with foreign competition again [after the end of the Napoleonic Wars], while small arms manufacturing and the metal working trades associated with it saw a precipitous decline in demand for their output. In view of this, it was perhaps to be expected that the representatives of agricultural interests in Parliament were sometimes found attempting to obstruct the restoration of convertibility and the deflation that had to accompany it. Nor, since metal working was concentrated around Birmingham, is it surprising that this important city became the centre of a dissenting and, for its time, quite radical body of economic thought. The principal, and certainly the most able spokesman of so-called *Birmingham School* at this time was the banker Thomas Attwood." (Italics in the original)

[46] Again, Attwood is speaking here in his own economic interest as he was himself a debtor. As Fetter, states: "As early as 1836, when the elder Matthias Attwood died, not only did the Attwoods have no net capital in the bank, but they were heavily in debt to it" (1964, Xxvii).

> one article and then upon another, without any correspondent fall taking place upon debts and obligations, it has the effect of destroying all confidence in property, and all inducements to its production, or to the employment of laborers in any way.[47]

In Thomas Attwood we can also find the sticky prices (wages) argument against deflation (Viner 1975, pp. 186–187). He argues that when there is a monetary deflation, prices must fall, but as wages do not fall, workers will become unemployed. His words resembling Christiernin's, he states that wages would only fall after an interval, when under the pressure of "intense misery" workers finally would agree to lower wages. As output and employment fall, a self-reinforcing downward spiral develops.[48] In a last effort to promote his policy recommendations, Attwood appeals to the ruling class. In a letter to the Earl of Liverpool he argues that price deflation would lead to misery and discontent in the population and that the social unrest might shake the throne of the king (Attwood 1819, p. 42).

Similar to Attwood's arguments are those offered by John Wheatley (1772–1832).[49] Wheatley does not see problems with growth deflation, i.e., falling prices caused by economic growth. Yet, he regards other incidents of price deflation as harmful, taking recourse in the sticky prices argument. Thus, he states that wages, rents, and taxes do not fall as long term contracts are difficult to change. This would cause distress to both farmers and manufacturers.[50] John Wheatley came from a prominent aristocratic military and landowner family. He had connections with West India trade and experienced personal financial difficulties.[51] In view of his family background, Frank Fetter speculates that Wheatley was especially concerned about the conditions of agriculture and the landowner (1942, pp. 369–370).

Wheatley argues that falling prices would be much worse than rising prices. However, he does not see a growth deflation but rather a price deflation caused by monetary deflation as problematic, thereby anticipating the current commonly-held view that there is good price deflation (caused by economic growth) and bad price deflation (caused by other reasons):

> When low prices proceed from an increase of produce, the amount of money continuing the same, they are good[;] they are good, because all receive the same income as before, and as that income will go so much further, all are benefited by the plenty that causes them. But when they proceed from a decrease of money, the quantity of produce remaining the same, they are an evil, because only those receive the same income who can legally demand a fixed sum; and all who derive a fluctuating income from agriculture and trade, sustain a loss according to their reduction. When they are occasioned by an increase of produce, the additional supply makes up for the deficiency of price, and the aggregate quantity sells for

[47] Quoted in Viner (1975, p. 186); italics in the original.

[48] See Humpfrey (2004, p. 28).

[49] See Viner (1975, p. 187).

[50] Similar sticky price arguments are employed by C.C. Western, George Julius Poulett Scrope (1797–1876), Thomas R. Malthus (1766–1834) and Henry Thornton (1769–1815). For the first three, see Viner (1975, p. 187), fn. 3. See also Thornton ([1802] 1978, p. 119).

[51] See Fetter (1942, pp. 358, 361).

as large an aggregate sum, as the smaller quantity at high prices, without any diminution of income taking place.[52]

Henry Thornton (1769–1815) fears a deliberately incited monetary deflation following a monetary inflation. He states that wages tend to adjust downward more rigidly than other prices resulting in distress for manufacturers. Workers would regard the price fall only as transitory and thus, not be willing to accept wage cuts. Thornton, in addition, brings up two other arguments against deliberate monetary deflation.[53] He argues that merchants in a monetary deflation would restrict their purchases in order to replenish their nominal cash balances that had fallen. This would have a depressionary effect on manufacturers. Then he refers to the inefficiencies that would be induced by the deflation-created idleness. Unsold goods would pile up to be dumped suddenly on the market when producers needed cash. He even opposes the outflow of gold through the specie-flow-price mechanism, (something that early classical economists thought to be the most natural process), and recommended the Bank of England to neutralize it through the issue of bank notes.[54] Concerning Thornton's interests as a banker, it is not so surprising that he worried about deflation.

George Julius Poulett Scrope [55] (1797–1876) is another author who feared a deflationary scenario. He writes that

epochs of general embarrassment and distress among the productive classes, accompanied...by a general glut or apparent excess of all goods in every market...are...occasioned by the force of some artificial disturbing cause or other. A general glut—that is, a general fall in the prices of the mass of commodities below their producing cost—is tantamount to a rise in the general exchangeable value of money; and is a proof not of an excessive supply of goods, but of a deficient supply of money, against which the goods have to be exchanged. ([1833] 1969, pp. 214–215)

Scrope implicitly assumes that prices of factors of production are sticky and cannot fall, while prices of consumption goods do fall. Therefore, prices of goods fall below their producing costs. Remedy in such a situation, from Scrope's point of view, is obviously an increase in the quantity of money.

Even strong proponents of the resumption of specie payment like David Ricardo or Edward Copleston (1776–1849) become less assertive about a pure gold coin standard due to their fear of deflation. Copleston emphasizes the agricultural distress caused by falling prices.[56] Ricardo[57] comes out in favor of a gold bullion

---

[52] Wheatley (1816), A Letter to Lord Grenville on the Distress of the Country, p. 29 as quoted in Fetter (1942, p. 374).

[53] See Humpfrey (2004, pp. 20–22).

[54] See Rothbard (2006b, p. 175). In the famous Bullion Report, Thornton also argues for a devaluation of the pound to prevent a price deflation. See Rothbard (2006b, p. 195).

[55] George Julius Poulett Scrope, a son of a merchant, also married into an aristocratic family.

[56] See Rothbard (2006b, p. 209).

[57] As indicated above, Ricardo, in his theoretical long-term analysis, is not deflation-phobic. Only when it comes to practical policies in his time, does he become somewhat deflation-phobic.

standard which is easier for the banking system to inflate than a gold coin standard as only a few rich traders can use gold in transaction and resume their deposits in specie.[58] Moreover, Ricardo apparently wants to prevent a price deflation. He writes that he would never advise a government to restore the parity of a strongly inflated and devalued currency to its old levels. In a passage in a letter to John Wheatley, dated September 18, 1821 he writes that he:

> never should advise a government to restore a currency which had been depreciated 30 % to par; I should recommend, as you propose, but not in the same manner, that the currency should be fixed at the depreciated value by lowering the standard, and that no further deviations should take place.[59]

From this letter, one can deduce that it is the sudden and strong deflation that Ricardo opposes.[60] He considers a large deflation of 30 % to be too much, generating distress via price stickiness. A small gradual deflation, he does not regard as dangerous.[61] We see, that after his experience of deflation following the Napoleonic Wars, even Ricardo, the resumption proponent, was not free from a deflation phobia.

In sum, before this period, next to no one had been worried about the phenomenon of falling prices in particular. The specie flows of the gold standard that would cause price deflation, apparently did not preoccupy theorists. The literature of the Bullionist controversy, however, brought up new arguments concerning deflation. Now, in the time of Britain's resumption of specie payment when prices in a contractionary recession fell and many manufacturers and agricultural interests[62] favored monetary expansion, the first theories about deflation appeared. Agreeing with these later arguments, Viner supports those theorists favoring an inconvertible paper currency to overcome the mechanisms of the gold standard (1975, p. 217):

> They presented valid and novel arguments for the economic advantages of the freedom afforded by an independent monetary standard to escape a deflation (or inflation!) induced by external factors, to cope with a deflation resulting from internal factors and intensified by the prevalence of rigidity downwards in the prices of the factors of production, and, in general, to provide a country with the quantity of means of payment deemed best for it as against having that quantity dictated to it by external factors beyond its control.

[58] See Rothbard (2006b, p. 207).

[59] Ricardo ([1821] 2004, p. 73).

[60] Also, Jean-Baptiste Say opposed the return to the old parity. He uses a legal argument, stating that debtors had to pay more than they owed if they had to pay back with the old parity. See Rist (1966, p. 184).

[61] See Humphrey (2004, pp. 23–24).

[62] Concerning manufacturing and agricultural interest groups, see Rothbard (2006b, p. 206). For instance, the landed aristocrat, the Earl of Carnavon denounced the Resumption Act of 1819, as well as lower farming prices, calling for monetary expansion and fiscal policies as a remedy.

2.3.3 *Later Classical Theories of Deflation*

Robert Torrens (1834/1970) is one of the late classical authors who wrote about deflation. He feared that a protective tariff from a foreign country could cause price deflation at home. In this case a lowering of domestic tariffs would aggravate the downward pressure on prices as metals would be lost. In particular, he writes:

> When, from foreign rivalry and hostile tariffs, a country begins to lose a portion of her former command over the precious metals, and to experience a contraction of the currency, a fall in prices, in profits, and in wages, and a falling off in the revenue, then, the lowering of import duties upon the productions of countries retaining their hostile tariffs, instead of affording relief, would aggravate the general distress, by occasioning a more rapid abstraction of the metals, and a deeper decline in prices, in profits, in wages, and in the revenue, accompanied not by a diminution, but an increase in the real extent of taxation. (Torrens [1834] 1970, pp. 28–29)

Thus, Torrens favors domestic tariffs. He hopes that those tariffs would bring back precious metals and thus prevent a price deflation. Torrens also employs the common arguments of increasing real burden of debts and sticky wages.[63]

John Stuart Mill (1806–1873) continues the tradition of Adam Smith, David Ricardo, and Jean-Baptiste Say who discuss reasons for economic growth, but are not worried about growth deflation. In 1844, he comes out against the proposal to increase the money supply along with increases in output and increases in the use of money. He calls such proposals, as made for example by Sir Robert Peel, as degrading the standard (1844, p. 581). Hence, he is not afraid of a price deflation that can occur when output is growing and the money supply is constant. Furthermore, Mill writes that the division of labor increases productivity[64] and describes how large scale production increases productivity.[65] He also states that the progress of industry and population makes the costs of production fall[66] and refers to the contemporary situation of the world without being worried about the price deflation. He does not mention deflation as a threat in these circumstances.

In sum, we can find two lines of thought concerning deflation in classical economics. Along one line of thought, authors such as Smith, Ricardo, Say, and Mill do not see problems with a price deflation or, at least, do not see them worth discussing in their theoretical works and treatises. In the other line of thought, authors, starting with Hume and Christiernin, and followed by the British authors after the Napoleonic Wars, are more critical of price deflation. They regard price deflation as something harmful. This line of reasoning is inspired by the historical events of their time. Sometimes they had personal ties to those groups that suffered losses during the price deflations. In the following section, I will turn to the theories

[63] See Humphrey (2004, pp. 38–39).

[64] Mill ([1848] 1965), Book I, Chap. VIII.

[65] Mill ([1848] 1965), Book I, Chap. IX.

[66] Mill ([1848] 1965), Book IV, Chap. II.

of deflation of early neoclassical thought. Then I will analyze two groups of thinkers that reach back to classical economics.

2.4 Neoclassical Theories of Deflation

2.4.1 *Early Neoclassical Theories of Deflation*

Alfred Marshall (1842–1924) continues the classical line of economists like Adam Smith, David Ricardo, Jean-Baptiste Say or John Stuart Mill who do not treat deflation critically. As does Ricardo and Smith, Marshall concentrates on long run equilibria in his theoretical analysis. Possible transitional problems during price deflation are not discussed. Thus, a critical treatment of deflation by Marshall cannot be found. Only indirectly does he refer to price deflation when he writes about economic progress and falling costs.[67] In this context he does not talk about possible problems connected with economic progress and falling costs. Hence, one might assume that Marshall did not see any problems resulting from price deflation.

In early neoclassical theory, there is an important treatment of price deflation by Knut Wicksell (1851–1926). His case is curious as at several stages in his life, he defends different and apparently inconsistent theories of deflation. In his famous article "The Influence of the Rate of Interest on Prices" (1907) Wicksell reveals his theory of inflation and deflation. When the banking sector lowers the rate of interest below its normal level, i.e., the existing rate of profit or the natural interest rate, a credit expansion will follow and prices will keep rising. When, on the contrary, the banking sector raises the rate of interest above the natural interest rate, all prices will keep on falling. Prices fall because credits will be restricted and entrepreneurs will have less money to bid for factors of production. In other words, a credit contraction ensues.

Knut Wicksell's assessment of price deflation is ambivalent and changes over time.[68] It seems that he did not hold a firm opinion on the issue of deflation. On the one hand, he argues that deflation leads to business stagnation, unemployment and falling wages ([1898] 1968, pp. 2–3). He also states that, possibly, the most important effect of a deflation would be its implications for taxation. Salaries of state officials would not decrease as quickly as other prices. Furthermore, the state's creditor would claim a higher real stake, which in the end would mean higher taxation to repay government debts. In 1908, he argues that a falling price level disturbs entrepreneurial spirit and destroys many companies. In 1919, he states that falling prices would have a negative effect on production.

On the other hand, Wicksell argues that an announced and perfectly anticipated deflation would not have real effects when it is taken into account in all economic

---

[67] Marshall (1920), Book VI, Chaps. XII and XIII.

[68] Concerning Wicksell's treatment of deflation, see Bioanovsky (1998).

contracts. Moreover, an unexpected but gradual deflation would not be too disturbing to the economy, either.[69] And after World War I he is in favor of a deflationary policy to bring Sweden back to the gold standard at the pre-World War I parity. He justifies his view by pointing out the importance of the constancy of the value of money for contracts. He takes recourse to economic history, stating that between 1873 and 1896, a long period of price deflation and a prospering economy had co-existed. Possibly inspired by the criticism of Eli Heckscher,[70] he argues that only companies with debts would suffer real losses in a general price deflation. Wicksell severely criticizes the view point that price deflation would lead to unemployment through wage stickiness. He wonders why workers would not be able to compare cost of living indexes with their nominal wages. Thus, he thinks workers, aware of the general price fall, would be willing to accept reductions in nominal wages. Wages would not be more rigid than other prices.

After the 1921–1922 Swedish depression, Wicksell's views concerning deflation turn more negative again. He explains the Swedish depression by the increase in real debts and by hoarding induced by the price deflation. As a consequence, Wicksell suggests indexing all money contracts. In sum, Wicksell argues that a perfectly anticipated deflation would be neutral. However, over time, he became influenced by historical events, and saw more practical problems with deflation like the effects of bankruptcy and hoarding, thereby, suggesting indexation of contracts.

The odd man out in this period is Silvio Gesell (1862–1930), who anticipates John Maynard Keynes in his theory of crises (2003, pp. 143–144): When production increases, and the stock of money fails to increase, prices tend to fall. As expectations of price deflation rise, money is hoarded or "buried." Consequently, the demand for goods falls and the economic crises begins.

Gesell warns that preventing economic crises would require that prices never be allowed to fall (2003, p. 150). In order to achieve this, Gesell proposes his famous "Freigeld" (2003, pp. 179–240). The Freigeld is an inconvertible paper money that loses 0.1 % of its worth every week. With this measure, Gesell thinks that individuals will no longer hoard their money at home, as the money is losing value, but spend it as quickly as possible, thus preventing crises. The government issuing agency would then easily be able to stabilize the price level (2003, p. 187).

---

[69] An announced deflation cannot be gradual according to Gustav Cassel who argued that when a central bank would announce such a policy, demand would immediately contract and accelerate the fall in prices. The central bank would lose the control of the pace of the process. See Bioanovsky (1998, p. 248).

[70] See Boianovsky (1998).

2.4.2 *Deflation and the Productivity Norm*

One important group of theorists does not see problems in a price deflation caused by economic growth: the productivity norm theorists. Proponents of the productivity norm argue that price-level changes should take into account changes in productivity.[71] When productivity declines, prices should respond with a rise, and when productivity increases, prices should fall as a consequence. One of the first proponents of the productivity norm was Samuel Bailey (1791–1870).[72,73] He argues that changes in the price level stemming from monetary causes would be harmful and lead to an unjust redistribution, while those redistributions caused by changes in productivity would not be unjust. Bailey was mostly interested in the question of justice in debtor-creditor relations. With a productivity norm, creditors would also participate in a productivity increase.

Later Alfred Marshall (1842–1924), Francis Edgeworth (1834–1926) and Robert Giffen (1837–1910) also embraced the productivity norm and did not see any problems with the contemporary fall in prices caused by economic growth.[74] Other prominent defenders of a productivity norm were Ralph Hawtrey (1879–1975) and Dennis Robertson (1890–1963). Hawtrey argues that a price index should reflect changes in the real costs of production. Otherwise, prices would deceive entrepreneurs and could cause economic booms or depression. A rise in productivity accompanied by prices that do not fall could lead to an unwarranted encouragement of entrepreneurs. Moreover, Hawtrey argues that there is no reason to exclude receivers of fixed income from productivity increases by monetary policy.[75] Arthur Pigou (1877–1959)[76] likewise sees no problem for the industry due to a productivity-caused deflation nor anything unjust in the redistribution from debtors to creditors.[77] Other economists in favor of a productivity norm were the Swedish economists Bertil Ohlin (1899–1979), Eli Heckscher (1879–1952),

---

[71] See Selgin (1995, p. 707).

[72] This implies that the productivity norm goes back to times of classical economics. It is discussed in this paragraph because in neoclassical economics, the productivity norm still plays a prominent role.

[73] See Selgin (1995, pp. 708–709).

[74] See Selgin (1995).

[75] See Selgin (1995, pp. 714–715).

[76] See Selgin (1995, p. 717).

[77] Pigou plays another important role in respect to deflation theories as the "Pigou-effect" is named after him. In a 1943 article "The Classical Stationary State," Pigou argues that if the price level falls, real wealth, defined as government bonds and money supply divided by the price level, increases. Feeling richer ("wealth effect"), economic agents would increase consumption and thereby stimulating output and employment. The Pigou-effect was intended as a critique of Keynes' *General Theory*. Through price deflation and the "wealth effect" an economy would be self-correcting when aggregate demand falls.

Gunnar Myrdal (1898–1987), and Erik Lindahl (1891–1960); the Austrian economists, Gottfried von Haberler (1900–1995) and Friedrich A. von Hayek (1899–1992)[78]; as well as the American economists James Laurence Laughlin (1850–1933), Simon Newcomb (1835–1909), and Frank Taussig (1859–1940).[79]

Taussig, for instance, argues that the money paid back to the creditor could buy more goods and services than when the contract was settled. However, due to the productivity increase, debtors would be able to pay back monetary units with a higher purchasing power. Their monetary income would not have fallen. Creditors should not be prevented from participating in productivity improvements.

As can be seen, especially in the nineteenth and early twentieth centuries, the productivity norm had numerous followers. Yet, after the Keynesian revolution, ever fewer economists defended the productivity norm. In contrast, the number of economists joining the zero inflation or price level stability camp, discussed in the next section, grew ever larger. Recently, the productivity norm was rediscovered by George Selgin (1997). In this respect, the productivity norm theorists are intimately connected with the free banking theorists, forming part of the Austrian School of economics, which is in favor of a fractional reserve banking system without a central bank. Free banking theorists are, thus, intellectual heirs of this tradition. They also regard falls in the price level caused by economic growth as not dangerous and recommend that increases in the demand for money or changes in the velocity of money be counteracted by changes in the supply of money.

2.4.3 *Price Level Stability and Deflation*

Indirectly, there are many authors who oppose price deflation as they argue for a stabilization of the general price level. Such proponents include among others Knut Wicksell (1851–1926), Gustav Cassel (1866–1945), Irving Fisher (1867–1947), Josiah Stamp (1880–1941), John Maynard Keynes (1883–1946) (at least in some of his writings), Carl Snyder (1869–1946), George Warren, and Frank Pearson, as well as contemporary economists like Robert Barro, Robert Black, Kevin Dowd, and Robert Hetzel.[80] They argue that the stability of output prices is necessary for general macroeconomic stability. In fact, they argue that stable prices would be necessary for rational economic actions.

---

[78] See the second edition of *Prices and Production* (von Hayek 1939, p. 124). Concerning the evolution of Hayek on this point from a proponent of a constant money supply to a proponent of policies which advocate adjusting the money supply to changes in the velocity of money, see Selgin (1999).

[79] See Selgin (1995). The list given by Selgin must be considered with caution. It is true that the mentioned authors saw no problems in a price deflation caused by economic growth. However, not all of them explicitly follow Selgin in his view that changes in the demand for money must be necessarily counteracted by monetary policy. As one example, see Hayek in his earlier works.

[80] See Selgin (1995, p. 705). According to Hülsmann (2006, p. 72), St. Thomas Aquinas was the first philosopher who postulated a stable purchasing power of money.

There are five basic arguments provided for price level stability or zero inflation.[81] First, unanticipated price level changes would lead to unfair redistribution of wealth. Second, falling prices would hamper business and entrepreneurship and, therefore, should be prevented by expansionary monetary policy. Third, "menu costs" occur when prices are changed and price level stability, as it is argued, would minimizes the "menu costs." Fourth, the ability to predict the price-level is desireable. This would be the case under a zero inflation norm. A similar argument maintains that long-term uncertainty is to be reduced by stabilizing the price level. Thus, economic agents could better rely upon contracts in fixed money terms without having to fear unpredicted changes in the purchasing power of money. Finally, there is a fifth argument offered for a stable price level: the danger of monetary misconceptions. Thus, modern price stability champions or zero inflationists have put emphasis on the "money illusion." In a money illusion economic agents confuse general price changes with relative price changes. When local prices rise they do not take into account that the general price level has changed. In order to avoid the money illusion zero inflationists want to avoid change in the price level altogether.

There are additional arguments for price level stability. The industrialist and banker Josiah Stamp (1932, p. 5) argues that price level stability could solve the most pressing social problems (of his time). Warren and Pearson write: "One of the most important problems in all human relationships is the establishment of reliable measures"(1933, p. 150). Regarding the problem of redistribution by price changes, these authors go so far as to state: "The solution of the problem of a stable measure of value will go far in establishing peaceful relations among men" (1933, pp. 151–152). From the argument for price level stability it follows that price deflation should be prevented. These authors advocate preventing price inflation as well. However, it seems that at least some of them regard price deflation as worse than price inflation and therefore the reason why these authors promote price stability policies.[82] Along this line, Warren and Pearson write: "Any given amount of deflation is far more serious than the same amount of inflation" (1933, p. 180). Not surprisingly, these authors try to prevent all price deflation independent of its cause. Thus, Warren and Pearson explicitly discuss the allegedly negative effects of a price deflation caused by increases in productivity (1933, p. 156).

Let us now turn more closely to probably the most prominent proponent of price level stability: Irving Fisher. He has probably developed the most elaborate case for a stabilization of the purchasing power of the dollar and has analysed deflation vigorously. Therefore, we will take a closer look at his theory of deflation. He defines "relative deflation" as occurring when the circulation of money decreases relative to the circulation of goods, and when the price level falls (1928, p. 35). "Absolute deflation", in turn, is a per capita decrease of circulating money (1928, p. 38). Fisher regards the dollar as the money yardstick that—as every standard—

[81] See Selgin (1995, pp. 706–707) and Dowd (1995).

[82] Josiah Stamp is such a case (Stamp 1932).

must be held constant. Thus, he regards inflation and deflation as equally harmful and delivers four typical arguments against deflation. He calls the redistribution between debtors and creditors a social injustice. He regards this redistribution as equivalent to a redistribution in society that occurs in a bank robbery. He also makes the argument (1928, pp. 91–92) that a money illusion occurs when business men calculate their profits in constant dollars. He argues, consequently, that in a deflation, entrepreneurs would unduly contract their business. He also states that workers become unemployed in a deflation (1928, p. 97). He, furthermore, argues that the before mentioned cases, i.e., the social injustice, the problems for businesses, and unemployment would cause social discontent with negative effects on economic output, in the form of strikes, sabotage, riots, violence and even Bolshevism (1928, p. 98, 103).

In his "Debt-Deflation Theory of Great Depressions" [1933] and *100 % Money* ([1935] 1945), Irving Fisher offers us his famous debt deflation theory. He argues that a euphoria caused by new opportunities with expected substantial profits, for example, induced by the development of new technologies, brings about an over-indebtedness. This over-indebtedness tends to lead to a liquidation that will alarm either debtors or creditors or both. Nine consequences will ensue: (1) distress selling created by debt liquidation; (2) a contraction of bank credits as bank loans are paid back and the velocity of money circulation is reduced; (3) a fall in the general price level caused by distress selling and contraction in bank credits; (4) bankruptcies and another fall in the net worth of businesses; (5) the decrease in profits; (6) as a consequence, a reduction in output and trade and increase in unemployment; (7) pessimism and lack of confidence; (8) subsequent hoarding and a further reduction of the velocity of money circulation; and (9) disturbances in the interest rates, namely the fall of nominal interest rates and the increase of real interest rates (Fisher 1945, pp. 122–123; 1933, p. 1). In the cumulative downward process, debts and deflation aggravate each other. The liquidation of debts will make the price deflation harsher and the price deflation makes it more difficult to repay debts as the purchasing power of the dollars rises even more. The liquidation feeds itself. Thus, the forerunner of the price level stability theorists, Irving Fisher, provides us with a vast array of arguments against price deflation and develops his influential debt-deflation theory. Unsurprisingly, Fisher had strong personal interests in monetary inflation.[83] During the Great Depression he agitated for inflation not only to reinflate stock prices, but also to be able to pay his debts, and save his wife's family fortune, which was mainly invested in the major American company Allied Chemical. He would have been ruined by debt-deflation.

A somewhat similar approach is represented by monetary disequilibrium theorists like Leland B. Yeager (1986).[84] According to Yeager, a monetary disequilibrium occurs when there is a shortage or surplus of money at some given price

[83] See Rothbard (2002, pp. 453–456).

[84] Another case is Clark Warburton. See Cargill (1979, pp. 439–440). Warburton argues that prices are sticky in the short run, especially wages. A decrease in the money supply or a failure to adopt

level, which is regarded as rigid (1986, p. 370). Hence, we are confronted with the old price rigidity argument once again. Yeager writes that in a monetary disequilibrium, prices will change and "[t]hese price changes *tend* to correct or forstall the monetary disequilibrium but do not and cannot occur promptly and completely enough to absorb the entire impact of the monetary change and so avoid quantity changes" (1986, p. 373).

Yeager names three reasons why prices do not change immediately: First, there are fixed money contracts like wage and debt contracts that cannot be changed easily. Second, there are "menu costs" corresponding to the posting and negotiating of new money prices, which makes prices sticky in the short run. Third, sellers might be reluctant to lower (or change) their prices and do not easily see why they should accept lower ones. Yeager characterizes this taking of the lead in a downward price adjustment as a public good (1986, pp. 376–377). Sellers might even be aware of a monetary disequilibrium, for instance, a money shortage, and that prices must fall to correct it. But no seller wants to be the first in lowering his own product price but would rather that others cut their prices first.

As a consequence, Yeager argues that macro-economic disturbances could be reduced or avoided by avoiding those monetary disequilibria and adjustments in the general price level. Thus, Yeager argues that the nominal stock of money must be manipulated in a way so that the general price level remains constant.

2.4.4 Keynes on Deflation

Modern theories of deflation begin with John Maynard Keynes (1883–1946). Actually, he did not come up with many new arguments against deflation. Rather, he took the old ones, combined them, and developed a line of reasoning that would later come to be called the liquidity trap argument.[85] I will also analyze his influential theories concerning deflation in detail and then also consider the work of his adversary, the very influential economist Milton Friedman (1912–2006).

From the beginning of his career, starting with *A Tract on Monetary Reform* (1923), Keynes was deflation-phobic. We can find almost every important argument against deflation in his works. First, he regards price deflation as leading to an unjust redistribution which would harm borrowers ([1923] 2000, p. 39). Keynes clearly sees the redistribution going on in a price deflation, stating that price deflation always "involves a transference of wealth from the rest of the community to the *rentier* class.... In particular it involves a transference from all borrowers, that is to say from traders, manufacturers, and farmers, to lenders, from the active to the

the money supply to decreases in the velocity of circulation means a decrease in spending. Due to sticky wages, this leads to a decrease in business profits and, thus, to a further fall in total spending.

[85] The concept of the liquidity trap was formalized in Hicks' (1937) classic article "Mr. Keynes and the 'Classics:' A Suggested Interpretation." The term liquidity trap, however, was first coined by Dennis Robertson, although in a different context. See Boianovsky (2004, p. 92).

inactive."[86] He seems to imply that the economic function of lending would be less "active" or productive than the production or trading of other goods aside from future monetary units. Interestingly, in the context of redistribution, he explains the fact that we have had historically more periods of price inflation than periods of price deflation ([1923] 2000, p. 9) by "the impecuniosity of Governments and and the superior political influence of the debtor class." From the perspective of interest groups, it is thus clear for Keynes why the world has experienced price inflation. Price deflation is neither in the interest of a highly indebted government nor of the influential debtors class, consisting of big business.

Second, he ([1923] 2000, p. 144) argues that everyone will try to postpone their expenditures. Third, we find the sticky price argument when he writes that problems will occur when business and social arrangements inhibit prices from falling quickly enough ([1923] 2000, pp. 161–162). In *General Theory*, he argues that wages are sticky ([1936] 1964, pp. 232–233).

Fourth, he argues that deflation "means Impoverishment [sic] to labour and to enterprise by leading *entrepreneurs* to restrict production, in their endeavor to avoid loss to themselves; and is therefore disastrous to employment."[87] Keynes argues that the expectation of price deflation hampers production for two reasons. First, it increases the real interest rate. The real cost of borrowing or the real burden of debt increases as money that must be paid back has a higher purchasing power. Second, as production takes time, and prices continue to fall there will be losses for businesses paying their production factors in the higher, still rigid prices and selling at the lower new prices. Thus, when the deflation is expected or anticipated, production will be inhibited ([1923] 2000, pp. 32–37, 144). Keynes' view stands in contrast to other authors who regard anticipated deflation to be less harmful than he does.

The argument concerning social unrest is also not overlooked. Fifth, Keynes argues that deflation leads to social instability.[88] In 1931, Keynes makes a sixth argument, identifying another consequence of price deflation, that is nowadays often used as an argument against it, namely that it "threatens the solidity of the whole financial structure" (1931, p. 176).

Another point should also be made that Keynes regards price deflation as more harmful than price inflation, "because it is worse, in an impoverished world, to provoke unemployment than to disappoint the *rentier*."[89]

In 1930, Keynes continues his case against deflation, in *Treatise on Money*, repeating that price deflation would be more harmful than price inflation:

> Since neither economists nor bankers have been quite clear in their minds as to the character of the causal process through which a reduction in the quantity of money

---

[86] (Keynes [1923] 2000, p. 143); Italics are in the original.

[87] (Keynes [1923] 2000, p. 39); Italics are in the original.

[88] See Keynes ([1923] (2000, p. 143); See also Keynes ([1925] 1963, p. 247).

[89] See Keynes ([1923] 2000, p. 40); Italics are in the original. See also p. 4.

> eventually leads to a new equilibrium at a lower level of money earnings and of price, they have been apt to contemplate a deflation too lightheartedly (1971, p. 244).

He concludes his analysis: "I am doubtful, therefore, whether those are right who believe that a period of deflation generally does less harm than a period of inflation" (1971, p. 245). Keynes argues that if the money supply or the velocity of circulation falls, investments fall below savings. Windfall losses result, inducing entrepreneurs to reduce their spending on factors of production. Spending less, the owners of these factors will further reduce profits or increase losses. Prices continue to fall with the downward process ending when investments are finally equal to savings (1971, pp. 241–245).

Influenced by the developments of the Great Depression, Keynes continues his anti-deflation path in 1936, with the publication of *General Theory*.[90] His recommendations for getting out of the Great Depression are clearly anti-deflationary as revealed in his endorsement for expanding the money supply and engaging in expansionary fiscal policy.[91] In the *General Theory*, Keynes argues that in the case of economic growth there are two options: Either one allows prices to fall and keeps wages stable, or one allows wages to rise and keeps prices stable. He argues that the second options would have the advantage of avoiding unemployment, reducing the burden of debt, and providing psychological encouragement that likely would be due to rising nominal wages.

As a seventh argument against deflation, which we find in the *General Theory*, Keynes revisits Mercantilist hoarding theories, particularly those which saw hoarding as something to be avoided.[92] Keynes argues that with lack of effective demand (consumption and investment expenditures) caused by hoarding, an equilibrium with unemployment will prevail.[93] When sudden crises of confidence occur, the individual will not spend a larger part of his income on investments nor on consumption, but simply "hoard" the money. In other words, the "propensity to hoard" or the liquidity preference increases.[94] This, via the multiplier, would have "disastrous, cumulative and far-reaching repercussions" (Keynes 1964, p. 161). Hence, Keynes defends the Mercantilist anti-hoarding theories that make the demand for increases in cash balances responsible for economic crises. Monetary policy cannot stimulate the economy in a deflationary crises as the new money is hoarded and the nominal interest rate is close to zero. He is, thus, the father of the famous liquidity trap argument against deflation. In sum, many of the main arguments against deflation can be found in Keynes' writings.

---

[90] Keynes ([1936] 1964, p. 271, 291).

[91] See Skidelsky (2002, p. 99).

[92] See Keynes (1964, pp. 344–345).

[93] See Keynes (1964, p. 30).

[94] See Keynes (1964, p. 207). Later this concept became famously known or described as the liquidity trap. For Keynes, the liquidity preference and propensity to hoard are essentially the same thing (1964, p. 208).

2.4.5 *Friedman on Deflation*

Before analyzing contemporary deflation theories, I will first turn to Nobel prize winner and influential economist Milton Friedman (1912–2006).

Friedman's view on monetary deflation can be inferred from his writings on the Great Depression. Friedman feared monetary deflation, in that he saw the monetary deflation of the Great Depression as the main cause of its severity.[95] According to Friedman, the Federal Reserve had not tried hard enough to prevent a reduction of the money supply, i.e., had allowed the money supply to shrink. The Federal Reserve allowed bank runs to occur and did not provide them with sufficient liquidity by granting the credits or by buying open market purchases. This caused the failure of banks and the reduction of the money supply as well, creating problems for other banks of which some also went bankrupt. As the money supply fell even further, businessmen could not get loans for investing or went bankrupt as loans were not renewed. Friedman alleges the Federal Reserve's inactive policy made the Great Depression far worse than it would have been. Otherwise, an ordinary recession would have followed the stock market crash. For him, a monetary deflation is a scenario which must be prevented.

2.5 Latest Theories of Deflation

2.5.1 *Fractional Reserve Free Banking School*

One contemporary deflation theory is proposed by the Fractional Reserve Free Banking School branch of the Austrian School. These economists are basically modern proponents of the productivity norm. For instance, George Selgin (1997) argues that growth deflation is something good and not harmful to the economy. Price deflation caused by economic growth would pose no problem for the economy. Any changes in the purchasing power of money caused by the goods side and not by the money side should not be counteracted by monetary policy.[96] A price change caused by productivity changes would contain important information about the price of outputs relative to inputs for economic agents and a counteracting monetary policy would undermine the accuracy of those price signals (1997, p. 23). Thus he writes: "…the price level should be allowed to vary to reflect changes in goods' unit costs of production. I call a pattern of general price level adjustments corresponding to such a rule for individual price changes a 'productivity norm'"(1997, p. 10)

---

[95] See Friedman (1968, p. 3) or Friedman and Schwartz (1971, p. 407).

[96] This is the difference of Selgin's position as compared to the view of the zero inflationists who advocate reducing any change in the general price level no matter what its cause is.

While productivity caused price changes should not be counteracted, price deflation caused by changes in the velocity of money should be counteracted by adjustments in the quantity of money. Selgin goes on: "Under a productivity norm, changes in velocity would be prevented (as under zero inflation) from influencing the price level through offsetting adjustment in the supply of money" (1997, p. 10). And he adds that the productivity norm "calls for monetary expansion to prevent any deflation not consistent with improvements in factor productivity" (1997, p. 59). This is so, because shifts in aggregate demand caused by a change in the velocity of money could lead to monetary misconception. For instance, economic agents might misconceive the general fall of the price level caused by a decrease in the velocity of money for a decline in the real demand for particular goods and services they provide.

Another author in this line of thought is Steven Horwitz. He explains in further detail why decreases in the velocity of money or increases in the demand for money should be counteracted by an increase in the money supply:

> During the time it takes the price level to fall, firms will find themselves with unintended inventory accumulations, implying that *desired* saving (holding of gold) is not equal to *desired* investment. This further implies that increases in the money supply would be warranted in order to bring desired saving and investment back together.... [T]here will be downward pressure on prices and, barring perfect price flexibility, a drop in output and employment. Free banking theorists argue that free banks will respond to this increase in demand by producing more bank liabilities, thus preventing the fall in output and employment that would otherwise result. (2000, p. 227)

Horwitz, like Selgin employs the additional argument that there is a prisoners' dilemma with regard to which producer lowers his prices first in the situation of an increased demand for money: "[G]iven wage stickiness, it is in no producer's interest to be the first to lower his prices.... [F]inding the newly appropriate level of prices is a Mengerian discovery process and not an instantaneous shift" (2000, p. 229).

In sum, fractional reserve free banking theorists do not fear growth deflation but price deflation caused by an increase in the demand for money, or cash building deflation. For his policy recommendation of only counteracting changes in the demand for money, Selgin coins the term "productivity norm." The free bankers, as well as productivity norm proponents, are therefore less deflation-skeptic than the many of their fellow economists who might recommend preventing any price deflation. However, except for growth deflation, free bankers recommend counteracting other causes of deflation. The solution they offer is a fractional reserve free banking system (Selgin 1997, p. 67).

2.5.2 *Liquidity Trap Theorists*

In the economic mainstream, there are basically two main strands in contemporary deflation theories. The first strand can be represented by economists who in some way are inspired by Keynesian theories like Ben Bernanke, Lars E.O. Svensson, Marvin Goodfriend, or Paul Krugman. The first group fears that price deflation might put the economy in a liquidity trap and opposes all price deflation categorically. It represents the deflation phobia in its clearest form. The second strand has representatives like Claudio Borio, Andrew Filardo, Michael Bordo, John L. Lane, and Angela Redish.[97] Inspired by the Chicago School, the second group is more free market oriented. Bordo, for instance, received his doctoral degree from the University of Chicago. This group distinguishes between two types of deflation: good deflation and bad deflation. Its views are briefly presented in the section following our consideration of the liquidity trap theorists.

This first group of theorists fears a liquidity trap. For the liquidity trap group, deflation "is seldom benign" and even when stemming from a positive supply shock, can lead to a deflationary spiral of prices and output.[98] Svensson (2003, p. 145) states that it is uncontroversial to hold that a liquidity trap and deflation should be avoided. According to this view, unanticipated negative demand or supply shocks may cause recession and deflation. Also substantial realized or anticipated negative aggregate demand shocks like bursts of asset price bubbles, doubts about government policies, or corrections of overly optimistic expectations would lower inflation and output and their respective forecasts (Svensson 2003, p. 146). In this situation a central bank should lower interest rates to stimulate aggregate spending. However, there is a negative premium for deflation in the interest rates. In a price deflation nominal interest rates are already very low. It might be impossible to lower interest rates sufficiently as nominal interest rates cannot fall below zero. The central bank, as feared, has "run out of ammunition." The real cost of borrowing will be on a level higher than is necessary to stimulate the economy.

Liquidity trap theorists argue that there is no way out of this situation via conventional monetary policies. The central bank can buy bonds from the public and enlarge the money supply, but the public will hold onto the money it receives, instead of spending it. Bonds and money are essentially conceived of as perfect substitutes as the nominal interest rate is zero. The recession and deflation can then be prolonged. In other words, the economy is stuck in a liquidity trap. The ineffectiveness of monetary policy is seen as a main threat of deflation.[99] Considerable intellectual effort is spent in finding ways out of a liquidity trap via inflation of the money supply.[100] These recommendations imply measures that give more spending power to politicians. Therefore, politicians have an incentive to adopt the

[97] For a book of selected essays that stand in this tradition, see Burdekin and Siklos (2004a). Good deflation is caused by a positive supply shock and bad deflation by a negative demand shock. In particular, see the Burdekin and Siklos (2004b) and Bordo and Redish (2004).

[98] See Kumar and colleagues (2003, p. 5 or p. 9). On p. 12, these authors state that temporary price declines due to economic growth may not entail significant costs. This seems to imply that even with a positive supply shock, significant costs might exist.

[99] See Kumar et al. (2003, p. 13); Krugman (1998, p. 137).

[100] See Krugman (1998), Goodfriend (2000), Svensson (2003), and Leigh (2004).

point of view of liquidity trap theorists and avert the danger of deflation. They are given an excuse to increase spending and to inflate the money supply.

In addition to the liquidity trap problem, Svensson names other negative consequences of a prolonged deflation: (1) an increase in bankruptcies as the real debts of companies increase; (2) financial instability due to the deterioration of commercial banks' balance sheets; and (3) unemployment in cases where nominal wages are rigid downward.[101] Kumar and colleagues add another point: Credit intermediation might be distorted by deflation as collateral loses value (2003, p. 5). All this may lead to a deflationary spiral as declining prices lead to the expectation of further falling prices and further decline in aggregate demand. Thus, these theorists argue for an inflation rate that has some buffer against the danger of price deflation.[102]

2.5.3 Good-Versus-Bad Deflation Theorists

The second group of contemporary deflation theorists is inspired by the Chicago School and is more free market oriented. Because this group views deflation as being good at times, and not at others, they might be called the Good-versus-Bad deflation school. The Good-versus-Bad deflation school, to a certain extent, rehabilitates deflation. Thus, it is argued that a mild deflation would not always be more harmful than a mild inflation (Borio and Filardo 2004, p. 1), an assessment contrary to that of the liquidity trap theorists. For Good-versus-Bad deflation theorists, deflation has basically two causes.[103] One cause is economic growth or positive aggregate supply shocks. There are high profits, asset prices, and rising real wages accompanied by a strong financial sector. This deflation they consider to be good deflation. The other cause is a negative demand shock with a non-vertical aggregate supply curve. As these negative demand shocks would have negative output effects, this type of deflation is considered to be bad deflation. Furthermore, these theorists argue that deflation produces only negative consequences when it is unexpected.[104]

---

[101] Svensson (2003, p. 147); It should be pointed out that by criticizing the negative consequences of deflation, Svensson takes a stand against all kinds of deflation. For instance, a positive supply shock, or more specifically, continuous economic growth, might cause a prolonged price deflation also.

[102] For example, Svensson (2000, p. 30), justifies an inflation targeting of 2 % instead of 0 % by the allegedly negative effects of price deflation. Krugman (1998, p. 161), even argues that when an economy is in a liquidity trap, it is stuck there, because the "economy needs inflation." He, p. 181, suggests a price inflation rate of 4 % for 15 years for Japan.

[103] See Bordo et al. (2004, p. 15). This is the main difference between the two groups. The liquidity trap group does not differentiate between causes of price deflation, but, in contrast, states that "[d] eflation is, in almost all cases, a side effect of a collapse of aggregate demand—a drop in spending so severe that producers must cut prices on an ongoing basis in order to find buyers" (Bernanke 2002, p. 2).

[104] Rational expectation theorists like Sargent and Wallace (1976, p. 175) argue that fully anticipated price changes would not have any effect on the real economic activity. This implies

Borio and Filardo even distinguish three types of deflation: "the good, the bad and the ugly."[105] Good deflations are caused by productivity increases. Bad deflations are caused by nominal rigidities, while ugly deflations disrupt the economy in a self-reinforcing spiral.

That this group is more friendly towards price deflation can also be inferred from the optimal deflation rate for which Bordo and Filardo argue (2005, pp. 804–806). After reviewing Milton Friedman's argument for a negative optimal inflation equal to the real interest rate, they name disadvantages of deflation, like price stickiness, nominal wage inflexibility, redistributive losses, and financial stability. After pondering the arguments, they write: "In general, the optimal inflation rate should be low, possibly as low as a moderate deflation" (p. 806). Thus, they regard it as possible that a moderate price deflation would be optimal for an economy. This position is one with which the liquidity trap theorists would never agree.

2.6 Conclusion

Theories of deflation have flourished during times when price deflation has occurred. The first treatments of deflation begin with the Swedish experience in the eighteenth century. A cluster of treatments follows during the suspension of specie payment in Great Britain from 1797 until the 1830s. Later, during the price deflations of the second half of the nineteenth century the subject is addressed again.[106] The discussion receives new impetus in Sweden and Great Britain after World War I when these countries pursued deflationary monetary policies. Then, in the Great Depression, a new anti-deflation climax is reached when Keynes made his case against deflation. After World War II price inflation becomes a main problem in the eyes of economic theorists who did not regard deflation as a subject worthy to study in depth. This has changed recently with the price deflation in Japan and with fears that a price deflation could occur in Europe and the U.S. And so papers and articles on the subject of deflation flourish once again.

These theories often were developed during deflationary periods and concerned the problems of individuals who suffered losses during those periods. In fact, deflation theories were sometimes inspired by interest groups that had suffered losses in the price deflations. And in some cases, theorists had links to those interest groups or personal interests in inflation. In fact, negative theories on deflation thrived when some people most urgently wanted monetary inflation. Naturally, over-indebted companies, banks and governments feared price deflation. Prior to

that a fully anticipated price deflation would have no adverse effect on economic activity. The public's expectations are "rational" if they "are formed using the appropriate data and objective probability distributions" (p. 175). The view that an expected deflation would be "neutral" to the economic progress is widely held today.

[105] See Bordo and Filardo (2004, p. 7); and (2005, p. 1).

[106] See Sect. 5.1.7.

the twentieth century some of the anti-deflation economists had links to interest groups and the economic establishment. In the twentieth century, the state emerged as the largest debtor in the economy and most professional economists have often been and are government employees or have some connection to the state. Moreover, the majority of monetary economists are employees of monetary authorities or central banks or banks that, naturally, fear price deflation. Also, many university professors dealing with monetary economics receive part of their income from research conducted on behalf of monetary authorities. The prevailing negative view on deflation can hardly surprise considering these economic interests.

One also finds a tendency that deflation was more positively viewed in the past than it is today.[107] Or in other words, the assessment of deflation by economists has become more negative, though it has slightly improved in recent years in the writings of the the Good-versus-Bad deflation theorists. One reason for this negativity is probably that until the twentieth century, price deflation caused by economic growth was common. This kind of deflation was widely appreciated and could be seen by everyone. Arguing that it would be harmful, would have been more difficult in this context. Yet, in our world of continuous price inflation, assessments of deflation have turned more negative.

Instead of ordering the theorists chronologically, one might also try to group modern theorists according to their deflation phobia. The most deflation phobic theorists, like Keynesian-inclined theorists, want to avoid every type of deflation and recommend positive price inflation rates. By recommending positive price inflation rates, they want to make sure that the price inflation rate does not come too close to zero. They see an asymmetry in the effects of price inflation and price deflation. Price deflation is regarded as worse than price inflation.

Then come the price stabilization theorists who recommend avoiding any type of price deflation as well. However, they are not so deflation phobic as the Keynesians[108] and argue for a price inflation rate of zero. They see both price inflation and price deflation as bad. There is no necessary asymmetry in their assessment of inflation and deflation.

Good-versus-Bad deflation theorists regard a price deflation caused by economic growth as good and other types as bad or even "ugly." A similar position is held by the productivity norm theorists. They allow for a negative price inflation rate, i.e. price deflation, if it is caused by economic growth. They recommend preventing price deflation if it is caused by increases in the demand for money. Productivity norm theorists from the fractional reserve free banking school do not fear monetary deflation if it occurs within their preferred system. They actually recommend monetary deflation when the demand for money falls.

The most deflation-friendly group consists of Austrian economists in the Misesian tradition. I have analyzed the individual deflation theories of Ludwig

[107] See also Bordo and Filardo (2005, p. 811).

[108] Those economists regard price stability as dangerous for monetary policy due to the liquidity trap problematic. They argue for a positive inflation rate. See Goodfriend (2000, p. 1007).

Table 2.1 Theories of deflation compared

	Fear price deflation caused by growth	Fear price deflation caused by an increase in the demand for money	Fear price deflation caused by credit contraction
Liquidity trap theorists (Keynes, Bernanke, Krugman)	Yes	Yes	Yes
Price level stabilization theorists (Fisher, Barro)	Yes	Yes	Yes
Good-versus-Bad deflation theorists (Borio, Filardo)	No	Yes	Yes
Productivity norm theorists, fractional reserve free bankers, monetary disequilibrium theorists (Hawtrey, Pigou, Selgin, Yeager)	No	Yes	Not within fractional reserve banking system
Mises	No	No	Yes (in some of his writings)
100 % reserve Austrians (Salerno, Hülsmann, Rothbard)	No	No	No

von Mises, Murray N. Rothbard, Friedrich A. von Hayek, Jesús Huerta de Soto, and Hans Sennholz elsewhere (Bagus 2003). They do not see difficulties in a price deflation caused by economic growth and an increased demand for money. However, in some circumstances they regard monetary deflation as harmful and want to prevent it when it comes to monetary reform (see Bagus 2003).

In this overview, I have not elaborated much on Austrian theories of deflation. Yet, in the following section, I will develop a theory of deflation with its causes and its consequences within an Austrian theoretical framework. As we will see, this Austrian theory of deflation significantly contrasts the theories of deflation just discussed in this chapter.

Table 2.1 ranks theories on price deflation according to their adversity towards price deflation.

Chapter 3
Causes of Deflation

3.1 Growth Deflation

3.1.1 Economic Growth and Prices

One possible cause of a price deflation is economic growth. A growth deflation is a price deflation that occurs due to a growing economy.[109] A growing economy is an economy where the amount of goods and services produced increases over time.[110] This growth, i.e. the production of additional goods and services, leads to money prices that are lower than they would have been, had those goods and services not been produced.

Theoretically, all additional goods and services might be exchanged in some form of barter.[111] Yet, producers tend to produce goods and services to buy money, the most marketable good. Then they are able to exchange the money against the goods and services they most urgently want in a quick and efficient way. In other words, producers do not produce goods and services to engage in barter or to use

[109] Concerning growth deflation, see, for instance, Salerno (2003, pp. 83–84), Hülsmann (2003a, pp. 51–52), or Thornton (2003, p. 6).

[110] This is a very rough definition. And it contains at least two caveats. First, from the subjective perspective of the individuals the quantity of production is not important. Rather it is important for them, that goods and services are produced that well satisfy their subjective wants. Second, there is no way to measure this material growth as one cannot add different physical objects. For example in a modern economy good X is produced in a higher quantity and only one good Y in a lower quantity. Then what is the economy's growth? And can it be stated at all, that there is growth? Nevertheless, it is not necessary to measure growth. And it is useful to speak of economic growth, when the majority of production of goods and services increases. The reason why this definition is useful, is that economic growth can lead to a general fall in prices, i.e., a price deflation and thus help us to explain this phenomenon.

[111] Anderson shows that the extension of barter or credit in a modern society is often underestimated [1917] 2000, pp. 173–178.

P. Bagus, *In Defense of Deflation*, Financial and Monetary Policy Studies 41,
DOI 10.1007/978-3-319-13428-4_3

these goods and services themselves. Rather, they produce in order to buy money for those situations in which it would be too expensive or even impossible to engage in barter.

In a growing economy, the marginal utility of goods and services produced for the producers will be lower than without the growth. Producers, increasing their production, are ready to accept lower money prices than without the growth of their production. In other words, their minimum selling price falls. Therefore, we face a situation, in which producers who have a falling marginal utility for their products, are willing to accept lower money prices than those prices would have been without the growth. However, the minimum selling price is rarely relevant for the market price when there is substantial production. Rather, the marginal consumer determines the price of the product. As production increases, new marginal consumers must be found in order to sell this additional production. These consumers will only buy the product at prices that tend to be lower than they were before. These price falls are anticipated by the producers. The producers plan to sell more, even though this might involve lower prices, intending to be more than compensated by the higher quantity, they sell. Thus, producers consciously aim at producing and selling more than their competitors at lower prices in order to increase profits.[112]

An increase in production might not only occur because established producers increase their production. New producers competing for a market share might also appear. All these producers of goods and services are competing with each other to buy money. And in a growing economy, potential money buyers possess and can offer more goods and services against money than they would have if the economy had not experienced growth. As the marginal utility of the goods produced tends to be very low for the producers, they will start outbidding each other in order to obtain money units. Producers are willing to offer more goods and services for a given sum of money units than they would have offered otherwise.[113] Or stated differently, they are willing to sell a given amount of goods or services for less money than they would have sold it for had the economy not experienced growth.[114] The exchange demand for money increases.[115] This leads to higher prices of money, i.e., money prices of goods and services become lower than they otherwise would have been. If there are no counteracting forces like an increase in the quantity of money working at the same time, the competition of producers to buy money will imply falling prices, i.e., a price deflation. Another possible

[112] See Selgin (1997, p. 31).

[113] On this point, see Salerno (2003, pp. 83–84).

[114] That does not imply that they earn less revenues than before, since they sell more goods at a lower price. Their revenues might increase, decrease, or stay the same.

[115] Rothbard distinguishes three parts constituting the demand for money: the exchange demand for money, i.e., the demand of sellers for money who want to buy all other goods with it; the reservation demand for money, i.e., the demand for money by those market participants who already hold money (everyone's post-income demand for money); and the demand for non-monetary uses of the money stuff. See Rothbard (2001, pp. 662, 665).

counteracting force might also be the increased use of compensatory devices or clearing houses that reduce the amount of money necessary to make exchanges.

It must be pointed out that not all prices will be influenced at the same time to the same amount or even in the same direction. Neither would all producers have to increase production for a price deflation to result. Were only a few producers to increase their production, the prices of other producers would still be influenced. In cases where the production of a particular product increases and the price of this product falls, this price fall may mean a reduction in costs for other enterprises that use this product. As their costs fall, the rate of profit in those lines of production using this product increases. Therefore, entrepreneurs will increase production in those lines of production to take advantage of the higher rate of profit in those lines. As production increases in those lines, prices of their products will be lower than without this increase. However, production in other lines of production must be restricted, of course, to make this increase possible. As the output of those lines of production is restricted, prices will be higher there than without that restriction. In this way the initial increase of production spreads through the economy over time and changes relative prices.

3.1.2 The Reasons for Economic Growth

After stating the effect of economic growth on prices, one has to explain why economic growth occurs. How is it possible that the amount of goods and services produced increases? The only ultimate cause that makes economic growth possible are human beings. The ingenuity and creativity of each entrepreneur in creating profit opportunities and moving toward those opportunities with his very being, makes the production of new and more goods possible. In short, the entrepreneurial function is the origin of economic growth. All barriers to it inhibit economic growth, and consequently, the removal of such barriers animate economic growth. There are three main ways in which the entrepreneurial function may cause economic growth: (1) innovations; (2) an increase in the division of labor or an increase in population; and (3) savings and capital accumulation.[116] I will discuss all three of these, beginning with the role of innovations.

[116] Mises (1998, pp. 512–513) names some other reasons. The reductions of institutional disturbances (crime, wars, sabotage) and the improvement of natural conditions also allow for growth. However, these reasons are either one-time effects or are necessarily limited. Once all crimes and wars would end, there would be no further increase in production. Similarly, at some point there might be a limit for the improvement of natural climate that might spur production. In contrast, there is virtually no limit for growth caused by capital accumulation, innovations and increases in the division of labor (caused by population growth).

3.1.2.1 Innovations

One reason for an increase in the production of goods and services, i.e., a growing economy, is the implementation of innovations. An innovation is a new method, object, or technique made possible by the innate creativity of the acting individual. In the use of an innovation, producers engage in new production processes. An example of such an innovation might be one which allows the production process to be shortened.

Often, some form of savings is necessary to provide for the research required for innovation. Savings may consist of providing capital to engage in the research, like the building of a laboratory and the funding of scientists. However, savings are not always necessary to develop innovation. For instance, an entrepreneur might instantaneously come up with an idea that serves to make production more efficient.

In certain cases, the use of innovations requires an increase in net savings. Other innovations can be employed with the same amount of savings, and some do not require any new savings at all. It is important to point out, that in the last case, savings are not a necessary condition to implement the new production process. Resources are only rearranged in a way that allows for higher production in the same or shorter amount of time. An example would be that of an entrepreneur who only rearranges the workers, or other factors of production he uses, leading to the same (or increased) production in a shorter time period than without the innovation. In this case, he does not need any new net savings.

Moreover, some innovations may be implemented with a constant amount of savings, i.e., as when the consumption-savings ratio of income remains constant. In other words, these innovations need savings, i.e., an abstention of consumption, for their implementation but no net increase in savings. For instance, an innovation might be financed with retained cash-flow. Or that is to say, entrepreneurs can incorporate new technology via amortization funds. Thus, a new fall in time preference rates or increased net savings are not a necessary condition for economic growth. For instance, it may happen, that an existing research laboratory, financed out of existing operations and not out of an increase in net savings, develops an innovation. This laboratory builds a machine that uses the same quantity and quality of materials as the older machines but produces more physical products in a given period of time. Then production can be increased without making an increase of net savings necessary. As the old machines wear out, they are substituted by new ones, financed out of the very gross savings that would have bought the old machines, if the invention had not been made. Now the newly-developed machines are being used instead of purchasing the old machines, increasing physical output without lengthening the structure of production. Recall that the laboratory was part of the existing structure of production.

Yet, many innovations, especially new technologies, require an increase in the savings-consumption ratio for their implementation. In reality, many technologies are not used due to a lack of savings. As Mises points out, in the developing countries, the highly efficient production techniques that are in use in the Western world cannot be employed due to a lack of savings and capital accumulation.[117] Hence, a lack of savings poses often a narrower limit on production than technological knowledge.

A very important example of innovations that with or without requiring additional savings, lead to an increase in production, are those innovations allowing for a more productive use of natural resources.[118] Technological innovation might indeed multiply the types of usable resources. With the increase in knowledge in the use of natural resources, production increases. For instance, until it became known that petroleum could be used to run a motor, petroleum was not in such great demand as it is now. Furthermore, with the invention of the motor, useful resources for mankind increased.

In sum, innovation is one cause of an increase in production.[119]

3.1.2.2 Increase in the Division of Labor

A second reason for the growth in an economy is an increase in the division of labor, as the division of labor makes production more productive.

There are several reasons for the division of labor to increase. The necessary condition for division of labor to occur is that people become aware of its advantages and engage in specialization.[120] The most important reason for subsequent increases in the division of labor is capital accumulation which makes an increase in the division of labor possible, through the use of new tools, machinery, and factories.

In addition, restrictions and barriers on the division of labor might be abolished, thereby enabling a higher division of labor. Obvious barriers are usually international trade barriers and regulation of industries and professions. However, restrictions on the division of labor can also consist of transportation or transaction costs. For instance, the wide-spread use of the Internet has lowered traditional transportation costs and transaction costs quite considerably, thereby allowing for a higher division of labor. Thus an innovation can open new ways for cooperation.

[117] See Mises (1998, pp. 492–494).

[118] As George Reisman points out, there is a limitless potential of natural resources (1999, pp. 63–66) which can be created by progressive technologies incorporated in new capital goods.

[119] Of course, not all innovations lead to an increase in production; it may well lead to the substitution of old products by new products that were not possible without the innovation. In most cases innovation will lead to new products that now compete with the old ones. This competition also leads to a tendency of prices to decrease. People spend more money on the new high quality products, and have less money to spend on the old products.

[120] Beside its higher productivity, there is another reason for the division of labor which has its origin in different psychological utilities or disadvantages of different types of labor. One person might just hate to hunt while another person finds berry collecting very boring. In this case, both can profit from a division of labor.

However, innovations may not only lower transaction costs but may also engender other new ideas and products, creating additional possibilities for cooperation.

Another important reason for an increase in the division of labor is population growth. Population growth allows for a more sophisticated and intricate division of labor or knowledge. Specifically, more human beings are available to create and divide the knowledge necessary to engage in production and coordinate society. Moreover, population growth itself is an independent reason for economic growth, as the new population begins producing goods, services, and innovations.[121] As the population keeps increasing, the division of knowledge can increase further as does production. This process of a continual self-reinforcing expansion of population and knowledge has been coined by Jesús Huerta de Soto as a "Social Big Bang."[122]

3.1.2.3 Increase in Net Savings

The final reason for economic growth is an increase in net savings.[123] Why does an increase in savings lead to an increase in the production of goods and services? When there are savings, consumption must be restricted. Individuals are only willing to restrict consumption, if they are able to obtain a higher value in the future for the resources currently at their disposal. One saves in order to consume more in the future. This is implied in the universal concept of time preference which states that we want to attain our ends rather sooner than later.[124] It is time that separates us from our ends, which means that if we save time reaching one end, we dispose of additional time to attain other ends. This implies that a producer attempts to produce a given amount at given monetary costs in the shortest time possible.

Savings can increase, leading to an increase in investments in several ways. An individual can just refrain from consumption and save the money, leaving more consumer goods available for investments. To state it differently, these consumer goods can be used to sustain workers in the processes of production until other consumer goods are finished being produced.[125] Another way of increasing savings is changing one's demand. An individual demands fewer consumer goods in order

[121] Concerning population growth and growth, see Kuznets (1965, p. 124).

[122] See Huerta de Soto (2001, p. 82), ft. 54.

[123] It is not necessary that time preference rates decrease to make a higher net saving in real terms possible. Time preference manifests itself in the ratio of consumption to savings. If the economy is on a path of growth, regardless of the cause, be it innovations, a past decrease in time preference rate, population growth, etc., then real output grows as well. If social time preference rate remains constant, net savings in real terms will increase, making a further lengthening of the structure of production possible. This, in turn, will again lead to a higher output, making higher net savings possible, and so on.

[124] Concerning the concept of time preference, see Huerta de Soto (2006a, pp. 270–272) or Mises (1998, pp. 480–485).

[125] For the subsistence fund theory see, for instance, the Austrian economist Richard von Strigl (1934).

to invest in higher stages of production. Instead of consumer goods, the individual demands factors of production for the investment project. In this case, factors of production will be directed from the production of consumer goods to investment in the higher stages of production.

Thus, an increase in net savings implies an increase in possible net investments. Those processes which are known to be the shortest, most productive in terms of value, and least risky, will be used first. As a result, an increase in investments will be used for several types of processes. The investment funds can be used to finance projects that seemed too risky without additional savings. Or they can be used to finance additional projects of the same length as existing ones, thus widening the structure of production. Or they finance projects that take a longer time to complete than existing ones, thereby lengthening the structure of production. Therefore, an increase in savings and investment makes the production processes more capital intensive.[126]

Due to time preference these processes are not only more time consuming, but they are also, or at least are expected to be, more productive (in the sense of producing more goods than before or producing new goods not otherwise possible without prolonging the production process).[127] This is so, because if the more roundabout processes were not more productive than the shorter production processes, due to time preference, the shorter processes would be preferred. Thus, by the additional savings and investments, the structure of production of the economy has become more capital intensive and the production in real terms has increased.[128]

For an increase in net savings or for positive net investments it is not necessary for the time preference rate to fall continuously.[129] When the economy is growing, be it by a fall in the time preference rate and more net savings or be it by an increase in the division of labor or by innovation, then more goods or goods of higher quality are produced. More goods or higher quality goods will be available to spend on consumption or investments. When the ratio between goods spent for consumption and investments remains the same, this is a deliberate entrepreneurial decision to invest more. Then there will be an increase in net investment allowing for a lengthening of the structure of production and further economic growth.[130]

---

[126] See Rothbard (2001, pp. 486–491) concerning capital accumulation and the length of the structure of production.

[127] It is conceivable that by capital accumulation only qualitatively better goods are produced instead of more goods. In this case there can also be price deflation. The better goods substitute for the goods of lesser quality whose prices fall. This case might also occur with the other causes of growth.

[128] Note that these longer production processes might require homesteading and use of new natural resources. That means that an increase in natural resources in itself is not a reason for growth. Rather, a cause of economic growth is an increase in savings that makes more of the same natural resources and hitherto unused natural resources available.

[129] Salerno claims this (2001); He seems to imply that time preference directly determines the absolute amount of savings instead of the proportion between consumption and investment.

[130] Roger Garrison (2001, p. 55) calls this phenomenon "secular growth".

3.1.3 *Interrelation Between the Causes for Economic Growth*

I have now explained the potential causes of a growth deflation. It should be added, that the aforementioned three reasons for economic growth are interrelated and influence each other. Higher savings and capital accumulation allow for the implementation of innovations. Large scale production is made possible by capital accumulation and makes increases in the division of labor and the implementation of sophisticated tools and machinery possible.[131] Savings allow for better education and more highly qualified workers,[132] also enabling a more sophisticated division of labor or knowledge. As the division of knowledge increases and grows more sophisticated, it is more likely that the number of innovations also increases. Therefore, these three processes often reinforce and rely upon each other.

As these effects build upon each other, the process of economic growth also entails an accumulative effect. Another factor adding to this accumulative effect is the spread of innovation. When there is economic growth the prices of certain factors of production tend to fall, spurring production again. For instance, due to its increased production, the price of microchips has continuously fallen over the past decades. Due to the fall in the prices of microchips, microchips have become employed in both existing and new production processes. The innovation spreads into additional lines of production. Without new net savings, the capital stock becomes even more efficient. This extended use of microchips not only provides the basis for new innovations and a higher division of knowledge, but it also has another effect. As production in those lines involving microchips become more efficient, the prices of their particular products fall. Thus, the lower prices of these particular products enables the use of these factors in other lines of production including the production of microchips. As a result, production in these other lines becomes more efficient, leading to lower pricing. This allows for wider use, more efficient production, etc. Thus, economic growth is a cumulative and reinforcing process.

3.2 Cash Building Deflation

After discussing growth deflation and its possible causes, I will now turn to another kind of price deflation, namely cash building deflation. I will discuss the possible reasons for a cash building deflation and point to its consequences for the structure of production.

[131] See Reisman (1999, pp. 127, 141).

[132] This is sometimes called an increase in human capital.

3.2.1 Cash Building and Prices

In a cash building deflation the demand for money increases. Any increase in the demand for money leads to a higher purchasing power of money than would have been otherwise. Therefore, in the absence of counteracting effects on the purchasing power of money, an increased demand for money causes price deflation. I will now analyze the reasons and effects for changes in the demand for money. It should be made clear from the outset that when we consider the demand for money we will only look at the components and effects originating on the monetary side and not on the goods side. A change in the demand for money originating from the goods side is caused by a change in the production of goods. It is a different type of real demand for money. Indeed, an increase in production can also lead to price deflation, as was discussed in the previous section.

3.2.2 Types of Money Demand

The demand for money stuff can be divided into industrial demand, the demand for a medium of exchange,[133] the demand for storage of wealth, and speculative demand.[134] These subjective reasons can not be observed by an outsider. However, the motive can be revealed later. For instance, if someone increases his money stuff demand and later uses the actual money stuff to build an item, the demand for money manifests itself as an industrial demand for money at the moment this can be observed. Yet, if someone increases his cash balance, another person cannot discern motive by this action alone, i.e., whether this was caused by an increase in the exchange demand, in the industrial demand, in the wealth storage demand, or an increase in the speculative demand. In the following section, I will discuss the four reasons for the demand of money stuff.

3.2.2.1 Industrial Demand for Money

Individuals who demand money stuff for industrial purposes either want the money stuff for production purposes or wish to use the money stuff in a form different than the standardized form used for exchange (gold coin, bank note in a fiat standard, etc.). In the case of a fiat paper money the industrial demand is normally not

[133] A medium of exchange is a good that is demanded in order to exchange it again for other consumer or producer goods.

[134] There is also a small demand for money as a consumer good. A person who puts a note or coin in a frame and gains satisfaction from looking at or touching this particular monetary unit, demands this unit as a consumer good. However, this kind of money demand is normally very small. Therefore, I will not analyze it in more detail.

relevant.[135] In the case of a commodity money the industrial demand can be important and indeed lead to a price deflation or an increase in the purchasing power of money. For example, in an economy that uses gold as money, people's subjective valuations might change in a way that they value gold jewelry higher in relation to other goods than before. Or they may want to use it for a new medical treatment. As a consequence, the demand for the money stuff increases. Thereby, the price of the money stuff and the purchasing power of money will be higher than without this increase in the industrial demand of gold. We will not analyze this cause of a price deflation further, as today in a world of fiat paper monies, this cause of price deflation is only a very remote possibility.

However, in a hyperinflation, when money is abandoned as a medium of exchange, the industrial demand for paper money actually can become important and may become the main reason for even demanding the money at all. For instance, the money stuff used during the period of hyperinflation in Germany in 1923, paper money, was burned in ovens and used to heat houses and apartments. At any rate, these cases are rare, and the industrial demand for money is usually only a very small part of the money demand. It is difficult to see how an increase in the industrial demand for money would have a considerable influence on the purchasing power of money. There is no particular reason why the majority of a particular population might suddenly value industrial money stuff significantly more highly than it did before.

3.2.2.2 Exchange Demand for Money

The second component of the demand for money is the demand for money as a medium of exchange. Basically, one reason exists why any media of exchange including money, which by definition is any *commonly* accepted media of exchange, are even used at all: Media of exchange facilitate exchange.

It should be noted, that these exchanges can also be intertemporal. Thus, money can be used to settle debt obligations. In order to pay the debt, when it becomes due, the debtor will demand a nominal sum of money.

---

[135] In a fiat monetary system with token coins, it is possible that these token coins attain a higher industrial value than their nominal value due to the inflation of the currency. For instance, in recent years in the U.S., the one penny coin's industrial value became higher than its nominal face value. Consequently, these coins, made of 95 % copper, disappeared from circulation, as predicted by Gresham's law. Since 1982, the penny has been made of 2.5 % copper and 97.5 % zinc. In this case, the industrial demand for the pre-1982 token coins became relevant. See Alec Nevalainen (2007). Coinflation.com. http://www.coinflation.com/ (accessed Oct. 14, 2007).

The Origin of Money

I will now analyze a well-known case of an increase in the demand for money as a medium of exchange. This case occurs when a commodity emerges as money, i.e., as a general accepted medium of exchange. Carl Menger (1871) was the first to describe this process in full detail. In a barter economy some entrepreneurs become aware that some commodities are exchanged more often than other commodities.[136] These commodities are more marketable than others. Therefore, they demand those commodities, not to consume them or use them in a production process, but rather to sell them against things they need. An exchange demand for the commodity emerges. With the additional exchange demand for the commodity, the price of the commodity will be higher than without the exchange demand. Thus, there is a likely increase in the purchasing power of the commodity. That means that the origin of money is closely linked with a price deflation. Or in other words, prices in terms of the commodity tend to be lower.

As the first entrepreneurs begin using the medium of exchange successfully, its price begins to increase even more. Other entrepreneurs notice the success of those who first use the commodity as a medium of exchange. As a consequence, they will imitate this first wave of successful entrepreneurs. The demand for the money-to-be increases further, and prices in terms of the medium of exchange tend to fall. Thus, the commodity becomes even more attractive as a medium of exchange because more people use it and its price continues to increase.

Curiously, those favoring a modern economy based on the division of labor made possible by money, yet wishing to prevent price deflation because they see it as dangerous, find themselves in an almost self-contradictory position. This is so, because a situation in which money never experiences price deflation is next to impossible. Desiring such a scenario is unrealistic. The demand for the money stuff increases as the commodity demand will be accompanied by a demand to use it as a medium of exchange. Moreover, the possibility for the division of labor increases and spurs economic growth. Thus, money is "born" in a process that very likely involves price deflation. This price deflation indicates to the entrepreneur that it is a good medium of exchange and speeds up the triumph of a medium of exchange as money. Very likely, media of exchange that experience no price deflation will lose in the competitive process against those which do.

[136] One characteristic necessary for a commodity to be exchanged more often and with a low spread between the bid and ask price, is its capacity to serve as a suitable storage of wealth. Then a producer can sell his goods against this commodity, store this commodity, and when he is in need of something later, use it at a good price as a medium of exchange. Thus, the exchange demand and the demand as a storage of wealth are intimately related.

Uncertainty and Cash Balances

I have explained that one demand for money is for the purpose of exchange. But why is money held in one's cash balance? Why do people not just lend their money out until the moment they need it for an exchange? The motive for holding a reserve of money is uncertainty.[137] Money is an institution that serves to reduce the uncertainty of the future, in that money is the generally accepted medium of exchange. Thus, it can be used to buy virtually any marketable good or service: One can use money to exchange it against the vast majority of goods, services, and assets that are offered in the market place. Moreover, the spread between the bid and ask price for money is very small even for large quantities, which implies that it can be bought and sold without incurring great losses. Therefore, individuals often choose to hold money in reserve. With money in their cash balances, they can later buy the goods, services, and assets of which they are currently not aware. Or, perhaps they are aware of these goods, services, or assets, but uncertain of whether they will require them for future use.

If there were no uncertainty and all future purchases in quantity, quality, date, and place were known, there would be no need to hold a cash balance.[138] The cash balance of a person is the reserve of money that she holds at any point in time.[139] One could loan the money out until the exact date when it would be needed, assuming that it would be possible to find someone who is in need of this money until this date. But as economic agents do not know of all the purchases that they may wish to make in the future, they prefer to hold some money in their cash balances in order to be able to respond immediately to unexpected changes. Thus, they are able to offer money in exchange for a good or service that they may later want or need.[140]

Obviously, individuals are uncertain about their own future financial needs. This fact is grounded in human action itself. The inherent creative character of the category of action makes the future uncertain. An individual does not know what kind of means and ends he will discover. His value scale is constantly changing. As a consequence, some ends become more important to him, as others fall in their relative importance. In those cases it is better to have some money at hand. Profit opportunities might arise unexpectedly. Then money is needed to exploit them. For instance, when new products appear on the market, a sufficient cash balance is useful for buying those new products. Prices also might change unexpectedly. Goods that the individual did not expect to rise in price, might rise in price. When the individual still wants to buy those at a higher price, a sufficient cash

---

[137] See Mises (1998, pp. 399–400). As Mises has pointed out, the cash holdings do not have to consist only in money proper. They can also consist in money substitutes that are accepted as if they would be money proper (1924, p. 113).

[138] See Mises (1998, p. 414).

[139] See Rothbard (2001, p. 174).

[140] See Rothbard (2001, p. 228). Also Mises (1998, pp. 399–400).

balance is needed. Moreover, some specific prices might fall unexpectedly, and the individual may want to buy a product he did not plan to buy, otherwise. Likewise, a sufficient cash balance is needed for this unexpected profit opportunity as well.

When individuals regard their circumstances as becoming more uncertain, they may choose to maintain a higher balance of cash. For instance, when people arrive at a place that they do not know well, their uncertainty increases. This is often the case in moving to or vacationing in an unfamiliar area. Here these individuals have less knowledge of the available means, ends, and profit opportunities that might occur. As they become familiar with their surroundings, they may reduce their cash reserves.

Another reason to hold a cash balance is the possible occurrence of emergencies. An illness or accident makes payment for operations, medicine, or important tools lost in an accident necessary. Thus, individuals often hold cash balances for cases of emergency, and when they expect the probability of such emergencies to rise, they may increase their cash balances even further.

What is true for individuals is also true for companies. Companies holding a comfortable cash balance enjoy an advantage vis-a-vis their competitors. Especially, in times of recession or any unexpected fall in demand they do not have to fire sale their assets. Furthermore, they can afford unexpected expenditures.

Level of Cash Balances and Uncertainty

As we have seen, an individual may wish to hold a certain cash balance for several reasons. But how high will levels of an individual's cash holdings actually rise? This question must be answered with recourse to subjective valuations. If the individual considers the marginal utility of an increased cash balance to be higher than the marginal utility of a good, or service he owns, he will sell this good, or service in order to buy the sum of money. And if the marginal utility of a good or service is dearer to him than the marginal utility of holding the corresponding sum of money in his cash balance, then he will buy this good or service and sell the money. An individual forgoes consumption and the buying of factors of production when he holds a cash balance. The individual will always add or subtract from his cash balance until he has found the cash balance that he in his particular situation and circumstances regards as appropriate and optimal.

It is important to note that when individuals demand cash balances, they demand a nominal sum of monetary units in consideration of their purchasing power.[141] The exchange services of a monetary unit depend upon the amount of goods and services it can buy. If an individual wants to be able to make more purchases in the

[141] See Rothbard (2001, p. 680). Also see Mises: "The services money renders are conditioned by the height of its purchasing power. Nobody wants to have in his cash holding a definite number of pieces of money or a definite weight of money; he wants to keep a cash holding of a definite amount of purchasing power." (1998, p. 418)

future for cases of emergency, he wants an increase in real cash balances, his stored purchasing power. Increasing his cash balance nominally is not helpful if this does not allow him to make more purchases in cases of either emergency or profit opportunities.

3.2.2.3 Wealth Storage Demand for Money

A motive for holding money which is slightly different than uncertainty is the motive to store wealth, the third component of money demand. Here it is not the uncertainty about future money needs that induces the money demand but the convenience of storing wealth in cash. Indeed, wealth can be stored easily in money. Money can be directly exchanged when necessary. It can be sold instantaneously at a good price in great quantities. In other words, money is the most liquid good. For every good there is a spread between the bid and ask price on the market. When higher quantities of a good are sold, this spread tends to increase. The more liquid a particular good is, the slower the increase of the spread. The advantage of money is that this spread increases very slowly as higher quantities of money are exchanged. This is so, because the marginal utility of money diminishes extremely slowly.[142] Money's liquidity makes it very suitable for storing wealth.[143]

3.2.2.4 Speculative Demand for Money

The fourth component of the demand for the money stuff is speculative demand.[144] As there can be speculation for any good, there can also be speculative demand for money.[145] In this case, money is demanded with the intention to resell it later at a higher price. So the subjective reason for this demand is not industrial use, uncertainty, or wealth storage, but rather the expectation that money could be sold for a higher price in the future, which thereby guarantees a greater command of non-money assets in the future.[146] This future price must be sufficiently high to justify the holding of the money in the mean time due to the praxeological category of time preference. If the purchasing power of money does not rise quickly enough,

[142] See Rallo (2005).

[143] Before a money debt becomes due, the debtor normally begins to accumulate the amount of debt. He accumulates that amount normally in money as it is a good storage of wealth. It should be noted, that this demand for money on the part of the debtor is a demand to store a nominal sum of money until it becomes due. Of course, the time between the beginning of the storage of that sum and the payment of the debt can be very short.

[144] See Mises (1998, p. 423).

[145] In an economy of several media of exchange the speculative demand can be considerable. For instance, in our fiat paper world the speculative demand for foreign exchange is far higher than the exchange demand.

[146] See Hutt (1956, p. 198).

other investments could be more profitable and yield a higher profit. Logically, the speculative demand for money rises when the purchasing power of money is expected to rise and it falls when the purchasing power of money is expected to fall.

The amount of money speculation depends upon the money standard. This amount is relatively small in the case of a 100 % reserve commodity money. Commodity money production, such as gold production, has historically been relatively stable. As economic growth has been relatively stable as well, no great increases in the purchasing power of money can be expected. An exception might be in the case of war when the demand for money surges. In any case, the role of money speculation remains relatively small.

In a commodity money standard with a fractional reserve banking system, the amount of speculation is greater than it would be in a 100 % reserve commodity system. This is so, because to a certain extent, the fractional reserve banks can expand the money supply via credit expansion. These credits can also be contracted again, giving rise to a higher volatility of prices, and thereby making speculation more profitable.

Speculation is the highest in a fiat money system where money and money substitutes can be produced at negligible costs. As fast as the money supply can expand, it can also contract.[147] The money supply often depends on the whims of politicians. Thus, the potential for fluctuations of the purchasing power of money in a fiat money system is much higher than in a system in which commodity money is standard. Therefore, the potential gains for money speculation in an economy using a fiat money standard are also much higher than potential gains would be in an economy with a commodity money standard. Thus, money speculation attains an important role in a system with a fiat money standard.

3.2.3 Increased Demand for Cash Balances

In this section, I will discuss in more detail the reasons for an increase in the demand for cash balances, which is sometimes called "hoarding." In particular, I will analyze the reasons for increases in uncertainty as well as for the speculative demand for money. Furthermore, the effect of cash building on the structure of production is examined.

3.2.3.1 The Term "Hoarding"

Whether it be to prepare for a more uncertain future, to participate in monetary speculation, or to increase monetary wealth storage, the desire to hold a higher real cash balance implies a refraining from consumption or investment in production

[147] We will discuss the process of credit contraction at length in Sect. 3.3.

facilities. Three kinds of cash building derive from these purposes. The first can be called uncertainty cash building, the second speculative cash building, and the third qualitative cash building. From the outside they cannot be distinguished. Accordingly, they are sometimes indistinguishably named by a single term: hoarding. This term is problematic. First, distinguishing between "hoarded" money and "circulating" money is impossible. Every monetary unit, except those that have been voluntarily or involuntarily given up,[148] form part of a cash balance. One cannot use money without holding a certain amount of it. All monetary units (with the exception of lost ones) are in some pocket or cash account and move in an exchange from one cash balance to the next, without ever "circulating" or being without an owner.

Second, the term "hoarding" seems to imply some idleness. However, this is not true. Money is never idle (except maybe the money on the floor of the ocean).[149] It performs an important service for the person holding it in her cash balance.[150] In cases of uncertainty or where storage is a motive, money serves as a security. This is a service valued by its holder, otherwise the person would not hold money as her cash balance. Money held in a cash balance allows an individual to be prepared for an uncertain future, i.e., for emergencies, unexpected price changes, the emergence of new products, unique opportunities, and changes in one's own value scale, etc. In this sense, the money provides the service of security. Hoarding may be also seen as a kind of protest of consumers against a structure of production that is not directed to their needs.[151] When after an artificial boom the structure of production is distorted and produces capital and consumer goods that people do not want, they react with hoarding. The hoarding induces an adjustment of the structure of production.

In the case of speculative demand, a cash balance is maintained not for use in an unexpected situation, but rather to make a real profit by selling the money unit at a price higher than for which it was bought in the first place. Therefore, the money is

[148] Just think of a sunken Spanish galleon filled with gold bullion, or consider some fountain in which individuals throw coins to enjoy luck in the future.

[149] See Rothbard (2001, p. 666); William H. Hutt emphasizes that the holding of monetary units is a service for the money holder: "The notion of *idle* money seems to have risen out of the age-old fallacy that money performs its services by circulating, whereas in reality its services, which are performed simply by its being possessed and *ready for circulation*, cease for the one holder the moment the ownership is transferred to another because the purpose of having invested in it has ceased for the transferor and is about to begin for the transferee" (1977, p. 258). The service that money provides is essential: Money simply is the best protection against uncertainty. See Hoppe (2009).

[150] See Hülsmann (2003a, p. 49).

[151] Rallo (2012).

not idle, but rather in the process of generating an entrepreneurial profit for its owner. In other words, it is an investment. The investment is not in production facilities but in the money itself.[152] The expected profit is valued by the money holder, otherwise the person would not hold the money as her cash balance. William H. Hutt's point is relevant here:

> Money so conceived is as productive as all other assets, and *productive in exactly the same sense*... money assets offer prospective yields just as the rest of the assets possessed by individuals, firms, banks or governments. As objects of investment, they are chosen for the same reason that other objects are chosen. Thus, if their marginal prospective yield at any time is below that of other assets, it will pay to part with some of them, and if it is above, it will pay to acquire money assets up to the point at which the marginal prospective yield has fallen to the rate of interest. [Italics in the original] (1956, p. 197)

When prices are expected to fall investment in money tends to rise. Investment in money is, of course, also an economic activity. Thus, economic activity does not decrease when investment in money rises, as prices are expected to fall. Economic activity is just of a different form, in line with consumer preferences. It would arbitrary to say that this type of economic activity would be bad and harmful, but investment in production facilities would be better. In any case, it speeds up the adjustment to the expected change in prices. Moreover, in a commodity standard more resources will be shifted toward the production of the money stuff inducing economic activity, for instance, in the mining sector.

But is investment in money equivalent to saving? We have to distinguish between savings which is a stock variable represented by cash holdings and saving which is the part of income not consumed in a given period. Investments in money, i.e. cash holdings, are savings. But do they represent an increase in saving? The answer depends upon where the resources used to invest in money stem from. If the resources were formerly used for consumption purposes, this abstention from consumption is additional saving. The resources become now available for production projects. If, in contrast, the resources were formerly used in production projects, the disinvestment in them is not equivalent to an increase in saving. Rather it is a reflection of a higher time preference and the desire for a shorter structure of production.

I will now turn to the reasons for and results of an increase in the demand for money. The results of and reasons for an increase in the speculation demand for money, for qualitative cash building and for a desire of a higher real cash balance due to uncertainty motives will be discussed in further detail. They have in common their regard by an outsider, who does not know the motives of these actions, as intentions of cash building. Thus, I define cash building deflation as an increase in the purchasing power of money caused by efforts of economic agents to increase their cash holdings.

---

[152] Rothbard distinguishes the post-income use of money as threefold: money use for consumption, investments, and adding to one's cash balance (2001, pp. 664–665). As adding to one's cash balance should also be regarded as an investment it would be more precise to say that one can use money for consumption, investment in real factors of production, or investments in money.

3.2.3.2 Uncertainty Cash Building

Reasons for Uncertainty Cash Building

When the future is expected to become more uncertain, people try to increase their real cash balances. An exception is the case in which the uncertainty of the future of a fiat monetary system itself increases. When the future of a fiat money system becomes more uncertain and people try to reduce their cash balance, a scenario in which fiat money is rejected may develop. However, aside from these doubts concerning the future of the monetary system itself, an increase in uncertainty leads to an increased demand for cash balances.

We will now turn to the specific reasons, why perception of uncertainty might increase. In principle, as we deal with subjective feelings, anything could induce such a perception. However, in reality, certain events are more likely than others to induce an increase in uncertainty. As Joseph Salerno points out, "[c]ash building usually stems from a more pessimistic or uncertain attitude toward the future caused possibly by the onset of a recession, a natural disaster or the imminent prospect of war" (2003, p. 85). Other causes for a more pessimistic or uncertain attitude toward the future include high unemployment rates or asset price crashes.[153] This more pessimistic or uncertain attitude, might also be caused by an expected increase in internal political violence and a failing confidence in banks. In the following sections, I will analyze these possible causes of increase uncertainty about the future.

Business Cycle Recession

In the onset of a recession people often become more pessimistic. In a fiat money system, this pessimism might lead to doubts concerning the future of the monetary system, as well. This can lead to a reduced demand for money or an abandonment of money. If, however, no concerns about future of the monetary system arise, for example in an economy using a commodity standard, the demand for money to hold as a cash balance increases. This is so, because in a short recession, or even a longer one, individuals may be unemployed or experience reduction in their income, etc. They might even expect social unrest due to the recession. As a result of this, political changes and policies might occur which change such a situation considerably. In order to be prepared for theses uncertainties it seems to be wise to

[153] Mark Thornton writes: "This type of *cash-building deflation* is a natural reaction to the outbreak of war, civil war, or natural disaster. It also occurs with the onset of recessions, higher unemployment rates, stock market crashes, or even with widespread speculation that prices will fall in the near future" (2003, pp. 6–7). The last reason Thornton names is the speculative demand for money which we will discuss later. Speculative demand is not necessarily linked to a more pessimistic outlook of the future.

increase the cash balance and thereby liquidity,[154] be it by refraining from consumption or by withdrawing investments.[155] In the latter case, some malinvestments incurred during the prior boom might be liquidated in order to add to one's cash balance. Alternatively, people may simple increase their cash balances because the supply of goods that the distorted structure of production brings forward does not correspond to people's preferences. This speeds up the recovery.[156]

Prospect of War

In the prospect of war—be it foreign or civil war—people are likely to increase their cash balances as well.[157] A war might destroy their holdings, assets, or leave them with out employment. They might become injured and killed, or so may family members and friends. Moreover, property rights become very insecure when a foreign invasion looms. Prices are likely to oscillate strongly. In these instances, people increase their real cash balances. Individuals might also lose confidence in money substitutes and increase their demand for money proper.[158] Fiduciary media may be sold to buy foreign media of exchange or gold. For example, in the wake of

---

[154] This motive of an increase in liquidity in a recession is especially important for businesses. As George Reisman has pointed out, the increased demand for cash balances "operates to make any given quantity of money stand in a higher ratio to the value of other assets and to spending for goods and labor. It thus operates to increase the degree of liquidity in the economic system and finally to put an end to the desire further to increase cash holding. To say the same thing in somewhat different words, it operates to increase the so-called quick ratios of corporations and all other businesses and to place them and everyone else in a financially stronger position, in which their cash reserves stand in a higher ratio to their current liabilities, and in which, therefore, the general state of financial solvency is better assured" (1999, p. 693).

[155] Once the economy is in a recession, the demand for money is likely to increase even further. As Rothbard states: "Another common secondary feature of depression is an increase in the demand for money. This 'scramble for liquidity' is the result of several factors: (1) people expect falling prices, due to the depression and deflation, and will therefore hold more money and spend less on goods, awaiting the price fall [analytically this is an increase in the speculative demand for money]; (2) borrowers will try to pay off their debts, now being called by banks and business creditors, by liquidating other assets in exchange for money; (3) the rash of business losses, and bankruptcies makes businessmen cautious about investing until the liquidation process is over" (2000, p. 15). These causes are, however, not directly related to a more pessimistic attitude, but rather to the dynamics of the recessionary process itself.

[156] Austrian economists such as Jesús Huerta de Soto, Murray Rothbard, and Guido Hülsmann have argued that boom bust cycles, and thus also recessions, are ultimately caused by a government privilege given to bankers: the privilege of maintaining fractional reserves. Thus, for these economists, this increase in the demand for money is ultimately caused by a government intervention.

[157] There is a case when in the prospect of war, people might actually reduce their cash balances. If people expect to die in the war soon, for example in an atomic war or a hopeless siege, then they will reduce cash balances and a price inflation will follow.

[158] Money proper, or money in the narrow sense, is commodity money, credit money, and fiat money when they are used as media of exchange. Money substitutes are claims to money proper

the Austro–Hungarian ultimatum to Serbia in 1914, the demand for gold skyrocketed.[159] Gold may also be taken out of the country to be kept in safety.

The monetary units added to the cash balances are likely to stem from disinvestment in capital goods instead of from the reduction of consumption. In times of war, people attempt to secure provision of consumer goods first. Thus, the structure of production is flattened. Another advantage of increasing cash balances via disinvestment in capital goods is that when the capital goods are consumed they cannot be destroyed by war anymore.

Prospect of Internal Political Violence

In the case of the prospect of war, external political violence is feared. However, expectations concerning future internal political violence can also become more pessimistic as perceived uncertainty increases. People might expect social unrest, violations of property rights, and in general, increased government interventions in the economy.[160] This political violence might affect their health, work, income, the price system, etc. Uncertainty has increased for these individuals because political interventions have become more probable, making future prices and provision of products more uncertain. They do not know what exact form the intervention will take, nor what its effects will be. In this situation, people might limit their consumption or withdraw their investments in order to increase their real cash balances and prepare for such interventions, before they become visible and their effects felt. As in the other cases, the increased demand for money cushions the adverse effects of undesired events and their effects.

Distrust in the Banking System

When distrust in a fractional reserve banking system occurs, for whatever reason (the aforementioned reasons included, i.e., war and natural disasters) people generally prefer to increase their real cash balances of money proper. Doubts about the liquidity of the banking system may mean certain money substitutes (such as demand deposits) will no longer be regarded as part of the individual's cash balance. As a result of this lack of trust, cash balances are reduced immediately, in a subjective sense. This is because people fear they cannot exchange their money substitutes for money proper in a fractional reserve system. Subsequently, the price of money substitutes will fall. In order to compensate for this, individuals will likely try to increase their cash holdings of money proper. When the convertibility of

---

convertible at face value on demand. Money proper plus money substitutes are money in the broader sense.

[159] See Palyi (1972, p. 27).

[160] Robert Higgs (1997) has coined the term regime uncertainty which describes a pervasive lack of confidence among entrepreneurs in their ability to foresee the extent to which future government actions will intervene with private property rights. Thus, regime uncertainty may induce a cash-building deflation.

money substitutes into money is suspended by the authorities (often allegedly only temporarily), the fear becomes reality and the demand for money proper increases further. We see this in Palyi's description about World War I and the financial instability following its end: "The demand, the 'scramble,' for gold, the monetary as well as the private hoarding demand, increases greatly when the currencies are 'off gold,' as indeed they were throughout the war and beyond as long as the monetary insecurity continued" (1972, p. 28).

Moreover, when the financial system seems to be unstable, perceived uncertainty increases. People might not only be unable to get their money proper, but bank failures and credit contraction might take companies down with them also. Thus, over-all bankruptcy could increase and people might temporarily become unemployed, suffer reductions in income, etc. Therefore, if financial instability is feared, people will increase their demand for money proper and decrease their demand for money substitutes. They will try to exchange their money substitutes into money proper. They will try to get cash at the bank—be it gold in a gold standard or paper money in a fiat money standard. This might trigger a credit contraction and a reduction in the money supply. In this case, the cash building triggers a bank credit deflation that will be discussed in further detail below. The behavior of increasing cash holdings is wise, as people prepare themselves for the events to come after the instability or breakdown of the financial system. They themselves speed up the breakdown of the unstable system and amplify the problems for the banking system by increasing their demand for money proper.

Natural Disaster

When people expect or experience a natural disaster they are likely to increase their cash balances as well.[161] They do not know what has been or will be destroyed by the natural disaster. Their own assets might be destroyed making purchases necessary or they might become unemployed and temporarily be without income. Prices might rise and vary strongly due to the natural disaster. The social, economical, and even political environment might change. Therefore, it would be wise to increase one's cash holding in order to be prepared for such events.

Conclusion: Government and Nature

Except for the cases of natural disasters,[162] the aforementioned reasons for a general and strong increase in the demand for real cash balances are ultimately caused by government intervention. It is hard to see why in absence of natural

[161] A case might be when in the prospect of a natural disaster, individuals might actually reduce their cash balances. If people expect for certain that they are going to die in the disaster, for example due to the impact of a meteorite that destroys the earth. Then they may reduce cash balances upon which a price inflation will follow.

[162] A fractional reserve banking system results from government intervention as it receives receive privileges from the government. Such privileges may include a central bank as a lender of last

disasters and government intervention, the demand for real cash balances should change abruptly. Moreover, in all cases, the increased demand for money is individually beneficial and dynamically efficient in the sense that it creates the foundation for and provides new impulse for further entrepreneurial actions, allowing the economy to coordinate itself again.[163]

Result of Uncertainty Cash Building

We will now examine the specific consequences of an increased demand for real cash balances. The increased demand for real cash balances in a commodity standard, brings about an increase in the production of this commodity.[164] Factors of production are directed to producing the commodity, thereby counteracting the tendency for price declines. Nevertheless, we will assume a constant money supply in our analysis as we are interested in possible causes of price deflation. Thus, the analysis includes the case of an exhaustion of the production of a commodity and the case of a fiat money standard where the money supply is constant. In particular, we will examine if the actors involved achieve their aims and if this brings about a price deflation. We will distinguish three different cases: (a) The increase in the demand for cash holdings by some individuals is balanced by the decreased demand for cash holdings by other individuals. (b) The increase in the demand for cash holdings is not balanced by the decrease in the demand for real cash holdings by other individuals. (c) All individuals want to increase their real cash balances.

(a) *The increase in the demand for cash holdings by some individuals is balanced by the decreased demand for cash holdings by other individuals*

In this case, certain individuals want to increase their real cash balances while some want to decrease their real cash balances. The first group sells goods, services, and assets to buy money and to add to their cash balance. The second group does the opposite. They buy the goods, services and assets that the first group offers thereby reducing their cash balance. The purchasing power of money does not have to change in this process, even though relative prices are likely to change. In the end the first group will have a higher nominal cash balance and the second group a smaller nominal cash balance. As the purchasing power of money has not changed, the first group obtains a higher real cash balance and the second group a lower real cash balance. Thus, both groups attain their subjective ends.[165]

---

resort, legalized suspension of payments, or the toleration of ambiguous contracts concerning demand deposits and loans.

[163] For the concept of dynamic efficiency, see Huerta de Soto (2003, pp. 231–254).

[164] See Rueff (1947, p. 348).

[165] One specific example of such a scenario would be a gold standard in several countries. When the citizens of one country (group one) in net want to increase their real cash balances, for instance, because they fear a war, they will sell goods, services, and assets (inclusive rights) to citizens of

(b) *The increase in the demand for cash holdings by some individuals is not balanced by the decrease in the demand for cash holdings by other individuals*

Another case would be that the increase in the demand for cash holdings by one group is not totally balanced by a decreased demand for cash holdings by another group. That means that the nominal amount that group two is willing to give up is not sufficient to satisfy the nominal demand for money by group one at current prices. Would it be possible that both groups attain their ends in this case as well? Until a certain point group one will sell goods, services, and assets, and group two will buy them. But after a certain point, group one continues wanting to add to their cash balances through the purchase of goods, services and assets, while group two does not want to sell money any more as they are content with their cash holdings.

Now, group two will resist selling money from their cash holdings, because they want to maintain their real cash balances. This implies that they restrict their selling of money and sell their money only for more goods, services, and assets. Group one, in turn, will offer more goods, services and assets to buy money in order to increase their cash balances further. Hence, the purchasing power of money is higher than without the increase, and the money prices of goods, services, and assets tend to fall.[166] When there is a rise in the purchasing power of money and thus of the real value of the second group's cash balances, group two will sell money to group one whose members wish to add to their cash balances. Therefore, group two has reduced the real value of their cash balances not more that they wanted. At the same time the real value of the cash balances of group one also increases as does their nominal value. As a result, in this scenario the purchasing power of money increases and prices fall. The nominal cash holdings of group one increase while those of group two decrease. The real cash balances of group one increase while the real cash holdings of group two falls. Both groups attain their respective ends.[167]

(c) *All individuals want to increase their real cash balances*

Now, we turn to the last case. Here, all individuals want to increase their real cash balances. Obviously, no-one will want to give up monetary units and loose nominal cash holdings. Everyone wants to increase their cash holdings. If there is no increase in the quantity of money, it is impossible for everyone to increase their nominal cash balances. However, the real cash balances can be increased. Individuals are willing to give up more goods, services, and assets

---

other countries for gold. The first country will then have more gold and the second country will have less gold in exchange for more goods, services, and assets.

[166] We are assuming a free market. If prices are not allowed to rise or fall by government intervention, the typical effects of maximum and minimum prices follow. There will be shortages and unsold surpluses. For example, if prices of goods, services, and assets are not allowed to fall, in our scenario there will be surpluses of goods, services, and assets that could have been sold at lower prices. Likewise, there will be a shortage of money for those who want to increase their real cash balances.

[167] Again, in the case of a gold standard, groups one and two could be different countries.

to attain a monetary unit; and/or individuals will offer less monetary units than otherwise, for the same amount of goods, services, and assets. In an extreme case, individuals will simply stop buying goods, services and assets until their prices have fallen so much as to increase their real cash balances to their satisfaction.[168] They simply bid up the market value of monetary units in terms of all other goods.[169] There is a tendency of prices to fall due to a general abstention from buying, and thus, the real cash balances of individuals increase. These individuals have attained their ends, and there is a tendency toward price deflation.[170]

This process can happen very quickly. It all depends on the entrepreneurial capacities of the individuals involved. If sellers correctly anticipate the amount they have to reduce prices in order to find willing buyers, they will reduce prices immediately to that amount. There is no reason why they should not be able to anticipate those prices correctly and as quickly in any other market situation.

We should take note that the supply of services derived from cash holdings is not independent from the demand for holdings.[171] If the demand for cash

---

[168] Of course, there is a limit to which people stop adding to their real cash balances, which is a level of consumption necessary to survive. Hence, the demand for money is always restricted by this fundamental biological need (putting aside the extreme case of a person who wants to commit suicide and who before her death intends to increase her cash balance. This tactic does not make much sense, anyway, as her future will be quite certain). As Rothbard writes: "...[t]he demand for money could not be infinite since people must always continue consuming, whatever their expectations. Therefore, necessarily the demand for money could never be infinite. The existing level of consumption, in turn, will require a certain level of investment." (2001, p. 692)

[169] See Salerno (2003, p. 85).

[170] Salerno (2003, p. 85) notes correctly the positive welfare effects of such a cash building deflation: "Despite the reduction in total dollar income, however, the deflationary process caused by cash building is also benign and productive of greater economic welfare. It is initiated by the voluntary and utility-enhancing choices of some money holders to refrain from exchanging titles to their money assets on the market in the same quantities as they had previously. However, with the supply of dollars fixed, the only way in which this increase demand to hold money can be satisfied is for each dollar to become more valuable, so that the total purchasing power represented by the existing supply of money increases. This is precisely what price deflation accomplishes: an increase in aggregate monetary wealth or the 'real' supply of money in order to satisfy those who desire additional cash balances." To the same effect, see Šíma (2002, p. 11). He speaks of "hoarding" as a productive activity.

[171] See Hülsmann (2003a, p. 50). He adds that "[s]uch independence does indeed exist in the case of most other goods, and the reason is that in most other cases the amount of services to be derived from the good in question essentially depends on the good's physical characteristics. For example, the services typically delivered by a telephone do not depend at all on the demand for this telephone, or on the demand for telephones of this type...But in the case of cash holdings, supply and demand are not independent because here demand does depend on supply, and supply does depend on demand. If the quantity of money is increased, the purchasing power of each unit will decrease below the level it would otherwise have attained. This means that the services that can be derived from each money unit have decreased, and since money owners are only interested in the amount of these services, rather than in the nominal quantities in which these services are embodied, their demand for nominal quantities of money will be higher than it otherwise would have been." [footnote omitted]

holdings increases, and prices fall, the supply of services of monetary units increases automatically without any increase in the nominal supply. Therefore, even without an increase in the money supply, the increased demand for real cash holdings is satisfied. If an increase in the supply occurs—be it by gold production[172] or paper money inflation—it will not be spent until the real cash balances have increased in the desired amount. Thus, in a commodity standard, nominal and real cash balances increase. In a fiat money standard, however, the increase in nominal cash balances does not always bring about an increase in real cash balances. As more fiat money is produced, prices can increase substantially. As people start to expect further increases, they could cause a hyperinflation. In a hyperinflation, prices increase faster than the money supply increases, because people spend their money for goods, ever more quickly, at continually increasing prices. As prices increase faster than the nominal money supply, real cash balances fall. Further increases in the money supply bring about further decreases in real cash balances. In this case, the inflation has been self-defeating. Therefore, Guido Hülsmann's following observation applies only in cases of a fiat money standard and a hyperinflation:

> . . . [I]t is not only superfluous, but also quite nonsensical to "adjust" the supply of money to be held to changes in demand. An increased nominal supply, far from offsetting the increased demand it was meant, only causes a further increase of the demand for cash holdings. Far from equilibrating the supply of and demand for cash holdings, nominal supply changes merely elicit an additional nominal demand. (2003a, p. 50)

It is true, that to "adjust" the money supply to changes of money demand is superfluous. Yet, it is not nonsensical in the sense that Hülsmann maintains. For instance, in a commodity money standard, the new production of the commodity will be demanded by those individuals who want to increase their real cash balances. This increase in the money supply does not beg another increase in nominal supply. This is so, because the money will be added to cash holdings without increasing prices as much as they would have, if the demand for money would have remained the same. Prices also in this case are bid down relative to the level they would have reached in the absence of the increased demand for money.

3.2.3.3 Speculative Cash Building

Reasons for Speculative Cash Building

When people expect an increase in the purchasing power of money, they might consider investing in money and increase their speculative demand for money.

---

[172] In an economy with a gold standard, when the purchasing power of gold increases, more efforts are directed to gold mining. The gold mining satisfies the wants of consumers who want to hold a higher store of gold.

People might expect this increase in purchasing power for several reasons: a decrease in the quantity of money, a growth deflation, an increase in the quality of money, an increase in the demand for money caused by higher uncertainty etc. In all cases the adjustment toward the expected point will be more rapid than without the speculative demand.

I will now briefly turn to one situation in which the speculative demand for money plays a special role and has often been neglected: the origin of money.[173] It is a special case of the expectation of an improved quality of money. When entrepreneurs pick a commodity to use it as a medium of exchange, the demand for this medium of exchange increases. Its use becomes more widespread and its price increases. It is likely that the purchasing power of the medium of exchange that finally becomes money will rise considerably in the process of its evolution. Now, people who expect a certain commodity to become a generally accepted medium of exchange will invest in this commodity or to-be-money. This is the speculative demand for money. In the process of the origin of money the speculative demand for money will speed up the process of the developing of the medium of exchange. Through speculation, the purchasing power of the commodity will increase further until the expected point is reached. Thus, the commodity becomes more attractive as money and more widespread in its use. The process of the development or origin of money is thus, speeded up by the speculative demand. The benefits of a monetary economy can be experienced much more quickly due to the speculative demand.

Results of Speculative Cash Building

I will now examine the consequences of an increased demand for cash holdings due to speculation. First, it should be realized that every business person and consumer is a money speculator when it comes to deciding the amount of cash balance they want to hold. One cannot avoid being a money speculator. An individual will restrict his purchases if he expects the prices of goods, services, and assets he is interested in to fall, and if the price drop compensates him for the time he has to wait to enjoy the good, service, or asset. Moreover, if he expects the prices of the goods and services he sells to fall, he will rush to sell them now, before they have fallen.[174]

This will increase the speculator's cash holding. He "hoards" money expecting a future rise in the purchasing power of money, or at least a fall in the prices he is interested in.[175] For an observer, the same effect has occurred when the individual has increased his cash holding due to a desire to increase his real cash balances because he experiences an increase in uncertainty or wants to increase the amount of

[173] Concerning the origin of money, see Carl Menger (1871).

[174] Of course, the present selling capacity of a producer is limited by the stock he has at hand.

[175] See Rothbard (2001, p. 673).

wealth stored in money. The difference between the cases of increases in cash holdings is that the speculator, if he sticks to his initial plan, will spend the increase in his cash holdings when prices really have fallen to the expected level.

The effect of the speculation by the individual is that by restricting his purchases and rushing to sell his possessions, he exerts a downward pressure on prices. When, prices finally have fallen to the expected level, due to his additional purchases and reduced sales he will exert an upward pressure on prices. The speculator will reap a profit when his predictions turn out to be true. And he will suffer a loss if his expectation turns out to be false. Thus, in the speculative process the bad speculator tends to be eliminated and the good speculator is rewarded.

Of course, money speculation can lead to an increase of the purchasing power of money or a price deflation. When the effects of the actions of the speculators who expect falling prices is stronger than the effect of speculators who expect constant or rising prices, prices tend to fall. As Mises points out in regard to expectations of both rising and falling prices:

> But it is different if people believe that they are on the eve of big cash-induced changes in purchasing power. When they expect that the money prices of all goods will rise or fall, they expand or restrict their purchases. These attitudes strengthen and accelerate the expected tendencies considerably. This goes on until the point is reached beyond which no further changes in the purchasing power of money are expected. Only then does the inclination to buy or to sell stop and do people begin again to increase or to decrease their cash holdings. (1998, p. 423)

In other words, the adjustment towards the expected point in purchasing power is accelerated.[176] In principle, this point can be reached immediately. It depends on the entrepreneurial talents involved. Once the expected point is reached speculators will sell the money they invested in and reap their profits. This prevents a further rise in the purchasing power of money or price deflation.

As all speculation, money speculation is self correcting. Speculators try to anticipate the underlying non-speculative money demand.[177] Of course, herein they can err. If speculators are wrong in their expectations they lose money. Let us assume that some speculators have anticipated a fall in prices and have increased their cash balances. With this increase in their cash balances prices will tend to fall. If the anticipation was wrong however, at these lower prices, a shortage of goods occurs. There will be an increased demand for goods that will bid up prices again. Thus, the error is revealed and prices rise again, which persuades the speculators to reduce their cash balances, realizing a loss.

[176] See Rothbard (2001, p. 673).

[177] See Rothbard (2001, p. 674).

3.2.3.4 Qualitative Cash Building

Reasons for Qualitative Cash Building

An often neglected reason for an increased demand to hold money in cash balances is an increase in the quality of money.[178] The quality of money may be defined as "the capacity of money, as perceived by actors, to fulfill its main functions, namely to serve as a medium of exchange, as a store of wealth, and as an accounting unit"(Bagus 2009, p. 23).[179]

The quality of money has an impact on money's marginal utility and its ranking on the individual's value scale in relation to other goods. When the quality of money increases, monetary units tend to increase in their ranking in relation to other goods. The factors influencing the quality of money are manifold and have been widely neglected. They can be classified according to money's functions to serve as an unit of account, medium of exchange and store of wealth.

Money's function as a unit of account is rather stable and only put into question during hyperinflations. For this reason we will not analysis the factors influences money's capacity to function as a unit of account in detail here. More relevant and variable are the functions to serve as a medium of exchange and store of wealth.

In order to be a good medium of exchange a strong non-monetary demand is crucial. The non-monetary demand provides the money holder with an "insurance"against demonetization. When the non-monetary demand for the good increases, the quality of money tends to increase as well and with it money's demand. Furthermore, the more people accept the medium of exchange, the better it fulfills its functions as a medium of exchange. Other properties of a good medium of exchange are low transportation and storage costs, easy handling, divisibility, durability, resistance, recognizability and homogeneity. If any of these properties improves, the demand for money tends to increase.

Money is the most liquid good. People store their wealth in it, because when selling their products, people normally do not buy goods and services they need at the very same moment. A good store of wealth is, therefore, very important. To be a good store of wealth, a good must be have a high liquidity and hoardability. Liquidity refers to the costs of buying and selling large quantities of a good, while hoardability refers to the costs of buying and selling small quantities of a good.

The possibility of changes in the quantity of money is a crucial factor that influences the quality of money, because it affects money's capacity to function as a good store of wealth. In this regard the costs of money production are

---

[178] Also financial innovations (credit cards, ATM machines, MMMFs) and frequency of payment affect the cash-balance demand for money. However, financial innovations and a lower frequency of payment are the norm leading to a decreased demand for money. They are more relevant as causes of price inflation. Therefore, we will not analyze these causes in more detail.

[179] For a detailed analysis of the quality of money, see Bagus (2009).

important. In a free market environment with competitive money producers, money production costs are ultimately determined by subjective valuations. The higher the production costs of money in relations to its market price, the slower the stock of money will increase. Moreover, the already existing money supply in relation to its production is important for the store of wealth function of money. The higher the existing money supply in relation to money's yearly production the better the commodity can function as a store of wealth.

In a fiat money standard, however, the production costs of money are negligible and do not restrain money production. Here, the credibility of self-restraints of the money producer affect money's quality. The institutional setting of the currency, such as the constitution of the central bank, its formal "independence", its statutes and mandates become very important. Changes of these settings influence the quality of money and thereby money's demand.

The integrity of the monetary unit is also an important factor for the quality of money. Money's integrity may be changed in the case of coins by wear and tear or by a change in the redemption rate of a government-controlled commodity standard. For instance, when the government suspends redemption in specie, the quality of money falls. When the government resumes redemption in specie, the quality of money increases. The change in quality is abrupt in the case of redemption changes, because the nature of money titles changes. Inconvertible paper money represents simply a claim on an indeterminate amount, while a money certificate is a claim on a clearly defined sum.

Even when redemption is suspended indefinitely in a fiat paper standard, the assets of the central banks and the banking system still influence the quality of money. These assets back the liabilities of the banks. In case of a bank run or bankruptcy, these assets are taken over by the creditors and depositors of the bank. The better the assets, the better the quality of the monetary substitutes the banking system issues. Of special importance are the assets of the central bank that it can use to defend the value of the currency internally and externally. The central bank can use its assets to buy back its currency in order to reduce its quantity and prop up its value. The assets may even be used for a currency reform. Thus, it does matter for the quality of a currency, if the assets of a central bank consist in the majority of junk bonds booked at inflated prices or in gold.

Finally, the ideology, credit, status and policies of the government influence the quality of money as a store of wealth. A fiscally imprudent government may likely resort to a deterioration of its monetary standard to solve its fiscal problems. It may abandon a commodity standard, change the redemption rate or inflate the money supply. Thus, indirectly also the economic development and others factors that affect the taxation capacities and the fiscal status of the government influence the quality of money.

Results of Qualitative Cash Building

When the quality of money increases, the demand to hold money units tends to increase. The quality of money can increase, when its capacity to fulfill its exchange or wealth storage function improve. For instance, the non-industrial demand for the money stuff increases, more people start to use it, its production costs soar, divisibility is increased by a technological innovation, specie redemption is resumed, or the central bank gets "independent" etc. This list of reasons is not exhaustive and factors affecting the quality of money are legion.

The higher the quality of money is, the more buyers and sellers of money value the monetary unit in relation to other goods and services. They are willing to hold higher real cash balances. When the quality of money increases, purchasing power will be higher than without this quality improvement. As a consequence there is a tendency for price deflation.

3.2.3.5 Cash Building and the Structure of Production

Are there other consequences of increases in real cash holdings beside a tendency toward a lower price level? First, in an economy with a commodity money standard, more resources will be used for the production of the commodity, and the structure of production will change accordingly.[180] There are other consequences that are valid for all monetary systems. As people do not change their demand for money to the same degree and as they have different preferences, different goods will be affected differently by the increased demand for cash holding. Hence, the relative prices of goods will change and consequently the relative wealth position of individuals. But how will the structure of production change? On the one hand, this depends on the time preference of those who gain and those who lose in the process. On the other hand, this depends on the question from where the money used to enlarge the cash balance originates. Money income can be spent in three ways. It can be spent on consumer goods, factors of production, and additions to the cash balance. One use is consumption, and one is investment in factors of production. The other is an investment in money. Cash building can come from money that would have been used for consumption or from money that would have been used for investing in factors of production. If cash balances are increased by abstaining

[180] Hülsmann (2009) has elaborated on this point. When the demand for money increases, the purchasing power of money tends to increase. As commodity money production increases and bids away factors of production from other projects, the structure of production changes. It would be, however, arbitrary to say that the structure of production becomes less capital intensive, since the money production facilities also constitute capital goods. There is a small growth of the money producing industry (i.e. gold mines) and a corresponding shrinkage of other industries. If time preference rates and the amount of real savings remain the same, interest rates remain the same. Thus, I do not agree with Hülsmann who argues that interest rates necessarily increase due to the increased use of factors of production in the mining sector.

from consumption or by selling consumer goods, the structure of production will be extended and widened. More consumer goods are liberated and can be used to nourish a longer or wider production process. On the contrary, if cash balances are increased by abstaining from investing in or selling factors of production, the structure of production will be shortened.

It might be that both uses, the consumption and investment uses, are reduced in the same proportion. That means, that an increase in cash holdings and a price deflation is possible without leading to a less capital intensive structure of production. The direction in which the structure of production is changed depends on the question in which direction time preference has changed. If time preference increases, investment in factors of production will be reduced. If time preference decreases, consumption will be reduced relatively in favor of investment.[181]

Now, I will discuss both cases of increase in cash building and its effects on the structure of production in more detail. First, I turn to an increase in cash holdings caused by an abstention of buying consumer goods or a more intensive selling of consumer goods. As a consequence, the prices of consumer goods will tend to fall. In particular, they will fall relative to capital goods. Therefore, the profits in capital goods industries rise relative to profits in consumer goods industries. The resources (consumer goods) liberated[182] by the abstention from consumption will be redirected to sustain processes in the capital goods industries. As a consequence, the structure of production is enlarged and becomes more capital intensive and thus, more productive. In other words, the increase in cash holdings boosts capital accumulation indirectly. As the prices of capital goods (consumer goods used to sustain productive efforts) will not be as high as without the increase in cash holdings, there is an increase in the capital available for entrepreneurs to enlarge the structure of production.[183] There will be economic growth in the sense that the structure of production has become more productive. When the new longer, and more productive production processes are completed, there will be more of the same products or products of a higher quality available. Hence, there are two tendencies working in the direction of a price deflation: first, the increase in the demand for money; and second, economic growth.

It should be noted, that an increased demand for money (hoarding) by a reduction of consumption has the same effects on the structure of production as in the case of an increase in savings and direct investment: the structure of

[181] In this context, one has to keep in mind, that the speculative demand for money is also influenced by time preference, as the speculator has to wait to reap his speculative profits. His action is an investment. As his time preference rate decreases, the speculator will invest more and reduce his consumption. He might also invest more in money if the investment seems worthwhile to him. On the contrary, an increase in his time preference rate might induce him to sell all or part of his money investments.

[182] In Richard von Strigl's terminology, the subsistence fund used to sustain workers during roundabout productions is increased. Thus, longer production projects can be undertaken. See Strigl for the role of the subsistence fund for the structure of production (1934, pp. 1–52).

[183] See Mises (1998, p. 518).

production becomes more capital intensive. In both cases, consumer goods are liberated to enlarge and widen the structure of production. The difference to an increase in savings and direct investment is, that in the case of an increase in cash holdings by an abstention from consumption, the funds are not directly invested in an enlargement of the structure of production, but they are directed to this effect indirectly by a change in relative prices.[184]

Let us now turn to the second case where the increase in real cash balances is brought about by disinvesting and selling capital goods. In this case, prices of capital goods fall relative to prices of consumer goods, as do profits in capital goods industries in relation to profits in consumer goods industries. Resources are shifted towards consumer goods industries were profits are higher. The structure of production is flattened, becoming less productive. The quantity and quality of consumer goods will be reduced when the structure of production has been adjusted. There is an impoverishment of society.[185] Hence, there are two effects working in opposite directions on the purchasing power of money: first, the increase in the demand for money that tends to raise the purchasing power of money and second, the economic shrinking that tends to reduce the purchasing power of money.

It must be noted, that uncertainty cash building can have an additional effect on the structure of production. While qualitative cash building and speculative cash building per se are neutral on gross interest rates, uncertainty cash building tends to have an impact on the yield curve and, thereby, also on the structure of production.

As mentioned before, when uncertainty increases, people want to increase their liquidity position by increasing their cash balance.[186] They tend to cut back relatively more on longer term saving instruments than on shorter term, more liquid ones. Selling a 10 year bond, in order to buy more liquid 3-months commercial paper improves liquidity in times of uncertainty. Due to investment decisions aiming at higher liquidity, long term interest rates will rise relatively to shorter term interest rates. The yield curve gets steeper. In other words, when cash building is caused by a higher perceived uncertainty, people tend to increase their cash

[184] See Huerta de Soto (2006a, p. 448) and Mises (1998, p. 518). It should be noted, that entrepreneurs who lengthen a structure of production due to cash building by an abstention from consumption spending do implicitly assume that this cash building is not reversed until the lengthening of the structure of production is completed. If, in contrast, people dishoard their cash holdings by increasing consumption expenditures before the new projects are completed, consumer goods' prices rise relatively to capital goods prices redirecting production efforts. Furthermore, let us emphasize again that in a commodity standard the money producing industry (i.e. mining) increases relative to other sectors.

[185] See Huerta de Soto (2006a, p. 448), fn 47.

[186] Uncertainty aversion explains the tendency for a rising yield curve. People prefer to be more liquid rather than less liquid. Due to time preference they prefer to be liquid rather sooner than later. Shorter term loans, therefore, tend to have a lower yield than longer term loans that are more illiquid.

balances by abstaining relatively more from longer term investments. There is a tendency for the structure of production to become shorter.[187]

3.3 Bank Credit Deflation

3.3.1 Bank Credit Deflation and Prices

A bank credit contraction is a reduction in the volume of fiduciary bank credits. To clarify the concept, a few definitions are in order.[188] In a credit expansion, credits are granted out of the issue of fiduciary media. Fiduciary media are money substitutes that are not backed by reserves of money proper. In a fiat money system, legal tender notes are considered money proper. Bank deposits are, for instance, a money substitute. When the bank deposit is not backed by cash, it is fiduciary media. And credits granted out of the issue of fiduciary media are called circulation credits. When a bank grants credits by issuing bank deposits not backed by cash and this granting of credits is not just a renewing of credits that have already effected prices, wages and interest rates, it engages in a credit expansion.

In a credit contraction, circulation credits and, as a consequence, bank deposits are reduced. As bank deposits and bank notes are monetary substitutes, the money supply in the larger sense (i.e., money proper and monetary substitutes) is reduced. Thus, bank credit contraction is a monetary deflation.

A bank credit contraction can only occur if there has been a credit expansion. When there has not been a credit expansion along with a creation of fiduciary media, fiduciary media, logically, cannot be destroyed. It is also logical, that the credit contraction is necessarily limited by the amount of credit expansion and the resulting circulation credits. The credit expansion, by contrast, can be increased

[187] It should be noted that a shift from long-term to short-term saving instruments (bonds, loans, etc.) does not necessary affect the real structure of production. It is just a likely possibility. Indeed, long term investment projects may be financed by successfully rolling over short-term loans or bonds. Yet, in a situation where perceived uncertainty has increased and is not expected to be reduced soon again, it is doubtful that entrepreneurs will increase their exposure to the risky business of financing long-term projects via short-term debts. Most likely, the structure of production will get shorter, reflecting the increased uncertainty. The effect on the structure of production also depends on the type of uncertainty. For instance, uncertainty can be temporarily increased by a natural catastrophe or it can be increased for the long run by the change in the political regime. Uncertainty increases and as long-term projects tend to be more risky than short-term, there results a shorter structure of production. There is a relative increase in consumption and the production of consumption goods or liquid goods that can be easily converted into consumption goods. There are more savings which are used in a more conservative, i.e. short-term way. If entrepreneurs expect that consumption will increase in the near future, they will not try to roll-over the short-term savings. They will not invest in projects that take a long time but rather invest in short-term projects. The yield curve reflects these expectations.

[188] Concerning this terminology, see Mises (1998, pp. 432–434).

virtually without limits.[189] Normally, a credit contraction occurs after an expansionary boom and forms part of the recession.[190] When there is a credit expansion, the interest rate can be artificially lowered and an artificial boom occurs that sooner or later reverts into an economic recession. This is the Austrian business cycle theory (ABCT) which will be explained in the next section.

3.3.2 *Austrian Business Cycle Theory*

In order to understand the dynamic of a credit contraction in an economic recession, one must understand why and how economic cycles, i.e. recurrent booms and recessions, occur.[191]

The Austrian business cycle is caused by an increase in the amount of money by the banking system via credit expansion. In a credit expansion, banks create fiduciary media out of thin air by granting credits. The new fiduciary media is injected into the loan market and reduces the interest rates below the level they would have been otherwise. Thus, the credit expansion leads to an interest rate that is too low in comparison to the preferences of the market participants.[192] In other words, the availability of funds is not matched by the preference of market participants. Due to the relative reduction of the interest rate, entrepreneurs are led to think that the amount of savings has increased. In turn, they engage in new investment projects, beginning more investment projects than can be finished with available means of production. Investment projects seem to be profitable that would not have been profitable without the reduction of the interest rate. Interest rate reductions have more of an effect on investment projects that take more time to be completed than on projects that take less time to be finished. Moreover, the market price of capital goods increases as their future returns are discounted by a lower interest rate. Therefore, many investment projects requiring considerable time to produce consumer goods are begun. The crucial point is that investors are led to undertake more investment projects than otherwise, acting as if savings had increased, increasing the demand for capital goods.

---

[189] See Rothbard (2001, p. 867).

[190] It is also conceivable that a credit contraction occurs without a business cycle downturn. This occurs when interest rates are not distorted by the monetary changes.

[191] For an account of the Austrian business cycle theory see Huerta de Soto (2006a), Chaps. 5 and 6, Mises (1998), Chap. 20, or Rothbard (2001, pp. 850–879).

[192] Hülsmann (1998, p. 4) has argued that this is not necessarily so, because the impact of the new fiduciary media on prices might be anticipated by entrepreneurs and included in the interest rate as an inflation premium. Entrepreneurs can underestimate, overestimate, or estimate correctly the effects of the credit expansion on prices. Only if they underestimate the effect, will there be an artificially low interest rate as a result. The business cycle is underway and malinvestments are made.

When the owners of the factors of production get paid with the newly created money and spend their income in the old consumption-savings ratio, (i.e., they do not increase their savings), there will be a relative increase in the demand for consumer goods. Moreover, the supply of consumer goods slows down. This is due to the undertaking of investment projects that yield consumer goods only after a longer time period. The relative increase in demand for consumer goods and the relative decrease in their supply allow the prices of consumer goods to rise. Consequently, the increase in the consumer goods prices increases profits in consumer goods industries in comparison to capital goods industries. The interest rate will increase again to a level even higher than it had been without the credit expansion.[193] There are several reasons for this. When the credit expansion stops and has exerted its influence on prices interest rates will return to the old level. So there is a continuous upward pressure. Also, a price premium in the nominal interest rates may be included, taking account of the price inflation induced by the credit expansion. Moreover, the demand of credits will increase on the part of entrepreneurs who become aware that there are not enough savings available. Eager to finish their investment projects, they will bid up the interest rates. The increase in the interest rates will lower the present value of capital goods and make investment projects appear unprofitable that had looked profitable with the artificially lowered interest rates. Finally, losses in capital goods industries may arise as well. It becomes evident that not all investment projects that were begun can be completed with the available means of production and a recession sets in.

Mainly investment projects that consume much time, i.e., those in the higher stages of production, have to be abandoned and factors of production are then shifted back to less time-consuming projects, to the lower stages of production, which produce consumer goods more quickly and yield higher profits. Investment projects and companies go bankrupt and are liquidated. Other suffer severe losses. Capital values and asset prices fall. The recession ends when the investment projects come into line again with the preferred consumption-savings ratio of the market participants. The scarce factors of production in society have not been employed to the most urgent wants of consumers. Inconvertible capital goods are lost, and other capital goods can only be adjusted to consumer preferences, incurring high costs. Moreover, time has been lost in this adjustment of the structure of production.

[193] See Huerta de Soto (2006b, pp. 295–297).

3.3.3 *Reasons for Credit Contraction*

3.3.3.1 Introduction

In a recession, a credit contraction is likely to occur. Yet, this is not necessarily so.[194] A recession would occur even if there were no credit contraction. All that is needed to start a recession is a slowing down of the rhythm of credit expansion.[195] Historically speaking, however, often recessions have been accompanied by a credit contraction. In the following section, I will analyze what or who contributes to or triggers a credit contraction.

3.3.3.2 Fractional Reserve Banks and Credit Contraction

A credit contraction might be initiated by fractional reserve banks. The banks, as Mises points out, might become "frightened by the pace of the boom and begin to abstain from further expansion of credit" (1998, p. 559). They try to increase their reserves in order to be able to satisfy the expected increased withdrawal of deposits. There are several ways to do this. They can sell some of their assets, which drives their prices down. Or they increase their reserves by restricting circulation credit.[196] When credits are returned they do not renew or do not lend them again.[197] They

---

[194] See Rothbard (2000, p. 14).

[195] See Mises (1998, p. 566). It is possible that the boom continues for some time if new doses of credit are injected into the economy. Yet, ever higher doses of credit are necessary in order to keep the boom going. There are two main reasons for this. The first reason can be explained by the fact that the credit expansion begins to flow into the real economy at some point, and consumer goods prices start to rise relative to capital goods prices. More specifically, consumer prices rise for several reasons. At first, consumer goods prices rise, because incomes of the owners of the factors of production rise due to the new money spent in new investment projects. The owners of the factors of production spend this new monetary income partly on consumer goods. Moreover, during the boom phase new investment projects are undertaken. These projects take longer to yield consumer goods than the projects that were undertaken before. Hence, the flow of consumer goods slows down, resulting in a tendency towards higher consumer goods prices. In addition, due to rising stock prices, people might be induced to sell their stocks and take delight in increased consumption, since they regard their real wealth as having been increased. The second main reason for the need of ever higher doses of credit to keep the boom going is that the interest rate begins to rise due to several reasons as explained above. Without credit expansion the interest rate will return to its free market level. Moreover, a price premium will be bid into the interest rate. And entrepreneurs will be willing to accept higher interest rates and fight for the available credit in order to finish the initiated investment projects. Therefore, ever higher doses are necessary to lower interest rates artificially.

[196] See Mises (1998, p. 564). See also Huerta de Soto (2006b, p. 204).

[197] Business borrowers who are scared and demoralized by the recession may disinvest or liquidate their investment projects by paying back loans earlier and thereby, possibly induce a credit contraction. Note however, that banks could always attempt to create fiduciary media again, thus sustaining the money supply by granting credits again at lower interest rates or by buying

raise the interest rates to restrict the demand for credits. Therefore, money proper returns to the banks without being used to create fiduciary media, and bank reserves of money proper are enhanced. Why do banks become frightened by the pace of the boom at all? First of all, banks know from experience that after a sudden boom, there will be a recession. Second, they observe that the companies that they helped to finance will go bankrupt. Investment projects turn out to be unprofitable.

Third, a recession sets in and then banks become more cautious and restrict credits. Another event that can trigger a bank credit deflation is the bursting of an asset price bubble. When asset prices fall, the banks' assets lose value. Those assets were used to back up the credits. Banks restrict credits in order to improve their solvency. Thus, Kumar and colleagues state: "The impact of large asset price declines on balance sheets and aggregate demand is sometimes associated with deflation" (2003, p. 7).

But why do banks restrict credit when they expect a recession? In a recession, many malinvestments are liquidated and companies go bankrupt. For the banks, this means that many loans will turn bad, as their borrowers go bankrupt. When the borrowers cannot pay back the credits, banks will suffer losses. The reserves are reduced as there is no money flowing back to the banks. Moreover, other assets of the banks lose value. As a general pessimism spreads and many companies get into financial difficulties during a recession, stocks and securities will fall in price. Another reason for the fall in stock and security prices is the likely increase in the interest rates, lowering their net present value. This might spur distrust in the bank whose assets are quickly losing value. As a bank suffers severe losses—in that assets lose value and credits are not returned—the reserve ratio declines and depositors begin to worry about the solvency of the bank and try to withdraw their deposits. Then a bank run ensues. By restricting credits and raising its reserve ratio, the bank tries to prevent any liquidity problems.

3.3.3.3 Central Banks and Credit Contraction

Central banks can deliberately initiate a credit contraction as well. They have basically three options to make the banking system contract credit. First, the central bank can raise the minimum reserve quota. If banks hold lower reserves then the new minimum reserve, they will probably try to restrict credits in order to improve their reserves. When old credits are paid back, they use the funds to increase their reserves and do not renew the credits. Thus, the new minimum reserve is held. Banks could also sell assets, but only at prohibitive losses, if other banks also sell. Thus, they will probably restrict credits.

More usual are two other mechanisms which the central bank has to induce a credit contraction. For one, the central bank can raise the discount rate for securities

securities. It depends on the banks in this instance if they wish to increase their reserves and contract credit or not (Rothbard 2000, pp. 14–15, fn. 10).

or commercial paper. If they do that, banks have to pay higher interest rates for loans from the central bank that they back with securities. Banks use these loans to expand credits on the basis of the central bank money they receive. In order to be profitable, the banks have to charge a higher interest rate on the credits they create than the rate which they themselves pay to the central bank. When the central bank raises its interest rates, banks have several options. They can demand fewer loans from the central bank and create fewer credits than they did before. This is tantamount to a credit contraction in relation to the situation with lower interest rates. They can also demand the same amount of loans from the central bank, but raise their interest rates as well in order to remain profitable. At the higher interest rate there will be less demand for credits. Fewer credits will then be granted at this higher interest rate. Or there can be a combination of the two possibilities. In any case, credits are restricted.

The last option that a central bank has in order to incite a credit contraction are open market operations. The central bank can sell securities to banks. Thus, it reduces the banks' cash reserves. As the banks' cash reserves fall, they have to restrict credit, if they want to maintain their reserve ratio.

One question remains. Why would a central bank want to contract credit? Several reasons are possible and depend upon the doctrine upon which the central bank is founded. For instance, the first central banks might be installed to provide cheap credits to foster economic growth. Logically, these first central banks would rarely restrict credit at all. Or, a central bank in an economy with a gold standard might be installed to rescue banks. Thus, the central bank serves as a lender of last resort and, at the same time, controls the banks. In order to save the gold standard, a central bank might be forced to restrict credit as it loses its reserves, i.e., a central bank might want to stop the outflow of gold. The central bank might also want to restore a depreciated currency to its old specie standard.[198] By restricting credit, the amount of fiduciary media is reduced and interest rates increase. Due to the higher interest rates, gold is imported and savings increase. As a consequence, consumer goods are exported and imports reduced. Due to the reduction of fiduciary media, there is a downward pressure on prices.

The same is true in a fiat currency, when the central bank wants a stronger currency. By restricting credits, there is a downward pressure on prices, or in other words, prices will not be as high as they would have been without the credit contraction. There is a tendency that prices will be lower. This will be anticipated at the foreign exchange and the foreign exchange rate appreciates.

In additions to these doctrines, others provide explanations for why a central bank may decide to restrict credit. One belief is that a central bank must steer or fine-tune the economy somewhat. The central bank would have to provide a stable price level of consumer goods and foster economic growth without endangering the price stability.

---

[198] See Salerno (2003, p. 86).

When resources are idle, a credit expansion would be beneficiary in order to employ these resources. Production increases and price inflation does not become a problem. In other words, when the economy is slack the central bank would have to provide impetus to the economy by lowering interest rates and inducing a credit expansion. However, when resource are fully employed, there might be a inflationary pressure on consumer goods prices. Thus, when the economy is booming or "growing too fast," it is thought that the central bank must restrict credit in order to curb price inflation. Thus, in an expansionary boom, a central bank might raise interest rates. This might only lead to a decrease in the rate of credit expansion, though.

Another related doctrine of central banking can be credited to Milton Friedman. He recommends an increase in the quantity of money at a stable rate irrespective of business cycles in order to achieve a stable level of prices of final products.[199] A central bank that follows Friedman's advise would have to restrict credit if the money supply increases more quickly than at the prescribed rate.

A last reason for the central bank to restrict credit is the fear of an unstable banking system. This reason rests on the doctrine of the central bank as a lender of last resort and regulator of the banking system. The restrictive monetary policy is thought to improve the stability of the banking system or to prevent its collapse. In a recession with numerous bankruptcies and an asset price collapse depositors might lose their trust in the solvency of their banks. They might try to get their deposits. Bank runs might ensue. One bank's collapse can kick off distrust in other banks as well. Banks might also have given credits to the collapsed banks. Those credits turn bad. Thus, bank runs can spread and take the whole fractional reserve banking system down. Of course, the central bank will try to prevent that by providing liquidity for banks under pressure. This could have undesired side effects like inflationary pressure. Therefore, central banks do not want to get into such a situation where they have to save the system in the first place. When they think a boom is getting out of control, they induce a credit contraction that increases reserves and, therefore, the stability of the banking system.

3.3.3.4 Depositors and Credit Contraction

Depositors can induce a credit contraction as well. One possibility is that bank customers use a larger portion of their money outside the banking system.[200] They do not use the banking system but pay in cash. They pay more in cash than with credit cards, checks, etc. Then banks have less money proper to expand credits on top of them. Consequently, they have to restrict credits in order to maintain their reserve ratio.

[199] See Friedman (1969, pp. 46–48).

[200] See Huerta de Soto (2006b, p. 204).

Another possibility is that depositors lose their trust in their banks. They might remove their original deposits or they might remove the deposits that created the banks. They try to redeem them into cash.[201] The loss of confidence may happen because depositors fear an economic downturn, or they fear that banks may be holding many highly speculative or even nonperforming loans.[202] As a consequence of the withdrawal, banks have to restrict credits in order to maintain their reserve ratio.

Another more radical form of the last point occurs when depositors directly reduce the amount of deposits massively, thereby, causing bank runs. In bank runs, banks have to liquidate their credits and other assets immediately in order to pay out the deposits. They thereby reduce the amount of fiduciary media. They buy cash by selling their assets, causing asset prices to fall sharply. They hand over the cash to depositors while the deposits disappear. When the bank goes bankrupt, its assets are liquidated to satisfy depositors' claims. The claims that cannot be satisfied disappear. These fiduciary media cease to form part of the money supply. Bank runs can also spread, when depositors begin a bank panic. Without a central bank intervention, an important part of fiduciary media is likely to be destroyed.

3.3.4 Credit Contraction as an Accumulative Process

A recessionary credit contraction can become an accumulative process.[203] When credits are restricted, companies that relied on an ongoing credit expansion will enter into financial difficulties. When companies go bankrupt, banks' balance sheets will deteriorate. Asset prices are likely to collapse, as many companies are in financial difficulties. Moreover, in order to increase reserves, banks will begin to sell assets. As asset prices fall, the collateral that companies can offer when they demand new credits will fall. Their net worth will fall, as their obligations remain nominally constant and their assets decline in value. Banks will consequently demand higher interest rates. The higher interest rates reduce the net present value of assets and thus, lead, to further declines in asset prices. It can even come to a severe credit crunch, a credit crisis where no one is willing to give credits anymore, because it is uncertain that they can be returned. As fractional reserve banks fear that other fractional reserve banks will become insolvent, they will no longer even lend to each other. This will continue in a downward spiral of further financial difficulties, bankruptcies, and a further fall in asset prices.

Moreover, during a recession, individuals may try to increase their cash balances,[204] leading to a scramble for liquidity. Pessimism about the future may spread

[201] See Salerno (2003, p. 86).

[202] See Thornton (2003, p. 7).

[203] Concerning this process, also see Fisher's debt deflation theory (1945, pp. 122–123) or Huerta de Soto (2006b, p. 353).

[204] See Rothbard (2000, p. 15).

as people hold on to their cash, exerting a downward pressure on prices. In addition, the credit contraction adds to that pressure. Companies whose selling proceeds fall faster than their buying costs will find themselves in difficulties. Their real burden of debt increases. This deterioration of balance sheets will place these companies in further trouble in obtaining credits. Companies who cannot pay their debts become bankrupt. A distress selling in order to liquidate debt exerts more downward pressure on prices. Those bankruptcies add to the pessimism, to the increased demand for cash holding, and the deterioration of balance sheets. Due to the bankruptcies workers will become temporarily unemployed. If the labor market is regulated and inflexible, unemployment can last even longer. This will also add to the pessimism and will increase the demand for cash holdings.

As stated before, all of this is likewise problematic for the banking sector, which can add a further spin to the downward spiral. Assets decline in prices, loans turn bad, depositors remove money from their deposits and start to distrust in the banking system. A bank run can ensue that spreads into a bank panic. Credits are restricted and fiduciary media are destroyed. This, as well as the restriction of credits by still liquid banks, adds to the downward pressure on prices. It causes problems for companies in need of new credits and increases pessimism. As prices fall, real debts and the demand for money increases further, while asset prices are further reduced, leading to more bankruptcies, etc.

When does the downward spiral on a free market ends? In a free market, the downward spiral ends when several conditions are met. Prices have reached the level that people expected them to fall to and the price differential between selling and buying proceeds has increased again. "[P]rices and wage rates are so low that a sufficient number of people assume that they will not drop still more." (Mises 1998, p. 567). Malinvestments have been liquidated and the structure of production has been adapted to the most urgent needs of consumers.[205] Fractional reserve banks have been purged. Creditors that have profited by the price deflation increase their investments and spendings as they see the price differentials increase. Asset prices start to rise again as new companies in line with consumer preferences and not in need of fiduciary media begin to flourish. The surviving companies are released from the competition of the marginal companies that went bankrupt. The pessimism disappears.

But is it not possible that the expectational spiral overshoots a "freemarket equilibrium?" As Hülsmann states: "People might panic and hold on to their money even when prices have reached such a low level that it would be worthwhile to start spending money again" (2003a, p. 56). It does not seem very probable that

[205] As Mises states, this process of adaption can be delayed by psychological factors: "The process of readjustment, even in the absence of any new credit expansion, is delayed by the psychological effects of disappointment and frustration. People are slow to free themselves from the self-conception of delusive prosperity. Businessmen try to continue unprofitable projects; they shut their eyes to an insight that hurts. The workers delay reducing their claims to the level required by the state of the market; they want, if possible, to avoid lowering their standard of living and changing their occupation and their dwelling place" (1998, p. 576).

this scenario would occur where entrepreneurs would not make use of those profit opportunities. Even though not very likely, it is at least conceivable. As Mises remarks: "They [the people] have for the moment lost self-confidence and the spirit of enterprise to such an extent that they even fail to take advantage of good opportunities" (1998, p. 576). If this is the case, prices will keep on falling, leading to ever smaller notes and coins and eventually, by money competition, to one or several new monies. The real problem with this scenario is the word "overshooting" as it implies that the deflation runs too far.[206] The question is be which standard is runs to far. At least, from the point of view of cautious individuals the process has to run its full course. Moreover, it must first be pointed out that a contraction can produce "neither malinvestment nor overconsumption. No protracted scars are left. When the contraction comes to an end, the process of readjustment does not need to make good for losses caused by capital consumption." (Mises 1998, p. 565).

There will be no artificial lengthening of the structure of production that would make a liquidation of investment projects necessary. Inconvertible capital goods are not wasted, as happens in an artificial boom when they are not employed according to the most urgent wants of consumers. The structure of production might be shortened in relation to the structure of production that would have prevailed without the boom thus reflecting the pessimism and loss of inconvertible capital goods. It is, however, misleading to state, as Rothbard has that "[i]t may well be true that the deflationary process will over-shoot the free-market equilibrium and raise price differentials and the interest rate above it" (2001, p. 867). What kind of free-market equilibrium is it that does not take the psychological state, the pessimism, felt uncertainty, the expectations and feelings of the market participants into account? Of course, these factors influence time preference rates and, consequently the structure of production. They also influence which products are produced. Rothbard is comparing the state that prevails after a recession with a hypothetical state of affairs, assuming another state of mind for the market participants than they actually have. This is, of course, problematic. One might always refer to a hypothetical state and claim that the current state of future outlook is wrong. One could at all times claim that there should be more optimism about the future and therefore less consumption and more savings. But by which standard may a scientist judge that the outlook concerning the future is wrong? Important is that which happens in the market according to the current state of optimism or pessimism.

From the viewpoint of the market participants, the deflation is not overshooting a supposed free market equilibrium but rather, just running its course to the end. It goes to the point where people regard it as worthwhile to start spending money again. In their calculation they are affected by subjective factors like fear, pessimism, self-betrayal, non-acceptance of the necessity for lower living-standards, and discouragement. The needs to address fears and to not risk too much are important to them. From their perspective, it is not worthwhile to spend. There is nothing

[206] For instance, Rothbard uses the term (2001, p. 867).

irrational about this. The deflation will run so far as is optimal from the viewpoints of the market participants.

One should also recall that a bank credit deflation and a deflationary spiral can only occur after a bank credit expansion. There has been a maladjustment of the structure of production or in other words, an intertemporary discoordination in society. The towering of ever increasing debts must lead to a readjustment that can take place in two ways. One has been described above. It is the way of defaults and bankruptcies. It is painful for the owners of malinvestments but fast and efficient. It favors savers and prudent management of resources. It is educational and ends the feverish speculation of the boom that had corrupted moral standards. It is the way of deflation that would occur on the free market.

The second alternative is the depreciation of the currency in which the debt is paid, i.e., monetary inflation. In other words, the downward spiral might also be ended by government intervention that props up malinvestments and the fractional reserve banking system. The government intervention has, of course, important consequences. In order to stop or prevent a deflationary spiral, a central bank must initiate another credit expansion or increase in the money supply. This disturbs the quick liquidation of malinvestments and of the banking system. It prevents the structure of production from aligning itself with the most urgent needs of consumers and leads to new malinvestments and a new artificial boom. It makes further redistribution through an expansionary fractional reserve banking system possible. It continues the moral corruption through cheap loans, excessive consumption, and feverish speculation. At the end of a hyperinflation it may have destroyed not only savings but also traditional virtues of a whole generation.[207]

3.4 Fiat Deflation

3.4.1 Fiat Deflation and Prices

The government can also cause a price deflation. When the price deflation is caused by an infringement on property rights, we may call this phenomenon fiat deflation. There are at least three types of fiat deflation: Price decree deflation, coercive monetary deflation, and legal tender deflation.

[207] For the demoralizing effects of fiat money inflation see Hülsmann (2006).

3.4.2 Types of Fiat Deflation

3.4.2.1 Price Decree Deflation

Price decree deflation occurs when the government imposes price controls in form of maximum prices in the economy that are below current prices. In this case, for instance, the government decrees that all prices must be lowered by 10 %. (Or it might also decree that prices are lowered in various degrees). Pushing prices below their clearing point in a free market will lead to shortages. At the lower prices there will be more buyers than sellers. In such a scenario, where price controls replace the price mechanism on a free market, other mechanisms like lines in front of stores, friendship, or other non-monetary payments, will be used to distribute the scarce goods. Moreover, investments in the production of these goods would be discouraged and disinvestments will occur.[208] However, if some prices were held up artificially by government intervention before, the government price decree can dampen or eliminate the effects of the previous intervention. If, for example, the government had given a privilege to labor unions that made wages sticky and lead to wages above the market clearing price, the government decree of reducing wages (more than other prices) might reduce the problem of unemployment. Of course, the government can never possess the knowledge to obtain prices that would have occurred on the free market.[209]

3.4.2.2 Coercive Monetary Deflation

In the case of a coercive monetary deflation the government confiscates or destroys money or money substitutes.[210] The money supply is reduced by state force. There are three types of coercive monetary deflation: confiscatory deflation, fiscal deflation and bond deflation.

---

[208] For the effects of maximum prices, see Mises (1998, pp. 762–68).

[209] Concerning the knowledge problems of a central agency, see, for example, Huerta de Soto (2001, pp. 87–103).

[210] It might be added that, in theory, individuals might voluntarily destroy their money. For example, the use of a commodity money in industrial production can reshape it into a form in which individuals no longer consider it relevant for action. For instance, when in a gold standard economy, a rocket containing gold parts is sent to Mars, this gold, likely, would not be considered available any more. This free market monetary deflation has, however, no practical relevance, because it has never occurred to such an extent that it leads to a price deflation. Concerning this, also see Hülsmann (2003a, p. 55).

Confiscatory Deflation

In a confiscatory deflation the government expropriates money or money substitutes and freezes or destroys them. The money supply is reduced. Historical examples of confiscatory deflations are Germany in 1948,[211] Brazil in 1990, the former Soviet Union in 1990, Argentina during the 1980s, Ecuador in the late 1990s, and Argentina in 2001. Confiscatory deflation is often forced on the economy after a strong inflation that has been suppressed. A confiscatory deflation after an inflation, as Rothbard states, is therefore "a double destruction of property rights, the second one in the name of the free market and 'of combating inflation'" (1995, p. 239).[212] As Salerno states: "[confiscatory deflation] violates property rights, distorts monetary calculation and undermines monetary exchange" (2003, p. 96). The confiscatory deflation disturbs the market economy, as people want to keep using the money. They want to exchange and calculate with it, but to the extent it is confiscated they can not. They do not see other monies more appropriate to use. Nevertheless, as they are prevented from using the money, they might be forced to turn to other monies.

Fiscal Deflation

In a fiscal deflation the government taxes its subjects, and either destroys the tax revenues or uses them to increase bank reserves. The money supply is reduced and there is a downward pressure on prices. A fiscal deflation is similar to a confiscatory deflation. The difference is that a confiscatory deflation is normally a one-time measure. In contrast, a fiscal deflation is usually continuous. By taxation, the government first takes the money, and then in a second step destroys it. Taxation has the same adverse effects on market cooperation as confiscatory deflation.

Assuming constant tax revenue, another question concerns whether a fiscal deflation would be less harmful than using the tax money for other means. Or in other words, is it less distorting to destroy the taxed money or to spend it? Taxation distorts the free market economy in a two-fold way: first, when the income and assets of market participants are reduced; and second when the taxes are spent by the government, attracting resources and changing incentives. In a fiscal deflation

[211] As Hülsmann (2003a, p. 55) points out, confiscatory deflation often forms part of monetary reforms when the old money is confiscated and partially destroyed without being changed into the new money. This was, for instance, the case in the German monetary reform of 1948.

[212] There is a theoretical case where a confiscatory deflation after an inflation is no double destruction of property. When money is created by the government and given to people and before these people can spend it, the money is confiscated again, then the inflation and deflation have no effect and cancel each other out. When the inflation, however, runs it course, and the recipients of the new money and those whose money is confiscated are not the same people, or there is a difference in money received and money confiscated, redistribution occurs, effecting the real economy.

this second effect does not occur. Thus, it is less distorting to destroy taxes than to spend them.

The following is a typical case of fiscal deflation: During a time of war in a gold standard, banks are forced to finance government expenditures and buy government bonds. The banks, thereby, lose their gold reserves. At some point the government suspends specie payment. Following the war, a fiscal deflation is used to achieve the resumption of specie payment in a gold standard. In other words, a fiscal deflation might be used to improve the liquidity of the banking system. After the war, the government uses taxes to pay the bonds in gold to the banks and then the banks use the gold to increase their reserves; i.e., they do not grant new credits with the gold reserve. The amount of fiduciary media (and the money supply in the larger sense), thereby, is reduced and specie payment can now be resumed.

In this context, one also has to refer to fiscal deflation as a possible way to achieve a 100 % gold standard. Joseph Salerno proposes a plan in which the Treasury gives the tax funds, that it has at the central bank, to the banks who in turn are to increase their reserve ratio (2003, p. 92). Thus, the reserve ratios of banks are increased until they have 100 %. When demand deposits are backed 100 % by reserves, the dollar will be made convertible into the gold of the Federal Reserve System. In this process, the amount of gold available at the Federal Reserve is divided by the amount of dollars outstanding in order to define the new gold dollar. Salerno also sees in his plan the aforementioned advantage of a fiscal deflation (2003, pp. 92–94). By a fiscal deflation, the Treasury has less money to spend in nominal terms. Tax consumers, i.e., net tax recipients, receive less tax money, as it is destroyed, and are therefore, worse off. Tax producers, i.e., net tax payers, fare better; for although they have paid the same amount of taxes, prices are lower than would have been without the destruction of the money. They can more easily compete with tax consumers for resources as these have less money. Resources are reallocated to some extent from tax consumers to tax producers. Salerno names this effect the "rabattage effect" of fiscal deflation. He concludes that "[i]n short, at a given level of taxation, fiscal deflation lightens the fiscal burden on the market economy and diminishes the calculational chaos endemic in government expenditures, whereas inflationary finance intensifies the fiscal burden and promotes the spread of calculational chaos" (2003, p. 95).

The crucial assumption in Salerno's reasoning is the given level of taxation. Once taxes are collected it is less distorting to destroy the money than to spend it. Yet, that taxes are raised in order to destroy the money lowers social welfare, because people would have destroyed the money themselves if they had wanted to. They are forced to accept the results of such actions.

Bond Deflation

The last type of a coercive monetary deflation is a bond deflation. In this case, the government borrows money from the public and destroys the money.[213] Another possibility is that the government uses the borrowed money to increase the reserves of a bank, normally a central bank. The government gives the money to the central bank which does not put the money back in circulation again. The amount of fiduciary media (and the money supply in the larger sense) is reduced. The reduction of the money supply leads to a tendency for prices to fall.

The government will pay back the bonds by future taxation. This type of deflation is, therefore, also based on government force. Historically, it has been employed by governments after inflationary periods to get a currency back to the old par. It is harmful for the economy because it increases the future tax burden. It can also exert a downward pressure on prices. Entrepreneurs who did not anticipate this downward pressure, will lose, while those entrepreneurs will profit who anticipated the government's attempt to return to parity and thus, to honor old contracts.

Another effect of a bond deflation is that it increases the interest rate in the market, if its effects are not included in a negative price premium. It might be easier to anticipate the effects on prices by a bond deflation then by a credit expansion, because a credit expansion is something thought to be beneficial. There is the illusion that there are no problems with the lowering of interest rates.[214] The bond deflation is usually thought to be something harmful and its effects on prices might be rightly anticipated as the government normally announces its desire to destroy the money.

But let us, for the sake of the argument, assume, that the bond deflation leads to higher nominal interest rates. A first effect is that as interest rates are bid up, private bonds are crowded out. Companies trying to issue bonds have to pay higher interest rates. A second effect concerns the possible effects after a credit expansion. If the interest rate has been artificially lowered by a credit expansion before, the loan deflation might thereby counteract this lowering. This speeds up the necessary recovery and liquidation of malinvestments. A bond deflation leading to an artificially high interest rate is also possible.[215] This is the case, for instance, when there has been circulation credit that already has had its effects on price and wages rates. Entrepreneurs who relied on the existence of circulation credit will get into financial difficulty and the structure of production will be temporarily shortened.

[213] See Mises (1998, p. 564).

[214] See Hülsmann (1998).

[215] See Huerta de Soto (2006b, p. 350).

3.4.2.3 Legal Tender Deflation

The last case of fiat deflation is a legal tender deflation.[216]

> A legal tender is an economic good (typically a medium of exchange) that may be used to pay contractual debts even though the contract stipulated payment in terms of another good (typically another medium of exchange) (Hülsmann 2004, p. 34).

Thus, legal tender laws "establish an imposed equivalence (fiat equivalence) between the privileged medium of exchange—the legal tender—and other media of exchange" (Hülsmann 2004, p. 37). When this imposed equivalence does not respond to the actual free market exchange rate between the media of exchange, Gresham's Law comes into effect. The legally over-valued money drives the legally under-valued money out of the market. Let us suppose the case of bimetallism (which of course is a special case). Let us assume that gold and silver are legal tender and the free market exchange rate is 1/15. The fiat exchange rate is also 1/15. As long as the free market exchange rate does not change, everything is fine. But what happens if the free market exchange rate changes to 1/16? Then people stop using the undervalued metal, which is in this case gold. People that owe 1 ounce of gold will pay with 15 ounce of silver, which on the free market they could have bought with 1/16 ounce of gold. People will stop paying gold, hoarding it (or exporting it) and pay with silver. Thus, legal tender laws entail simultaneous inflation and deflation (Hülsmann 2004, p. 34). The legally over-valued money is produced and held in greater quantities than on the free market. However, there is a deflation of other media of exchange, that are legally under-valued. To some extent, or all together, those goods cease being media of exchange; i.e., their supply as media of exchange shrinks. To some degree, they are converted into consumer and producer goods instead of remaining media of exchange, and these goods may be exported. Thus, the total supply of media of exchange in the economy shrinks. For all exchanges, the over-valued medium of exchange or money is used, including those exchanges that formerly were conducted in the under-valued medium of exchange. Less media of exchange are used than would have been used on the free market. This reduction of the overall supply of media of exchange leads to prices that are lower than those that would have occurred without the legal tender deflation. There is a tendency towards price deflation. As Hülsmann states: "Hence, legal tender laws force the market participants to adjust to a more or less severe decline of the price level" (2004, p. 39).

For example in an economy with a metal money where the government debases coins, prices can be temporarily lower than without that debasement. The government normally will not be able to debase all coins at one time, as the production of the debased coins takes time. Thus the money supply becomes heterogeneous. The legal tender law makes the debased coins equal with the old full-content metal coins. Thus, Gresham's Law comes into effect. The old coins will be hoarded (or exported) and only the new debased coins will be used in exchanges. The

[216] On the subject of legal tender laws and deflation, see Hülsmann (2004).

Table 3.1 A taxonomy of deflation

Origin	Free market	Free market reaction to credit expansion	Government
Monetary side	Cash building deflation	Bank credit deflation	Coercive monetary deflation • Confiscatory • Fiscal • Bond Legal tender deflation
Goods side	Growth deflation	–	Price decree deflation

hoarded coins are demonetized in the sense that they are not used as a medium of exchange anymore. Therefore, the money supply shrinks: a monetary deflation sets in. Of course, there is the counter effect on prices. The debasement increases the money supply. As the production of the new coins takes some time, it is possible that in the beginning a price deflation occurs suddenly and only slowly, do prices start to rise again due to injection of new amounts of debased coins.

There is one interesting effect of the legal tender fiat deflation. Hülsmann argues that there is an incentive to replace the vanishing media of exchange with credit money and fractional reserve banking if the price deflation was not anticipated. This is so, because credit money and credit expansion allow higher expected income streams to be maintained: "Thus, sellers have an incentive to accept far more fiduciary media in payment for their goods and services than they otherwise would have accepted" (2004, p. 40). Of course, the credit expansion could lead to liquidity problems for the banking system. If however, there is a voluntary payment cartel between market participants beginning to accept fiduciary media to a greater extent, no longer using money proper outside the banking system, and more willing to accept bank notes or cashless payments, the problem is solved. Whether such a voluntary payment cartel works depends upon the specific historic circumstances. It is therefore possible that fractional reserve banking is promoted by legal tender laws due to their deflationary effects. Table 3.1 summarizes our taxonomy of deflation developed in this chapter.

Chapter 4
Consequences and Myths Concerning Deflation

4.1 Consequences of Deflation

4.1.1 Falling Prices and Human Action

In order to understand the consequences of price deflation, many economists have focused on a macroeconomic aggregate: price levels. They have considered its declines and its relation to other aggregates like the gross domestic product (GDP). This procedure, however, obstructs the view of consequences apart from those aggregates that are more or less meaningful. In other words, the aggregates obstruct the view on individual human action. It is individual human actions in the first place that lead to exchanges of things and thus to exchange relationships, i.e. prices. Looking at the movements of a statistical price level obstructs the analysis of consequences of individual price changes on human action. To understand the consequences of price deflation one has to analyze the consequences of a decline of individual price changes. This is what price deflation really means: the fall of a significant portion of individual prices. Of course, prices are always the result of a complex market process. It is within this dynamic of human interactions that one can determine which prices fall first, which fall later, which fall faster, which fall slower and to which extent. Which companies or individuals make higher or lower profits in a price deflation depends on this dynamic.

This dynamic is the opposite of the dynamic of the Cantillon effect. When, for instance, the government confiscates and destroys some money that would have been used to buy cars, then car prices fall and the car industry contracts. Workers and entrepreneurs in the car industry will have less money to spend. Their monetary demands will decrease, leading to falling prices in other specific areas of the economy. In this manner, the price decline spreads over the whole economy. Resources will be shifted from the car industry and industries—where prices fall most—to industries where prices fall to a lesser extent.

P. Bagus, *In Defense of Deflation*, Financial and Monetary Policy Studies 41,
DOI 10.1007/978-3-319-13428-4_4

Of course, to know why prices fall is also important. I have analyzed different reasons for such price falls in Chap. 3 and already have indicated some specific consequences of the different kinds of price deflation. Now, I will focus on the question of what a lower price means generally for human actions or individuals.

Obviously, prices fall during a price deflation. For the individual, however, it is not so important that prices are falling, but rather that they are lower than they could have been without the cause that led to the price deflation. What is the consequence that a price or many prices are lower than before or lower than they could have been without the cause that led to the price deflation? A price is an exchange relationship, which means that when a price is set, an exchange occurs. Assuming that people prefer more goods to less goods and more money to less money, we can deduce the consequences of lower prices. The buyer of a good or service against money prefers lower prices. Hence, he will be better off than he would have been with a higher price. On the other side of the exchange is the seller of the good or service that is buying the money. The seller prefers higher prices and will be worse off than he would have been with a higher price. Individuals complaining about price deflation are not complaining about falling prices per se, but rather about the fact that they are net losers. They would be in favor of a price deflation if their buying prices would fall and their selling price would remain stable. For example, fixed income groups would welcome price deflation.

The main consequence of price deflation is, therefore, that buyers of goods and services will be better off than without the price decline of what they demand and sellers of goods and services will be worse off than without the price decline of what they sell. As almost every individual is both a buyer as well as a seller of goods and services on the market and prices fall to different degrees and at different times, one cannot say a priori who will be a net winner and who will be a net loser of a price deflation. We only know that as with every change in the data of the economy a price deflation means a redistribution of wealth in the society. However, the amount of wealth or number of productive facilities is not directly affected by this.

One important implication of the price deflation is also, that the real debt burden increases. One has to sell more goods and services to obtain the money to repay the debt than without the price deflation. In this sense, creditors benefit and debtors lose. As many individuals are both creditors and debtors directly or indirectly through participations in companies or investment funds, one cannot say a priori who will be a net winner and who will be a net loser due to the increase in real debt burdens. Also fixed income groups tend to win in a price deflation as their income is not reduced but they can buy goods and services more cheaply. In the following section, I will look more closely at this redistribution process implied in price deflation and its other consequences. Then, I will analyze some common errors among economists about the consequences of price deflation. At the conclusion of this chapter, I analyze the reasons for the strong opposition toward falling prices.

4.1.2 Consequences of Price Deflation

4.1.2.1 Redistribution in Favor of Fixed Income Groups and Creditors

In general, those people benefit from a price deflation whose buying proceeds fall faster than their selling proceeds, while those people lose whose buying proceeds fall slower than their selling proceeds. Another cause of a change in relative wealth position is caused by changes in asset prices. Some asset prices fall slower than others. Thus, people gain or lose in their relative wealth position according to the extent of the decline in the prices of their assets.

In particular, a price deflation leads to a redistribution in favor of fixed income groups and creditors. Fixed income groups benefit because their incomes remain stable while their buying prices fall. Creditors benefit, because the money they receive as debt payments can buy more goods and services than without the price fall. Of course, if the price deflation was anticipated, the nominal interest rate will change accordingly. If the creditor wishes a real return on his capital of 5 % and he expects an increase in the purchasing power of money of 3 %, he will be willing to lend his money for a nominal interest rate of 2 %. The same is *mutatis mutandis* true for potential debtors. Thus, an anticipated price deflation does not change expected returns of both creditors and debtors.

Rothbard argues in a historical, not theoretical argument, that the redistribution might be seen as an advantage of a price deflation because we have experienced decades of price inflation:

> After our long process of inflation, a deflation would mean that the fixed-income groups or the relatively fixed-income groups—academics for one, the traditional widows and orphans, people on pensions, creditors—would finally get a little bit of their own back. I see nothing wrong with that. It seems to me that after decades of the compulsory redistribution of wealth from the fixed-income groups to the other groups, there is nothing wrong with a little bit of restitution. A little bit of "reparations" on behalf of those of us on more of a fixed-income level. So I think that there is a good in itself too—the prospect of a little bit of compensatory deflation. (1976, pp. 37–38)

In other words, those who have lost in the inflation are likely to win. Rothbard's argument is, of course, not an economic argument, per se, but one based in moral and ethical considerations combined with a historical analysis. It is, of course possible, that those who win in a price inflation position themselves in a way so that they win again in a price deflation.

4.1.2.2 Speeding up of the Recovery in a Recession

One type of monetary deflation that may also lead to a price deflation is the bank credit deflation. The bank credit deflation has an important effect. It speeds up the adjustment process. During the credit expansion, when the new money enters the loan market and artificially reduces the interest rate, more investment projects are begun that can be successfully ended with the scarce resources of society. Important in this respect, is that the price differentials or "natural rate of interest" on the market is artificially lowered. In a credit contraction or credit crunch the opposite effect occurs. The interest rate increases. Entrepreneurs have less funds to bid for factors of production. Factors' prices fall and price differentials and interest rates increase again, thus motivating investments. The price fall is stronger in the higher stages of production where the effect of a higher interest rate is felt more strongly.

Capital values are reduced in the higher stages of production and it becomes obvious that with the higher interest rate, many of the production processes already begun were never viable. They are liquidated. This is an adjustment to the higher interest rate that complies with the higher time preference of market participants. The market process, via credit contraction, makes it clear that many production processes were undertaken erroneously. This means that the credit contraction speeds up the shift of factors of production from the higher stages to the lower stages of production. The adjustment process of the market is speeded up (Rothbard 2000, p. 18).

The deflationary credit contraction makes the adjustment of the structure of production to consumers' wishes faster than otherwise. There is no lingering and reanimation of malinvestment, but rather an efficient and fast purging of them. Hence, Salerno regards a deliberate reduction of the money supply by a central bank as something beneficial (2003, p. 88). It stops the credit expansion and helps to liquidate malinvestments.[217]

This effect of a credit contraction, namely the speeding up of the readjustment process, occurs of course only, when there has been an artificial distortion of the structure of production in an artificial boom. If there has not been a distortion of the structure of production, for example, because entrepreneurs anticipated the effect on the interest rate[218] then there is no readjustment necessary. The redistributional effects of a credit contraction via bankruptcies of companies that relied on further credits etc., persist, of course also in this case.

There is another possible effect of price deflation in a recession, "namely, that deflation sugarcoats the pill of recession" (Rothbard 1976, p. 38). For example, in the Great Depression the cost of living constantly fell. Those people who did not lose their jobs, actually enjoyed a rising living standard. As prices fall, those people whose income is not reduced, actually benefit in the time of recession. At least

---

[217] Salerno offers also an ethical argument in favor of a deliberate credit contraction induced by a central bank. He regards the fiduciary media issued by the banking system as "counterfeit property titles" (2003, p. 88). The destruction of those counterfeit property titles he regards as beneficial and an obligation of the central bank: "Similarly, in carrying out a contractionary monetary policy, the central bank is merely ceasing to violate its contractual obligation to maintain the integrity of its depositors' titles to their stored money balances..." Salerno refers to the case of a commodity money. However, the argument can *mutatis mutandis* also be applied to a fiat money. He thinks, however, that a central bank in a fiat money regime would never adopt a contractionary policy. In a gold standard regime, Salerno (ibid.) also sees the contraction as a step in a transition process back to a 100 % commodity money.

[218] See Hülsmann (1998).

consumers experience an ease or consolidation by falling prices. Eliminating this price fall would had make the recession harder for those who have maintained their jobs.

4.1.2.3 Potential Effects of a Price Deflation

Price Deflation Might Increase Savings

In a depression some of the erroneously undertaken investment projects have to be liquidated, because there are not enough savings available to sustain them. Rothbard shows that due to a credit contraction, "time preferences themselves" may decline because the falling price level leads to accounting losses and understatement of profits, which may induce businessmen to increase their savings (2000, p. 18). This is so because "[b]usiness accounting records the value of assets at their original costs." (p. 17). What seems like losses and capital consumption, is not so in reality, because the prices of assets and capital goods, that must be renewed, have decreased. This is basically an accounting illusion that can lead businessmen to increase their savings in order to make up for perceived losses and capital consumption.

Related to this is the so-called wealth effect. Due to falls in the nominal value of income, assets, etc. individuals might believe they are poorer. Moreover, when asset prices collapse they get aware that they had invested in malinvestments. To compensate for the nominal reduction of income and the investment losses individuals might reduce consumption relative to savings.

These are possible psychological effects of a price deflation. In the case of an increase in savings, the recession is cushioned and the recovery speeded up. Less adjustments are necessary because it was precisely a lack of savings in relation to the undertaken investment projects that led to the recession.

Price Deflation Might Induce a Pressure to Break Price Rigidities

A price deflation can lead to a pressure to reduce institutional price rigidities. These price rigidities are often caused by state intervention or government privileges that make prices downwardly rigid. As prices fall and other prices are rigid downward, these downwardly rigid prices effectively become minimum prices, in other words, minimum prices over a market clearing price. The results are the typical consequences of minimum prices: (1) an over-supply that is not sold; (2) a misdirection of the producer's entrepreneurial spirit from producing the goods in question; and (3) a misdirection of the entrepreneurial spirit of consumers to searching for substitutes. In the field of the supply of and demand for labor services, more people try to work at those prices and entrepreneurs intend to substitute workers with machines. There will be unemployment. The unsold surplus arouses discontent of the sellers, potentially bringing down the government interventions and privileges. There will be pressure on politicians to remove these interventions that cause the price rigidities. In the case of labor services, the unemployed might pressure the government to break privileges for unions and revoke legislation which causes wages to be rigid downwards. It further might induce workers to leave the unions.[219]

Price Deflation Might Bring Down the Fractional Reserve Banking System

A price deflation might bring down a fractional reserve banking system. This is so, because a price deflation can lead to bankruptcies as the real burden of debt increases. Especially in a recession after an artificial boom, a credit contraction and bankruptcies due to the malinvestments occurs. As a consequence of the bankruptcies that are induced by the price deflation, loans that banks gave out will turn bad.[220] The stocks of the bankrupt companies that other banks hold will lose value, perhaps even to the point of becoming worthless. In general, the assets of banks will fall in value. In order to preserve solvency banks will restrict credits and put pressure on its corporate partners and other banks. The decline in one bank's assets' values might induce doubts in the solvency and liquidity of other banks. Due to the credit restriction, corporate partners might go bankrupt. Other banks also financing these corporations get into financial difficulty as well. Bank runs might occur. In a fractional reserve system, by definition, the bank cannot pay out all demand deposit claims that exist. The bank will go bankrupt. If one bank collapses this instability might spread to other fractional reserve banks due to their interconnectedness. The bankruptcy will induce fear about the solvency of other banks, further reduce the value of their assets' value, and lead to systematic bank runs. A bank panic ensues. This might bring the whole fractional reserve banking system down if the central bank fails to bail out the banking system. This possible consequence of price deflation is beneficial as it purges the old banking system making place for a 100 % gold standard as Rothbard points out.

> We were in the process of smashing the banking system, and then the various governors, and Hoover and Roosevelt came in with bank holidays and the Federal Deposit Insurance Corporation which bailed the banks out. If not for that bail-out, there was a golden opportunity to eliminate fractional reserve banking forevermore. There would not even have been the problem of a transition period because we were *in* a transition, it was just a matter of leaving the thing alone for a few months and the deed would have been done. Deflation would have helped in this process of smashing the fractional reserve banking system. Why it should have been smashed is that that system has been a constant threat and source of inflation and special privilege, the business cycle, and a whole craft of other evils. (1976, p. 39) (Ibid., italics in the original)

[219] See Rothbard (1991, p. 67).

[220] See also Sect. 3.3.4 on this cumulative process.

Also Salerno states that the failure of fractional reserve banks

> has the salutary effect on the economy and enhances the welfare of market participants. For it is initiated by a voluntary and contractual redemption of property titles to money by bank depositors who perceive that fractional reserve banks are no longer functioning to safely and securely store their cash balances. When any form that trades on its trustworthiness, be it a financial services firm, an armored car company, or a law firm, loses the confidence of its customers or clients that it is operating in their best interests, it will rapidly purged from the market by an adjustment process that reallocates resources and improves the welfare of consumers. (2003, pp. 86–87)

Beside the economic welfare arguments in favor of a collapse of single banks or of the whole banking system, there is also a legal or moral argument.[221] Huerta de Soto argues that depositors, historically, entrusted their money to the banks for safekeeping. Issuing fiduciary media is a violation of the essential juridical obligation of safekeeping. The bank issues more titles to money than it has money proper. If customers do not know about this, it is plain fraud. Even if depositors, that want to have their money safely kept and always available, know and approve of the lending out of their deposits, the contract is a "legal monster"[222] as there are contradictory legal aims. In this case, the contract is null and void. In the case of a central bank backing the practices of the bank, the contract depends on government interventions into the monetary and banking system. The collapse of such a fraudulent or legally problematic system is a possible consequence of deflation.

The collapse of the financial and monetary system and the adoption of a new currency would put an end to the continuous redistribution of income in favor of those with good connections to the monetary and political establishment and to the disadvantage of those without such connection. Of course, this institutional change would mean disruptions.[223] It would mean an adaption of the structure of production which is now geared to satisfy the needs of the inflation profiteers, indebted companies, consumers, and governments, as well as fractional reserve banks and their best customers. A disruption, though, is not something bad in principle.[224] Every change in the data of a market economy means a "disruption." An important question in this context is if the disruptions stems from a violation of property rights, or not. The disruption might also stem from a restitution of property rights or an abstention from further infringements on them. For instance, if slavery in a slave economy is abolished or communism is abolished, this will lead to disruptions. The same is true when a free monetary system is adopted. Instead of the preferences of the old establishment, now the preferences of the formerly exploited population determine production. The length and amplitude of the disruptions depend on how

---

[221] See Huerta de Soto (2006a, b), Chaps. 1–4. See also Rothbard (1991, 1998) for a libertarian ethical theory that implies that fractional reserve banking is fraud.

[222] See Huerta de Soto (2006a, p. 151). For a further discussion of the legal impossibility of a valid fractional reserve demand deposit contract see Bagus and Howden (2009, 2012a, 2013) and Bagus et al. (2013).

[223] See Hülsmann (2003a, p. 58).

[224] Hülsmann (2006, p. 66) speaks of an "creative destruction" reminiscence of Schumpeter.

well entrepreneurs anticipate how much each price will drop. Theoretically, this rock-bottom could be reached immediately.[225] There might also be temporary unemployment, but this is not necessarily so, because workers and entrepreneurs can reach a wage agreement that makes the operation of firms profitable. It depends upon the preferences and entrepreneurial foresight of both parties.

Price Deflation Might Reduce the State's Power

The medicine for the state is inflation.[226] Via inflation there is a constant demand for government bonds many of which are finally bought or accepted as collateral by the central bank. Thus, the state can indebt itself to a much higher degree than without the fiat money inflation. It can spend more and command more resources of society than without the inflation.

In a monetary deflation or credit contraction this way to finance government debt and government expenditures is disturbed. Due to the monetary deflation prices of government bonds tend to fall. Moreover, price deflation increases the real burden of debt and leads to a redistribution from creditors to debtors as was explained above. This has an important effect as historically the biggest debtor in an economy has been the state. The real burden of government debt increases and a higher percentage of government revenue must be spent on debt payments. This means that the government, if it is not to increase unpopular taxes, has to reduce is spending on other ends. It will, thus, centralize fewer functions than in times of inflation and give more freedom to private citizens. The welfare state must be reduced. This also has an implication for the institution of the family, as the welfare state has usurped many traditional functions of the family, like care and assistance for the elderly, help in emergency situations, help during unemployment and illness, etc.[227] To the extent that the state occupies these functions, families started to lose some of their traditional meanings. Reducing the size of the welfare state might result in a reversal of this trend.

For these reasons, deflation has been unpopular among interests connected with the state. Mises explains the popularity of inflation and the unpopularity of deflation by governments:

> Looked at from the fiscal point of view, inflationism is not merely the cheapest economic policy; it is also at the same time a particularly good remedy for a low state of the public finances. Restrictionism [monetary deflation induced by the government] ...demands positive sacrifices from the national exchequer when it is carried out by the withdrawal of notes from circulation (say through the issue of interest-bearing bonds or through taxation) and their cancellation; and at the least it demands from it a renunciation of

---

[225] See Hülsmann (2003a, p. 58).

[226] Inflation allows the government to ignore fiscal resistance to its spending. This is especially important in times of war when governments hide the real costs of war by financing it via the printing press.

[227] See, for instance, Carlson (2003).

> potential income by forbidding the issue of notes at a time when the demand for money is increasing. This alone would suffice to explain why restrictionism has never been able to compete with inflationism... But furthermore... an increase in the value of money has not been to the advantage of the ruling class. Those who get an immediate benefit from such an increase are all those who are entitled to receive fixed sums of money. Creditors gain at the expense of debtors. Taxation, it is true, becomes more burdensome as the value of money rises; but the greater part of the advantage of this is secured, not by the state, but by its creditors. Now policies favoring creditors at the expense of debtors have never been popular. Lenders of money have been held in odium, at all times and among all peoples. Generally speaking, the class of persons who draw their income exclusively or largely from the interest on capital lent to others has not been particularly numerous or influential at any time in any country. (1981, pp. 263–264)

Here Mises explains the opposition of the ruling elites to monetary deflation and price deflation. He also mentions the political reasons why this policy is unpopular among politicians.

In sum, state power is likely to be reduced in times of price deflation.[228] In fact, the modern welfare state might collapse under the pressure of price deflation, as the real burden of debt increases. In this sense, Hülsmann (2003b) speaks of a liberating deflation as it has the potential to bring down the welfare state as well as the state-privileged fractional reserve banking system.[229]

Of course this is unlikely to happen, because the state has the power to prevent price deflation by inflating the money supply. It is unlikely that the state will cease to make use of inflation as a way to finance its expenditures and promote price deflation.

4.1.2.4 Price Deflation and Habits

In world of continuous price deflation, the habits of consumers and entrepreneurs will be different than in a world of continuous price inflation.[230] Expecting price deflation, consumers and entrepreneurs would indebt themselves less than they would have without this expectation. Entrepreneurs would finance their ventures rather through equity or retained earnings than through loans due to the expectation of price deflation.[231] Thus, in their actions, entrepreneurs would be more independent from banks, which in many cases grant the loans to entrepreneurs.[232]

---

[228] See for instance Sect. 5.2 for the German bank credit deflation in the 1930s and the reduction of state expenditures like unemployment benefits, pension, state employee's salaries, etc.

[229] Hülsmann (2008, p. 16), therefore sates: "A frank and enthusiastic *endorsement of deflation* is, at any rate in our time, one of the most important requirements to safeguard the future of liberty."

[230] See Hülsmann (2006, pp. 175–181) for habits in price inflation.

[231] Of course, a negative price premium could be factored into the interest rate. Nevertheless, debts become more unattractive when prices are expected to fall as it gets easier to finance through equity or retained earnings that keep increasing in purchasing power.

[232] There are further implications of the lower debts. One can, for instance, maintain that, the higher the debt of a company, the higher the pressure on managers to work efficiently. One should keep in mind, though, that equity owners can control managers in different ways and provide them with incentives.

Entrepreneurs would become more dynamic, as they would be less dependent on the approval of conservative banks. Small companies or new companies would be at less a disadvantage vis a vis corporations with good connections to the banking industry, as credit financing becomes relatively less important.

Consumers will have an incentive to save long term in cash as they expect the purchasing power of money to increase. They will save more and indebt themselves less than without the deflationary environment. Consumers will also be more independent, in that they would rely less on financial intermediaries. Watching financial markets will be less important to them as cash savings automatically brings a return. Less energy will be spent on thinking how to invest money assets in order to preserve one's wealth. Real money wealth rises automatically. Financial self-reliance and independent thinking are the results.

4.2 Myths Concerning Deflation

4.2.1 Deflation's Bad Press

Interestingly, in the actual discussion, deflation is often only implicitly assumed to be harmful rather than demonstrated to be harmful.[233] Economists start with this hypothesis, because they probably do not want to make "open" value judgments. So they avoid them by use of implicit assumptions.[234] Assuming that deflation is undesirable, economists focus their discussion on the question if and how deflation can be prevented.[235] Usually, the arguments for why deflation would be bad are rather passed over. They are assumed to be self-evident. The importance of these arguments lies in the fact that they recommend expansionary monetary policies to prevent deflation. These arguments serve, thus, to justify monetary inflation. In order to address the validity of these arguments, this section will discuss the arguments against deflation in detail. In fact, there are many fallacies concerning deflation,[236] which will be corrected in the present section.

[233] See also Sect. 2.5 on this.

[234] See Svensson (2000, p. 31) or Bernanke (2002, p. 1).

[235] See Meltzer (2000, p. 71) or Goodfriend (2001, p. 1).

[236] Austrian economists, as well, diverge on the subject of deflation and some even propose an arsenal of interventions to fight it (Bagus 2003).

4.2.2 *Myth 1: Deflation Leads to an Arbitrary and Unfair Redistribution*

Economics is a value-free science.[237] Therefore, it seems unnecessary to deal with the argument that deflation should be avoided because it leads to an unfair redistribution. Yet we will see that this argument is sometimes used implicitly and that sometimes redistribution is openly criticized. Robert Kent provides us with a clear example of this particular error.[238] He claims that price deflation leads to an "arbitrary redistribution" of real income and wealth (1966, p. 458). Kent is correct that deflation leads to a redistribution of wealth, but why would that be arbitrary and unfair? Even if we, for the sake of the argument, assume that all price deflation is somehow "arbitrary" and leads to arbitrary redistribution of real income and wealth, it does not follow that it is harmful. Furthermore, would that not be an ethical value statement? Kent admits that "those who previously gained are likely to lose purchasing power" (p. 459).[239] Actually, those who gain during inflation and those who lose during inflation are not necessarily the same as those who lose or gain during a deflation. The ability to profit in either situation depends upon entrepreneurial skills. In other words, people who most accurately anticipate the rise in the purchasing power of money gain from the price deflation.[240]

DeLong (1999) claims that it is not an entrepreneurial task to anticipate price changes. Yet, this view is erroneous. Entrepreneurs try to anticipate all relevant future changes. Price anticipation is precisely the function of entrepreneurs. Especially important for them are the prices of their factors of production and their selling prices. And of course, entrepreneurs can be successful in anticipating price changes. Hence, in times of deflation, "...entrepreneurs *can* run a profitable business by bidding down buying prices or, if it is not possible, by abstaining from investment altogether" (Hülsmann 2004, p. 51).

Moreover, it must be recognized that any change in the economy has effects on the relative wealth positions of all market participants[241] and all human actions potentially lead to benefits to some individuals and disadvantages of others. That leads us to the question: Who decides which changes on the market are arbitrary and unfair and which changes are not?

---

[237] See Mises (1998, p. 10).

[238] See also Borio and Filardo (2004, p. 7); also see Stamp who writes that "[deflation] brings about the worst type of redistribution of income" (1932, p. 5).

[239] This has another implication. In an inflationary boom, the inequality in material wealth tends to increase, as some groups benefit at the cost of other groups. When those who profit in an inflationary boom suffer losses in a price deflation, the differences in material wealth are reduced.

[240] For instance, Bernanke considers the problems for debtors who did not anticipate the deflation (2002).

[241] See Hülsmann (2004, p. 45).

Mises remarks on the changing world that:

> In the world of reality all prices are fluctuating and acting men are forced to take full account of these changes. Entrepreneurs embark upon business ventures and capitalists change their investments only because they anticipate such changes and want to profit from them. The market economy is essentially characterized as a social system in which there prevails an incessant urge toward improvement. The most provident and enterprising individuals are driven to earn profit by readjusting again and again the arrangement of production activities so as to fill in the best possible needs of the consumers. (1998, p. 539)

Yet, it can be argued that fiat deflation, i.e. a price deflation caused by government fiat, is arbitrary because it is not initiated on the free market. From an ethical point of view, deflation that is caused by government intervention might be considered unjust.[242]

More precisely, government intervention that caused prices to fall would be unjust. Rather than claiming that its result, price deflation, per se is unjust. Deflation benefits some and harms others. As there are no interpersonal utility comparisons possible, we cannot say from a scientific point of view whether deflation is good or bad. We must state, however, that there is price deflation stemming from a violation of property rights and price deflation not stemming from a violations of property rights.

Of course, a redistribution will also occur in the case of a "liberating deflation" that purges an unsound banking system, e.g. by an abolishment of the amnesty for fractional reserve banks for the fraud of issuing fiduciary media. Fractional reserve banking is legally problematic, when banks issue more money titles than they have money and they promise, at the same time, to redeem them on demand. A sound and non-fraudulent banking system, is a 100 % reserve system. In this case, redistribution is not an arbitrary and unfair solution for it involves justice. Every punishment of criminals or the stopping of criminal activities will bring about a loss for the criminals and their trade partners, while their victims will win.

A crucial question is: Can "unfair" redistribution be prevented by inflation, i.e., an increase in the money supply? In practice, new money created out of thin air is injected through the banking system. Therefore, there is a redistribution in favor of the banks and the connected industries and individuals which get the new money first. They profit because they have higher sums of money to bid for resources before the prices have risen. On the contrary, there are people whose incomes rise only after there has been an increase in prices. Yet, why would this scenario be less unfair?

---

[242] For a libertarian theory of ethics that considers all government interventions as unjust as they are based on the initiation of violence, see Rothbard (1998).

4.2.3 *Myth 2: Deflationary Redistribution Necessarily Decreases Production*

Some argue that the redistribution which deflation causes would be harmful,[243] because through hurting debtors, entrepreneurs, businesses, or the financial system, overall production would fall. I will deal with these arguments one at a time, but it should be stressed here that redistribution or changes in the wealth positions of the market participants per se do not harm production at all. The production will be different though, since those, who benefit from the redistribution will have other preferences and talents than those who suffer a loss.

4.2.3.1 Financial Collapse and Production

The first variant of this argument states that if the price deflation was not anticipated and many debtors go bankrupt, the financial institutions of a fractional reserve system can get into difficulties (Keynes [1925] 1963, pp. 168–169).[244] Surely, it is true, loans that were given under the expectation of inflation can turn bad and harm banks' balance sheets. There is also a redistribution of wealth in favor of creditors. Furthermore, it is true, that the unsound monetary system, which rests on continuous inflation and benefits those who first receive the new money and money titles, could collapse. However, a new financial system based on 100 % reserve banking could emerge. It is hard to see why that would be an "adverse effect" (Bernanke 2002, p. 3) on the soundness of the monetary and financial system. Moreover, this new and sound monetary system would certainly spur production. Also, one always has to keep in mind the alternative necessary to prevent the price deflation: inflationary monetary policies. These policies even though not leading to a strong price inflation can severely distort the structure of production and lead to malinvestments when the interest rates are artificially reduced and a business cycle sets in. Banks and debtors are bailed out by the injection of newly created money or money substitutes, encouraging more risky behavior of them in the future. The inflationary monetary policies that prevent a price deflation and problems for the financial system also lead to a redistribution in favor of bailed out businesses and banks.

---

[243] (Keynes [1931] 1963, p. 177; or King 1994, p. 422); Interestingly, Keynes, himself, summarizes here the liberating effects of deflation and admits that the financial system would be liquidated and "[i]ndividually many of us would be 'ruined,' even though collectively we were much as before." ([1931], 1963, pp. 177–178).

[244] Hicks (1946, p. 264) argues that the increased fear of bankruptcy in times of price deflation would have a negative output effect as debts are harder to pay back. Again, the money saved to be able to repay the increasing debt burdens might come from reducing consumption spending. Therefore, investment might actually increase relative to consumption spending. This would lead to a more capital intensive structure of production and a higher output.

4.2.3.2 Entrepreneurs and Production

Another variant of this argument stresses that there would be redistribution at the expense of entrepreneurs. DeLong states that entrepreneurs are hurt by falling prices[245] and therefore production falls. Stamp writes that "slowly falling prices are a deadening influence on business itself" (1932, p. 4). Bye even states that: "When prices fall, however, the effects upon business men are very disastrous..." (1944, p. 220).

Warren and Pearson argue that as production takes time, and prices fall during the production time, long production processes will turn disadvantageous in times of deflation:

> The longer the period from the beginning to the completion of an article, the more serious are the effects of deflation. If the producer can sell his finished product in a few months after he has purchased the raw materials, he may succeed in spite of deflation. If the process of deflation requires one, two, or more years, as is true in agriculture, the results are exceedingly serious. (1933, p. 192)

Yet this mechanistic view of entrepreneurship is erroneous. Entrepreneurs can anticipate the price deflation and accordingly bid down the prices of factors of production, e.g. raw materials, and this they can successfully do independent of the length of the production process. It is certainly true, that price deflation can hurt entrepreneurs whose selling prices fall first while the prices of other goods and services they buy are still higher. Price deflation can also hurt those who have debts, but it does not hurt all entrepreneurs. DeLong's idea about the concept of entrepreneurship is obviously confused. Entrepreneurs try to anticipate the future prices of their products and bid for factors of production in relation to their anticipation. In this respect it is not important if general prices fall or rise. An entrepreneur can always thrive, also in a price deflation.[246] An entrepreneur can always err by expecting higher future prices for his products than will actually occur, and bidding too much for factors of production. He will, as a result, suffer losses. There is no systematical reason why entrepreneurs would err more in times of falling prices than in any other scenario. And as Mises points out:

> After all, the businessman's most important characteristic is flexibility. The businessman can operate at a profit, even if the general tendency of prices is downward, and economic conditions can even improve then too. (Mises 1978, p. 198)[247]

Especially, new and small companies may flourish during a price deflation. They have an advantage vis-a-vis big established competitors that face problems due to their debt burden. An economy were price deflation is not prevented by government intervention becomes much more dynamic as the prevention of price deflation

[245] See Delong (1999); For a similar view, see Keynes (1936).

[246] An example is the information industry and computer industry in the last decades that were able make profits and thrive with falling selling prices.

[247] Translation is from the German original (Mises 1931, p. 29).

favors the established business elite on cost of potential newcomers. Price deflation does not pose a problem for entrepreneurs per se, but a problem for the indebted business establishment.

Furthermore, in times of falling prices the essential price differential (the difference between buying and selling prices) does not necessarily fall but can actually increase and stimulate businesses if buying prices fall faster than selling prices do.[248] Moreover, if the price drop is unanticipated, the real rate of return, respectively the natural rate of interest, might not change due to the increase in purchasing power of the revenues. The anticipation of falling prices, in contrast, "lead[s] to an immediate fall in factor prices" and "partial anticipation speeds up the adjustment of the PPM [purchasing power of money] to the changed conditions" (Rothbard 2001, p. 697).

The myth that falling prices pose a problem for entrepreneurs might partly stem from the fact that most economists concentrate on one particular price index which is the consumer price index.[249] When they say that prices fall, they mean consumer goods' prices. All of the prices of the different factors of production are passed over. Asset prices, like stock exchange prices, are also passed over. Indeed, considering the vast amount of assets and different stages of production, consumer goods' prices constitute, a very minor portion of all prices in the economy and therefore, form a relatively small part of prices. For most companies consumer goods' prices are not directly relevant as they operate in higher stages of production. However, many economists only concentrate on the consumer price index. They look on an arbitrarily selected and very small number of prices, excluding from their index such important prices like asset prices and producer goods' prices. Then they infer from falling consumer goods' prices that entrepreneurs are in trouble as their selling prices fall. They neglect that the prices of factors of production can fall too and that the majority of entrepreneurs are not involved in the production of consumer goods but instead produce producer goods.

4.2.3.3 Debts, Bankruptcies and Production

Another variation of this argument sees the problem for businesses and production in the rising real debts and deterioration of balance sheets due to the collapse of asset prices.[250] But again, this simply leads to a redistribution that may not affect production at all. Surely, if a company rests on loans and invests in assets whose prices were inflated by credit expansion, problems can be expected. In such a case,

---

[248] See Rothbard (2000, p. 17).

[249] It must be noted, that it is illusionary to measure the changes in the purchasing power of money. Every individual would need his own index, which would be constantly changing. For a critique of index numbers, see Mises (1998, pp. 221–224).

[250] See Goodfriend (2001, p. 17); Cargill (2001, p. 116).

the company's real debt might increase to such an extent that it is forced into bankruptcy and its assets would therefore be turned over to the debtors.

As Rothbard states,

> It has often been maintained that a failing price level injures business firms because it aggravates the burden of fixed monetary debt. However, the creditors of a firm are just as much its owners as are the equity shareholders. The equity shareholders have less equity in the business to the extent of its debts. Bondholders (long-term creditors) are just different types of owners, very much as preferred and common stock holders exercise their ownership rights differently. Creditors save money and invest it in an enterprise, just as do stockholders. Therefore, no change in price level by itself helps or hampers a business; creditor-owners and debtor-owners may simply divide their gains (or losses) in different proportions. These are mere intra-owner controversies. (2000, p. 51)

There would be merely a change of ownership and a redistribution of the assets, from failed entrepreneurs to those who more successfully anticipated the price change. Successful entrepreneurs would now have the chance to use the assets in a way that better suits consumer wishes.

Yet, there is no need for the claim to be true that price deflation would lead to "changes in total productive activity and therefore in total output and employment."[251] The mere change of ownership inherent in all market economies from failed entrepreneurs to those that can satisfy consumer wants better does not have to change production. Actually, bankruptcy is a way to get rid of debts. If the production process is profitable, it will go on. The physical integrity of the redistributed assets is not inhibited at all by the change of ownership. And the opportunity costs of not producing and losing market share are high. When, for instance, Chrysler was taken over by Daimler, it did not mean that production of Chrysler cars had to fall. In such cases, the new owners are likely to change the production somewhat if there has been mismanagement by the former owners. They might also cut back on production and release workers in an attempt to restructure the company in favor of consumers wants. However, the new owners or their hired managers might increase production, as well.

Ben Bernanke argues that "bankruptcy imposes net social costs" (1981, p. 155). Thus, he is assuming an objective standard by which social costs and benefits could be identified, measured and added. However, only when they act do individuals have costs and benefits, which are subjective concepts. They cannot be measured, nor compared interpersonally, nor added, nor subtracted.[252] The concept of social costs on which this argument against deflation rests is, therefore, spurious.

Of course, it is true that every change of ownership implies some period of transition. George Reisman considers this period of transition a main disadvantage of deflation and he stresses the practical difficulties of mass bankruptcies during a deflation:

---

[251] See Kent (1966, p. 458); On this point, also see, Bernanke (1981, p. 155).

[252] On the subjective concepts of utility, value, costs, and benefits see Huerta de Soto (2001, pp. 41–50).

> ...[M]ass bankruptcies, which, given the inability of today's judicial system to keep pace even with its current load, would probably take a decade or more to get sorted out. That would mean that in the interval the economy would be largely paralyzed, because no one would know just who owned what.[253]

The ability of present-day judicial system to handle cases of mass bankruptcy is not, of course, a theoretical argument against deflation. For Reisman's argument deals with the practical difficulties a severe deflation might cause for the contemporary judicial system. Yet, there is no theoretical reason why there could not be a judicial system that could settle the lawsuits very quickly. That being said, let us deal with this practical argument. It must be stressed, that an increased demand for judicial services on the free market brings about an increased supply of those services. Yet, Reisman could contend, that we face a government monopoly of judicial services. Then, of course, government intervention ultimately would constitute the problem. However, politicians would likely come up with emergency measures if deflation-caused bankruptcies were to over-strain the judicial system.[254] For politicians are eager to search and find problems they can fix. In the absence of government intervention, the entrepreneurial function would be mobilized to solve the problem. Thus, the judicial system itself could come up with solutions for this problem.

It is true that the judicial sector would expand in the transitional period and attract resources. However, why would that be bad? From a value-free point of view, one cannot argue that the expansion of one industry or sector is bad. In our case we can only say that the expansion of the judicial sector is wanted by consumers who wish to settle their disputes. It is, therefore, productive. Moreover, in the transition period it is not in the interest of the parties involved to leave the assets idle. During this period, the assets of the bankrupt business are in use as well. As Robert Giffen states: "Contraction of currency and fall of prices, though they are painful things, do not stop production materially" (1971, p. 124). Giffen forgets to say, that while it might be painful for entrepreneurs who go bankrupt it might be very rewarding for those who have profited, i.e., those entrepreneurs who more accurately anticipated the price deflation.

One possible effect of the bankruptcy process is, though, that suppliers and customers lose confidence in the bankrupt company. Instead of dealing with a bankrupt company, they turn to competitors. The competitors that anticipated the price deflation and manage to stay liquid will gain at the expense of the bankrupt companies. They can thrive.

This loss of confidence is a psychological, adverse effect for the bankrupt company. If there are many bankruptcies, people might not have competitors to turn to, therefore choosing to stay and cooperate with the company. However, they

[253] (1999, p. 961); Also, Bernanke states that "[a]ministrative and legal expenses in bankruptcy are substantial." (1981, p. 155)

[254] Governments actually did that before. See Hamburger (1933) for blanke measures during the German Great Depression.

might also increase their cash balances, thereby putting a further downward pressure on prices. The downward pressure on prices will end, when the companies have finally changed ownership. People will anxiously cooperate at the lower prices and, reduce their cash balances again.

An additional argument concerning bankruptcy refers to a possible loss of knowledge and entrepreneurial talents. When the property of the bankrupt company is transfered to the creditors, the creditors might not have the capabilities of managing the company successfully. For example, when a farmer cannot repay his debts due to a price deflation, the farm is turned over to his creditors. The creditor might be a bank, which has no expertise in farming and does not know the particular circumstances of the farm. This being true, some replies are in order. First, the knowledge problem appears in every bankruptcy. It is the function of bankruptcy to change the control of resources from unsuccessful entrepreneurs to successful ones. The successful ones tend to have a better expertise than the unsuccessful ones.

Second, the knowledge problem does not change the fact, that the bankrupt entrepreneur has malinvested the scarce resources of society from the viewpoint of consumers. However, it must be noted that the bankrupt entrepreneur might have been brought into this position by government intervention. When there is a fiat deflation that causes bankruptcies, these bankruptcies are caused ultimately by the government intervention.

Third, the creditor can hire someone that has the specific knowledge to successfully manage the company. The creditor can even hire the former owner as manager. Fourth, one has to consider the alternative to prevent those bankruptcies. One alternative would be inflationary monetary policies to prevent those bankruptcies. Yet, these policies have severe consequences. They bail out bankrupt entrepreneurs, thereby leading to moral hazard. These policies penalize the successful entrepreneurs or creditors that could have taken over the bankrupt company. Furthermore, these policies can induce more malinvestments by artificially reducing the interest rates.[255]

Another possible effect during the transition period of a bankruptcy is that the bankrupt owner tries to disinvest and consume his capital or invest in other ventures, which leads to a different structure of production. This happens in every bankruptcy. Would it not be arbitrary to say that the needed transitional time to sort out a bankruptcy would be too long and therefore bad? And what is the optimal rate of bankruptcy in an economy? It must be pointed out that bankruptcy is not something bad per se. Hülsmann explains,

[255] It is true that the expansion of the legal sector bidding away factors of production from other ventures implies a reduction of other sectors. Real income in terms of goods and services other than legal services, therefore, falls slightly in the short-term. But this is not the end of the story. We should also keep in mind, that the medium and long-term growth prospects are greatly enhanced by these mass bankruptcies. People will be less willing to accept fiat money inflation and to incur in debts. The size of the state may be reduced significantly. There may even arise a free market monetary system.

> Bankruptcy fulfills the crucially important social function of preserving the available stock of capital. And it plays this role in all conceivable scenarios: when it results from fraud, when it results from insolvency, and when it results from illiquidity. (2006, p. 149).

Funds and assets are channeled from failed or fraudulent investors who have been misusing the scarce assets of society to those more honest and successful investors. In a free market consumers determine this rate of bankruptcy by their daily actions. Of course, government intervention can also cause bankruptcies, for example, by fiat deflation. In this case the amount of bankruptcies exceeds the amount that would have been optimal from the consumers' points of view. However, price deflation per se is not leading to more bankruptcies than on the free market but rather the government intervention is the cause of the increase in bankruptcies. Government interventions can lead entrepreneurs to commit clusters of errors in the form of malinvestments by facilitating credit expansion. Furthermore, government intervention can directly cause bankruptcies when it coercively deflates the money supply or lowers prices.

4.2.3.4 Price Deflation's Source and Production

It is also important to examine the sources of the price deflation before making any predictions about changes of production. First, a price deflation caused by an increase in productivity is indeed a result of an increase in total output. And this price deflation is also anticipated by the corresponding producers (Selgin 1997, p. 31). Those producers increase production and sell their goods lower than their rivals in the expectation of increasing their profits this way. They are aware of, anticipate, and deliberately cause the price fall. Second, a fiscal or confiscatory deflation, i.e. a destruction of money or money titles by the government, can flatten and shorten the structure of production due to an increase in the time preference rates (Hoppe 2001, p. 14). Third, a deflation initiated by the government through the loan market might lead to a shortening of the structure of production and therefore to reduction in total output. However, this intervention might also counteract the lengthening tendencies of a simultaneous credit expansion.

Regardless of which source is considered, a price deflation simply results in a redistribution of wealth. The preferences of the winners and losers cannot be known *ex ante*, and therefore, the effects on the structure of production and output cannot be predicted. The critics are right in that a price deflation results in economic changes. For all changes in economic data correspond to a change in the economy. But they give no explanation why changes should be prevented. Nor do they explain why the changes a central bank system induces via monetary inflation are somehow better than those made by the redistribution of wealth resulting from price deflation.

Again, the alternatives to price deflation should be kept in mind. Why would inflationary redistribution lead to an increase in production? The only thing we know for sure about the inflationary redistribution is that it will change the structure of the economy. An ongoing inflation in favor of some market participants will surely prevent some bankruptcies. In contrast, the inflation would hamper those businesses and households that are the last to get the new money because they have already faced a price structure driven up by the first recipients of the new money. While established industries might be bailed out, other companies are prevented from growing or coming into existence.

4.2.4 Myth 3: Deflation-Induced Price Instability Leads Necessarily to Chaos

One variant of this argument, and one of the most widespread fallacies in monetary economics, states that economic growth must be accompanied by a corresponding increase in the money supply; i.e., there must be an adjustment of the quantity of money to economic growth. This "adjustment" would prevent prices from falling. David Colander argues that "...if there's an increase in real goods but not a corresponding increase in money, there will be a shortage of money, which will hamper the economy."[256] Remarkable is that Colander fails to explain why it would hamper the economy.

He does not recognize that any quantity of money is suitable to fulfill the essential function of money as a medium of exchange (Rothbard 1990, p. 34). Any quantity of goods and services can be exchanged with almost any quantity of money. An increase in the purchasing power of money does not affect its usefulness as a medium of exchange. It is true that inflation may preserve businesses whose ventures rested on the expectation of higher priced products. In contrast, an inflation could cause harm to those businesses which had expected lower prices for their factors of production or which had lent out money. Moreover, the proposed inflation initiated through the loan market can artificially lengthen and broaden the structure of production by lowering the market rate of interest. Since real savings does not sustain this lengthening, the malinvestments must be liquidated at some point.[257] The initiation and maintaining of the unsustainable boom can hardly be called a "balance."

It is often assumed though, that price stability itself would be something desirable because it would balance the economy.[258] Therefore it is argued that "...[d]eflation is not price stability, and the absence of price stability is likely to increase information costs, interfere with the market mechanism and resource allocation, and make long-term planning more difficult" (Svensson 2000, p. 29).

Selgin provides a strong argument against that view. He argues that a stable and thus "certain" price level might be itself the source of misinformation as it does not

---

[256] Colander (1995, p. 519); See also Hahn (1956) for this argument.

[257] For more intensive accounts of the Austrian business cycle theory, see: Rothbard (2001) and Rothbard (2000, Part I), and Mises (1998) and Huerta de Soto (2006b).

[258] See Shiratsuka (2000, p. 16) or Dowd (1995, p. 722).

change despite changes in productivity, thereby distorting an important source of information for economic agents (1997, p. 45).

Moreover, when money is injected into the economy to attain price stability and prevent price deflation, this fact itself blocks the entrepreneurial function of dealing with possible problems of price deflation. When falling prices lead to problems in interhuman relationships, entrepreneurs are presented with an opportunity to solve those problems. For example, debts and salaries might get renegotiated in a way that satisfies both creditors, employers, debtors, and employees. Those involved in the negotiation will come up with solutions that take into account the specific circumstances of time and place, solutions that we might find difficult to imagine now because they would be created by entrepreneurs in these specific situations. In any case, it is problematic to base the argument against deflation on the assumption that these problems cannot be solved by spontaneous market processes, and then to call for a monetary inflation policy in order to prevent price deflation.

But let us focus again on the aim of price stability. Economic calculation can be successful under a stable, a growing, or a declining purchasing power of money. Also, even if we grant the argument that with "guaranteed" price stability, "long-term planning" is easier, it is not a conclusive argument against price deflation. Indeed, with price controls, long-term planning becomes easier as one source of uncertainty is reduced. Yet, even with government intervention, price stability is not guaranteed as a government might change its intervention at any point. However, just for the sake of argument, let us assume government interventions in voluntary exchanges are stable in the long run, making planning easier. We must then ask if this reduced uncertainty is a good per se. To answer this question it must be stressed, that many government interventions into the free market limit the array of possible human actions, which economic agents regard as beneficial and, could otherwise undertake. Since there are fewer actions possible, planning in this sense becomes easier. Yet, this ease in planning is not an advantage from the actors' or consumers' points of view, whose satisfaction of wants becomes limited.

Furthermore, stabilizing the price level does not reduce "information costs." They are actually increased. A quasi "aggregate price control" enforced by a central bank's manipulations of the money supply distorts the market prices. It becomes even more difficult to develop the knowledge or information necessary to successfully engage in business operations. The reason for this is that market prices become different than those that would occur in absence of that intervention and would have been based on consumer preferences. In addition, aggregate price controls inhibit necessary adjustments by rescuing businesses that would not be profitable without the manipulation of the money supply. If the new money flows into the loan market, there might be a misplanning in the form of malinvestments. "Businessmen, in short, are misled by the bank inflation into believing that the supply of saved funds is greater than it really is" (Rothbard 2000, p. 5). The resulting boom bust cycles make long-term planning more difficult.

In any case, there is no explanation why free market prices are bad and price controls good. As Mises points out: "All plans to render money neutral and stable are contradictory. Money is an element of action and consequently of change" (1998, p. 416).

Surely resources are allocated differently if there is government intervention. But it is hard to see how free market price changes interfere with the "market mechanism and resource allocation." Preventing price adjustments by inflation-targeting will make necessary readjustments slower, if the structure of production has been distorted. When the malinvestments become obvious, entrepreneurs might not even cut back production, because they rely on the central bank to fight price deflation.

Besides the argument that price deflation leads to a chaotic planning for entrepreneurs, there is a related argument stating that deflation leads to political chaos. Thus, Warren and Pearson argue that "[w]ith the collapse of commodity prices and the consequent difficulty of balancing the budget, the British have abandoned their policy of free trade for the protective tariff. In a further endeavor to curtail imports and improve the economic status of their producers, they have inaugurated a widespread advertising campaign to 'buy British'" (1933, p. 297).

Indeed, in times of price deflation there might be a tendency toward economic isolation as producers get into financial trouble and push harder for protectionist policies. However, this depends on the rhetoric of politicians and pressure groups, as well as the knowledge of the public about the theory of deflation. In any case, protectionist policies, and not price deflation, are ultimately responsible for economic isolation. Moreover, price inflation and competitive devaluations may lead to economic isolation as well.

Warren and Pearson also argue that in times of price deflation there would be a popular demand for a dictator (1933, p. 299). Hayek fears deflation in an economy with rigid wages can lead to unemployment that could be exploited by dictators like Adolf Hitler.[259] The argument that there may be high real wages during a deflation might be true, but during a time of inflation, or at any time, real wages may also be too high because of privileges given to unions or direct government interventions into the labor market. Moreover, the alternative to price deflation is the attempt to prevent it by monetary inflation. Monetary inflation could prevent a necessary readjustment of the structure of production, for some time. Yet, it would only postpone the readjustment and make necessary a more severe crisis in the future. In any case, monetary inflation would also lead to redistribution that could also be exploited by a demagogue or dictator who comes to power. In fact, any situation could be exploited by a demagogue. Much depends upon the education of the public about the consequences of deflation, as well as the public's love of liberty.

[259] Hayek (1979, p. 15).

4.2.5 *Myth 4: Deflation Leads Necessarily to Mass Unemployment*

This argument states that because wages are sticky, price deflation leads to a rise in real wages and therefore unemployment (Keynes [1936] 1964, p. 291; Svensson 2000, p. 29).[260] Yet, price deflation is not the ultimate cause of unemployment. Unemployment ultimately has only two causes. First, the unemployment is voluntary and the worker does not want to work for the wage which an employer is willing to pay for his work.[261] Or, in the second case, it is impossible for the worker to accept what would have been the employer's offer because of government interventions (minimum wage laws and union monopoly). If the nominal wage an employer is willing to offer decreases because of a price deflation, there will just be voluntary unemployment or unemployment caused by government intervention.

It is true that "contracts cannot be varied constantly," to reflect price changes; therefore, "costs tend to follow prices with some interval." It should be stressed that "...contractually fixed prices... are, in themselves, in no sense price rigidities. They concern agreements about the division of the value of output." Hence they can lead to a "speculative gain to the one party and speculative loss to the other" (Hutt 1995, p. 401). Therefore, constant changes in real wages (and all other real factor incomes) occur, but there is no systematic economic law that would say that these changes are always real wage increases. It is also possible that the parties of the wage contract will overestimate the price deflation. In this case, real wages would fall below the estimated height. Both employers and employees anticipate future prices and take them into account when they make long-term contracts. Surely they can err, but in both directions, while general prices are falling or rising.

In any case, inflation is not a remedy against overly high real wages due to union privileges, since unions are very unlikely to be deceived by price inflation all the time. They might try to anticipate the changes in the price level. As Mises observes in relation to the unemployment in Germany during the Great Depression:

> The attempts of labor unions to drive wages up higher than they would have been on the unhampered market and the efforts of government to alleviate the difficulties of various groups of producers have nothing to do with whether actual money prices are higher or lower. Labor unions no longer contend over the height of money wages, but over the height of real wages. It is not because of low prices that producers of rye, wheat, coffee and so on are impelled to ask for government intervention. It is because of the unprofitability of their enterprises. (Mises 1978, p. 198)[262]

It must be added that in anticipating changes in the price level, labor unions may also overestimate the price inflation. If they overestimate the price inflation, there might be more unemployment than before (Röpke 1995, p. 378; Hutt 1995, p. 400).

---

[260] For a discussion of price stickininess as a justification of credit expansion by a fractional reserve banking system see Bagus and Howden (2011, 2012b).

[261] It is also possible that a worker is still in the process of searching for better job opportunities.

[262] Translation of the German original (Mises 1931, pp. 29–30).

4.2.6 Myth 5: Price Deflation Can Put the Economy into a Liquidity Trap, i.e. a Disaster

A liquidity trap is "a situation of several years with persistent deflation, deflationary expectations, zero interest rates, and ineffective monetary policy" (Svensson 2000, p. 27). Later on, Svensson evaluates the liquidity trap as harmful: "Still, given the potential harm a liquidity trap may cause..., prepare for the worst." (p. 31). How does he come to this conclusion?

In a liquidity trap, goes the argument, the typical Keynesian stimulation—i.e., an increase in the money supply, which "leads to a lower interest rate, which [in turn] leads to higher investment and hence greater aggregate spending," (Krugman 1999, p. 2)[263]—does not work anymore. This is because in an economy in a liquidity trap, the interest rate, already near zero, cannot be lowered and there is virtually no investment. Open-market operations cannot increase investment, since "the private sector just holds the increased monetary base instead of bonds" (Svensson 2000, p. 28).

Foreign exchange interventions are probably ineffective as well, since foreigners who believe in a further appreciation of the currency will also simply keep the new money. That explains why "both Europe and the United States fear that they too may fall into liquidity trap" (Krugman 1999, p. 2).

There are so many errors in that argument that its critique must be split up.

One part of the argument is that, if the nominal interest rate is close to zero, a deflation inducing deflationary expectations will lead to high real interest rates (Taylor 2001, p. 41), because the nominal interest rate cannot become negative.[264] So if the deflation is expected to go on, "the real costs of borrowing become prohibitive." That "poses special problems for the economy and for policy" (Bernanke 2002, p. 3) because investments and spending decline. Indeed, with a perfectly anticipated deflation, the investment and spending would decline and prices would be bid down to the anticipated levels immediately. Far from being in a trap, from that point forward, no deflationary expectations would persist.

Thus, Rothbard refutes the argument that there are overly high real interest rates and states that the natural rate of interest, i.e. the essential price differential, need not to be changed by a general expectation of falling prices. "...[T]o the extent that [deflation] *is* anticipated, [entrepreneurs] will hold money rather than buy factors.

---

[263] This Keynesian reasoning is wrong, because an increase in the money supply through the loan market does not lead to more investments in form of real resources, but to malinvestments of these resources and higher nominal spending.

[264] It might be added, that it is contradictory to add as the costs of deflation both unemployment induced by wage rigidity and a fall in investments due to increases in the real interest rate (See Borio and Filardo 2004, p. 8). Only when the deflation is unexpected, wages will be too high due to price deflation. And only if there are deflationary expectation, real interest rates increase above the nominal rate.

This will *immediately* lower factor prices to their expected future levels..." (Rothbard 2001, p. 694). In this context, flexible factor markets are very important.

Partial anticipations accelerate the adjustment of the prices and reduce the purchasing-power component of the market interest rate. Of course, if not all entrepreneurs anticipate a price deflation, there could be loans with a positive nominal interest rate.

Therefore, a nominal interest rate close to zero in times of an anticipated deflation does not prohibit borrowing nor investing, since investments are determined by the natural rate of interest, i.e. the individual time preferences on the market.[265] As long as there remains a sufficiently high spread between the expected buying and selling prices, an expected fall in selling prices does not inhibit investments. This spread is determined by the time preference on the market. Also one has to take into account that low nominal interest rates, irrespective of them being high real interest rates, lead to higher market prices of capital goods as their future income stream is discounted by a lower interest rate. Therefore, market prices of capital goods will rise rapidly as interest rates approach zero and spur investments in the production of these capital goods.

Another part of the liquidity trap argument is that spending gets postponed because of the deflationary expectations (Cargill 2001, p. 116). Again, this postponing of spending, i.e., speculation, would accelerate the price deflation to the expected level and speed up adjustments. This "hoarding" would lead to the desired increase in real cash balances through falling prices without any change in real income, if the consumption/investment proportion stays the same. Therefore, this postponing does not necessarily imply a reduction of production. Once prices have fallen to the expected level, spending will set in. "Furthermore, the demand for money could not be infinite," (Rothbard 2001, p. 692) because everyone must consume sometime.

Moreover, to argue that in a price deflation people do not consume at all because tomorrow prices would be lower, would be the equivalent of saying that in a slight price inflation, people would not save at all, but consume their income immediately because tomorrow's price for goods will be slightly higher. In this context, it should not be forgotten that people prefer enjoying goods and services rather sooner than later. Thus, they will at some point start buying, even though they expect further increases in the purchasing power of money (Hülsmann 2006, p. 64).

Often, in the technology sector prices are expected to fall due to productivity increases. Imagine that prices in the whole economy are expected to fall. Similar to the tech sector today spending would not come to a halt. In some cases people could wait with their purchases in order to increase spending in the future. If prices are expected to fall due to increases in productivity, spending may be shifted from consumption to investment. Thus, consumption may fall marginally in a price deflation. As less goods are consumed, more goods and services are available for investment and extension of the structure of production. Investment projects that

[265] See Rothbard (2000, p. 40).

were not profitable before become profitable by the marginal decrease of consumption. As investments increase relative to consumption, production, instead of falling, actually tends to increase in a price deflation (Hülsmann 2006, pp. 64–65).

Another feared feature of the liquidity trap is that since the nominal interest rates are close to zero and due to the high real interest rates, the central bank has lost its power to use credit expansion to "stimulate aggregate demand" (Bernanke 2002, p. 3).[266] Strangely enough, that is supposed to be an argument against price deflation. In the eyes of the central bank, a process that leads to redistribution of wealth by credit expansion has become useless. Therefore, the central bank, in fact, might abstain from promoting further credit expansion. In this case, there will be no further distortions of the structure of production. Hence, there will not be further malinvestments that are ultimately doomed to be liquidated. In other words, the central bank will not initiate a boom bust cycle anymore.[267]

The economist who fears the liquidity trap because it hampers the opportunities of a central bank to "stimulate" the economy, does not see that in addition to its distributional effects, an increase in the money supply could lead to an artificial lengthening in the structure of production. This distortion must be corrected by the liquidation of the malinvestments sooner or later. The problem of a liquidity trap are not too high but too low interest rates.

In a liquidity trap economic agents are overindebted.[268] Higher interest rates lead to a lower capital value of old debts. Thus, higher interest rates allow to cancel old debts at a lower price, thereby reducing overindebtedness. Higher interest rates also accelerate the liquidation of malinvestments. Both the liquidation of malinvestment and the debt reduction help to decrease uncertainty and illiquidity of economic agents. Stable institutions and falling factors prices spurr confidence and investments. Thus, price deflation plays a crucial part in exiting a liquidity trap. Inflationary measures, low interest rates and government interventions delay the recovery.

---

[266] See also Svensson: "Fourth, and arguably equally important, the ineffectiveness of monetary policy removes all possibilities of using monetary policy for stabilization purposes" (2000, p. 29). It is hard to see why that would be bad, since "monetary policy for stabilization purposes" simply stands for interfering with market adjustments. And from the assumption that monetary policy making in times of deflation might be complicated, it does not follow that deflation is bad and must be prevented.

[267] Most writers still see a way to expand credit and get out of the liquidity trap. Finding a way out of the liquidity trap is actually the task that most writers want to solve. See, for instance, Goodfriend (2001, p. 24) and Cargill (2001, p. 131).

[268] It might be better to call the situation a illiquidity trap, since overindebted agents regard themselves as illiquid.

4.3 Theoretical Causes for Opposing Falling Prices

4.3.1 Bias Against Price Deflation

For a long time, there has been a bias against price deflation and monetary deflation. I have already explained in Chap. 2 the economic theories that regard price deflation as negative and how they increasingly become negative concerning deflation over time. I have refuted the main arguments against deflation in Sect. 4.2. I have also shown that these theories and arguments often arise in times of price deflation. Moreover, in Sect. 4.2.4 I have considered the argument that price deflation is bad, because it incites social unrest and political chaos. In Sect. 4.1.2.3 I have explained how price deflation can potentially reduce the power of the state and that its prescribed medicine, i.e. monetary inflation, is for the benefit of the state and connected groups. Thus, this might explain the anti-deflation bias of government-connected institutions, and interest groups like banks, or the educational system and the media. Now, it is time to explain in more detail the theoretical reasons for the opposition to price deflation. Special attention will be given to the question why price inflation is not so severely opposed as is price deflation.

4.3.2 Fallacious Theories and the Government

Theories influence the ideas that people have. If people hold the idea that something is bad for them, they will be opposed to this something. As shown in Chap. 2, most economic theories regard deflation as something harmful. Nowadays, economic research in this area is sponsored mainly by the government university system or the central bank, i.e., by two institutions that fear price deflation and benefit from monetary inflation.[269] The academic ideas concerning deflation are, then, brought to the general public via "second-hand dealers" of ideas, like the media and teachers. Thus, one reason why price deflation may lead to social unrest is that people are told again and again the price deflation is bad.

4.3.3 Deflationary Redistribution and Its Opposition

From a theoretical point of view, we understand why there might be reasons for people to be discontent in a time of declining prices. In every economic

[269] White (2005) describes the Federal Reserve System's influence on monetary research. He shows, that in 2002 the great majority of articles on monetary policy were published in FED journals or are co-authored by FED staff economists.

development winning and losing depends on the anticipation of future events and the coordination of one's action in function of this anticipation. In this case, winning and losing depends on the anticipation of falling prices and the exploitation of this anticipation. Falling prices imply losses for entrepreneurs who did not accurately anticipate the future, paying overly high prices for factors of production, i.e., factor prices that will lead them to incur losses. Also, those individuals lose whose real burden of debt is rising. During a price deflation debtors lose and creditors win.[270] In a deflation the pressure on debtors tend to rise slowly, which psychologically may cause malaise.

It should be added, that in a growth deflation this does not mean that producers will not be able to repay their debts and go bankrupt. Although the real value of the debtors' obligations increases, so does their real income, while the nominal payments remain the same.[271] This is so, because producers' productivity and their output increases. The prices of the products they sell are falling but they are selling a larger number of them, which might balance the price fall. Additionally, producers increase output precisely because they think by this they will maximize their money income. Hence, they do not necessarily get into problems in repaying their debt. Only producers whose selling proceeds fall faster than their buying proceeds will experience a fall in their money income.

4.3.3.1 Apparentness of Losses

The reason for the discontent lies in the difference of economic redistribution in times of price deflation, as compared to times of price inflation. The redistributional effects of price deflation are the reverse of those of a price inflation when the creditors lose and the debtors win as the real burden of debt is reduced. So why is there more opposition towards price deflation than towards price inflation? The effects are not exactly the opposite of those that occur in a inflation for several reasons. First, in price inflation the redistribution is obscured more than in a price deflation. In a price inflation creditors lose slowly, not abruptly, as the money they receive on their loans loses purchasing power. Creditors can buy fewer goods and services than they would have bought without the price inflation. This loss is hardly visible, almost unseen, because people do not know what they could have bought without the price inflation. On the contrary, in a price deflation the burden of real debts may become so heavy that the debt is renegotiated or the debtor goes bankrupt.[272] In the latter case the assets are turned over to the creditor. This is

[270] It is irrelevant if the price deflation had been anticipated. Debtors (and creditors) lose (and win) relative to a situation where prices had not fallen. They oppose the price deflation even though they anticipated it, because they lose relative to a scenario with higher prices.

[271] See Selgin (1997, p. 42).

[272] See on this point also Hülsmann (2008, p. 27). Felix Somary (1959, p. 185) makes a similar argument comparing the visibility of the costs of inflation and default.

not necessarily harming production, as only the ownership of productive assets is changed and during the bankruptcy process production can go on as before. One can even argue that it would be likely that production in the long run would be fostered by this redistribution. This might be so, because the redistribution goes from people who tend to save marginally less (higher time preference), debtors, to those who tend to save marginally more (lower time preference), creditors. Thus, total savings might be increased by such a redistribution.

The bankruptcy process, though, implies an important difference in the deflationary redistribution as opposed to the inflationary redistribution where there are abnormally few bankruptcies. The bankruptcy redistribution is highly visible and often a personal tragedy. The person who declares bankruptcy is probably more aware of his loss than the creditor who loses in a price inflation.

4.3.3.2 Spread of Losses

In price inflation the burden of loss is usually spread over many shoulders, over large parts of the population. Everyone that holds, or lends money is being affected. Therefore, with a slow and steady price inflation, resistance or social unrest is not as likely as with price deflation. This is so, because in a price deflation losses usually are not spread very much. The sellers whose selling proceeds are falling faster than their buying proceeds are fewer in number and better organized than the benefiting consumers. Moreover, usually one debtor, or debtor company has many creditors. That means that in a price deflation the gain is spread over many creditors while the debtor (or debtor company) assumes all of the loss and may go bankrupt. As the burden is not spread over the shoulders of many, social unrest is more likely to occur than during a price inflation.[273]

4.3.3.3 Organization and Power of Winners and Losers

Historically, the groups that lose in a price inflation are worse organized than the groups that lose in a price deflation.[274] In a price inflation, groups with a relatively fixed income as renters and creditors lose. As I explain in the previous section, these groups are quite large. They tend to be poorly organized, spreading the benefits of

---

[273] Public choice literature emphasizes the costs of organizing an interest group in order to seek wealth transfers through state intervention or to defend them against it. See Robert Ekelund, Jr. and Robert Tollison (2001). If the burden is spread on few shoulders it is easier to organize interest groups that seek wealth transfers because there is a higher incentive to do so. The protest against price deflation is also relatively easy to organize when, there is already an organized group, that is used for other purposes. See on this also the following section.

[274] For the public choice literature on the question why some groups can easier organize for rent-seeking purposes and have a higher influence than others, see for instance, Gordon Tullock (1967) or Mancur Olson (1971).

organizing across many shoulders, and making free riding easy. In contrast, the groups that lose in a price deflation are normally relatively small and can organize thereby relatively more easily.[275] This is so because the free rider problem is not so grave. The benefits from the organization of the group are high in relation to the personal costs that group members must assume.

Thus, the losing groups in a price deflation are normally well organized. Groups like indebted farmers, and businesses are in danger of losing considerably in a price deflation. This explains their strong opposition and successful organization. Those groups have typically also had the greater political leverage. Home owners even though not organized as well as farmers or businesses constitute an important political factor. Overindebted home owners may lose something essential in their lifes, which is their homes. Strong or even violent opposition may be expected by this group when they lose their houses. The farmers have managed to organize quite a substantial group, as their organization offers services that can be withheld from non-members.[276] Also business interests can be organized easily in small groups with strong common interests.[277] Businesses indeed have much to lose in a price deflation. Historically, the biggest debtors often are the business elite. They will strongly oppose a price deflation that can lead to their bankruptcy. They are normally very well organized with proven structure, are highly influential, and often "too big to fail", which implies a strong political influence. It is not surprising that they oppose falling prices since they suffer losses relative to other groups, and often suffer losses absolutely. In other words, they would profit by price inflation for which they are lobbying.

In general, the elites in our modern society benefit strongly from our current monetary system which is prone to inflation. In a system that is prone to price inflation, it does not make sense to save in cash and buy assets like real estate later. Rather, individuals indebt themselves in order to purchase assets. Price inflation later reduces the burden of the debt. Individuals can then pledge the purchased assets as collateral for further loans driving up assets prices even more, i.e. individuals that own assets may use them to purchase even more assets with newly created money. In such a world of rising prices, it makes sense for individuals and companies to indebt themselves. As a consequence, the elites in our society, wealthy asset owners, companies, financial institutions and governments have become ever more dependent on money creation to reduce their real debts.

A long and harsh price deflation would drive the majority of the financial system, the business elite and governments into bankruptcy.[278] Take the case of

[275] See for instance Olson (1971, pp. 5–52).

[276] Olson (1971, p. 132) explains that the free rider problem can be overcome in large groups if they offer as a "by-product" services from which non-members can be excluded. For farmers these services could be farming magazines, educational services etc.

[277] See Olson (1971, p. 143).

[278] Hülsmann (2012, p. 99) points to the fact that politicians of all parties independent of their ideology and notwithstanding their differences in other areas always coincide in their opposition to price deflation.

governments. Governments prefer to finance their expenditures via debts rather than via tax increases. Governments prefer debt financing, because tax increases are more impopular as they show more clearly the costs of government spending. The banking system may then directly or indirectly finance these debts via money creation. Indeed, today a large part of government debts are held by the financial system. A default of the government caused by a prolonged price deflation would lead to severe losses for the financial system.[279] Due to the interconnectivity of the financial system, the system could collapse. Credit contraction would follow and intensify price deflation. One bankruptcy would trigger the next. Eventually, all economic agents depending on further price inflation would have to default.

In sum, mass bankruptcies triggered by price deflation would hurt the interests of the banking system, indebted businesses and governments. Today's elites would perish, and new ones arise. As today's elites are well organized and maintain political and financial powers they have been able to avert price deflation.

The groups, however, that profit in a price deflation are larger and usually not well organized. The vast masses of workers and consumers tend to profit in a price deflation. Also savers and creditors profit in price deflation. However, as stated above, their gains tend to be spread over more shoulders than the losses. Thus, the winners of price deflation will not vehemently oppose the public pressure that those well organized and powerful groups in a price deflation will exert.

4.3.4 Money Illusion and Disillusion

Another reason why price deflation might be opposed is a money illusion.[280] When there is a price deflation, wealth and income in nominal terms might fall.[281] The money illusion can refer, therefore, to income and wealth.

Let us first turn to income illusion. People might feel poorer even though their real income has not changed or may even be increasing. Indeed, a psychological reason exists for the fact that falling prices are opposed more than rising prices. Many people are more concerned about their future as producers than their future as consumers.[282] Thus, when prices generally fall, people tend to overlook, that many

[279] It is true that banks being creditors also on the winning side in a price deflation. However, when a home owner defaults on his mortgage and the bank has to take over the house it suffers normally losses, especially in an environment where housing prices are falling sharply. A higher real debt burden tends to coincide with losses on banks' asset in a harsh price deflation caused by credit contraction.

[280] Bordo et al. argue that possibly this was the case for the 1880s and 1890s (2004, p. 16).

[281] This is not necessarily so in all deflation cases. In a growth deflation for instance, income in nominal terms might not fall for everyone as production is increased. Workers' discounted marginal value productivity (DMVP) might be constant as physical productivity increases. On the concept of DMVP see Rothbard (2001, pp. 387–409).

[282] See Stolper (1966, p. 137).

prices of the goods they buy, also fall. Rather they will concentrate on the price of the one good or service they sell. As this price, be it of labor services, or of a produced good, seems so essential for the future they will oppose the price fall. A worker, whose wage falls, tends to put more weight on his wage fall than on the fact that his consumption prices also fall. A producer, whose products' prices fall, might also regard this as to weight more than that the prices of his factors of production and consumption prices also fall. In both cases, the selling price is conceived in a sense as a very personal price. The fall of this personal price is opposed.

Let us now turn to wealth illusion. In a price deflation the prices of assets like machines might fall. Hence, businesses might suffer accounting losses, even though, they are not suffering losses in real terms. Yet, besides the accounting illusion there is also a disillusion caused by the fall in the nominal value of wealth. Due to the fall in asset prices, people might feel poorer. For instance, in a bank credit contraction during a recession, asset prices fall. There might be a stock market crash. When stock market prices plummet, stock market investors suffer regret. They suddenly become aware of the fact that they invested, to a large part, in malinvestments during the artificial boom. Of course, the malinvestments were committed probably a long time ago, but only now does it become obvious to them that these investments were actually malinvestments. Before the stock market crash, investors under an illusion of wealth were not aware of the destruction of real wealth in the malinvestments. Now, due to the asset price fall a painful disillusionment sets in.

Something similar to the stock market disillusion occurs when, in a price deflation, there is a bankruptcy due to an increase in real debts. The debtor loses everything and the creditor often can only recuperate part of his investment in monetary terms. In addition, sometimes the creditor has to wait a considerable amount of time until he recuperates his investment. Due to the bankruptcy, it becomes obvious that an inviable investment project has been undertaken. The destruction of real wealth becomes manifest in the bankruptcy. The illusion consisted in the fact, that before the bankruptcy, the individuals where not aware of the destruction of real wealth. They think that the bankruptcy destroyed the real wealth. Yet, the destruction happened when the investments were undertaken. It only finally becomes manifest in the bankruptcy.

There is another possible disillusion concerning the wealth of people. In a credit contraction, enforced by price deflation, problems can occur for a fractional reserve banking system. When depositors cannot recuperate their deposits in total or have to wait to withdraw them, they become discontented. They are now aware that their bank has used and lent out their deposits. Yet, the incapacity of the bank to pay them out is only a manifestation of redistribution that had occurred before.

In contrast, in a price inflation, the opposite can occur. People feel richer, because of accounting profits and increases in asset prices and nominal incomes. Optimism is widespread and everything seems to be possible. This explains why there is less opposition to a price inflation than to a price deflation. Hence, the money illusion and disillusion might also be a factor in explaining the social unrest.

4.3.5 Deflation and Recession

Deflation is also opposed because it simply often coincides with a recession and a bank credit deflation. Deflation is thus associated with recession. As stated above, in a recession it becomes obvious that the artificial boom was an illusion and that many malinvestments were committed. Thus, people in general do not fare well in a recession. It is not only a period of disillusion but also a period of social hardship caused by the adaptation of the structure of production. Companies go bankrupt. Capital is shifted, and many people become unemployed and must find work elsewhere.

People tend to see the price deflation as the cause of the recession, because in a recession there is simply sometimes price deflation at the same time. However, the opposite is true, the price deflation is not the cause of the recession but the consequence of the bank credit contraction, that itself has its roots in the bank credit expansion. People conflate price deflation with depression and price inflation with boom. Thus, the association of price deflation with recession, is one reason for the opposition to price deflation.

Chapter 5
Two Historical Examples of Deflation

5.1 The American Growth Deflation from 1865 to 1896

5.1.1 Introduction

From 1865 to 1896, the United States found itself in one of the longest periods of price deflation in history. As such, its history was, in part, shaped by continuously falling prices and is therefore a historical case of special interest. A main factor in this price fall was growth in the economic sector, indicating that an analysis of growth deflation is in order. This analysis will help to illustrate that falling prices do not pose any problems for economic growth.[283] Instead, in this particular case the economic development itself caused prices to fall. Furthermore, we will be able to see in general, that like changes in economic data, falling prices lead to a change in the relative wealth position of all market participants. When many prices fall over a longer period of time, there can be substantial changes in relative, or even absolute, wealth positions and redistributions from entrepreneurs who anticipated these changes to those who did not. We will also see that those changes in relative wealth positions led to social unrest on the part of those who saw their relative wealth position deteriorate. This group of entrepreneurs consisted of those mainly in the economic establishment, usually opposed to change, and highly indebted individuals or companies, whose real debt burden increased. Further, we will see that in the orbit of those groups economic theories were developed that justified inflation and denounced price deflation as harmful for the economy as a whole. This may serve, at least partially, in answering the intriguing question why price deflation

[283] A very popular argument against a 100 % gold standard is that such a system would hamper economic growth. When the supply of gold could not keep up with economic growth, prices would fall and lead to a recession. It is one of the most widespread myths among economists that the money supply must rise as fast as productivity to prevent price deflation. The American growth deflation illustrates that this argument is simply a myth.

P. Bagus, *In Defense of Deflation*, Financial and Monetary Policy Studies 41,
DOI 10.1007/978-3-319-13428-4_5

came to be feared instead of welcomed by many economists and journalists. This may also suggest why price deflation has been associated traditionally with recessions and viewed negatively.

5.1.2 The Monetary Institutions of the United States from 1865 to 1896

5.1.2.1 The Civil War Prelude: 1861–1865

In order to grasp the monetary history and the significance of declining prices, it is necessary to provide a short overview on the monetary institutions in place during the three decades following the Civil War. The monetary history of the United States from 1865 to 1896 can be split up into two conceptually different stages: the greenback era and the gold standard deflation era. However, the greenback era really began with the suspension of specie payment by private banks on December 30, 1861, i.e. before 1865.[284] By the suspension of specie payment, banks apparently were breaking private contracts in violating their obligation to redeem on demand bank notes and demand deposits into gold. The government failed to enforce these private contracts. On the next day the Treasury itself suspended specie payments on its Treasury notes.

How did the private banks come to suspend specie payment? The suspension of specie payment was caused by the start of the Civil War. The Civil War would lead to a vast increase in government expenditure from $66 million in 1861 to $1.30 billion 4 years later.[285] In the fall of 1861, the U.S. government had issued an enormous loan to be purchased by banks. The government insisted on being paid out in specie, thereby draining on the banks' reserves. As the Civil War military affairs proved to be more difficult for the U.S. government than expected, it raised new taxes and tariffs and increased its debt even further. As a consequence of the expectation of an increasing federal deficit, debts and shrinking bank reserves, the confidence in the banks' notes was reduced, and people began to hoard gold. They started to redeem their bank notes into gold threatening the liquidity of the banking system. As a result, banks were losing specie every week in late 1861 ($7 million in New York alone[286]) and the gold in the vaults was reduced constantly. Suspension of specie payment became unavoidable.

As funds for the war effort diminished government officials became reluctant to increase taxes further, as this would have raised resistance against the war effort. At the advice of representative and banker Elbridge G. Spaulding, the government

[284] For a short summary of the greenback era see Studenski and Kroos (1963, p. 143–146) or Rothbard (2002, p. 123–159).

[285] See Rothbard (2002, p. 123).

[286] See Studenski and Kroos (1963, p. 143).

began issuing non-interest-bearing Treasury notes, which were declared legal tender for all private and public debts but could not be redeemed in specie. This was settled in the Legal Tender Act of 1862, which authorized the printing of $150 million of new "United States notes." These notes, a fiat-paper money, were called greenbacks.[287] From the beginning, it was hoped that eventually (after a successful war) they would be redeemed in gold. Moreover, the notes could be converted at par into interest bearing government bonds. The government's plan was to reissue the notes again once converted into bonds. However, the public did not respond to this option and the convertibility into bonds was suspended in 1863.

As resumption was suspended, Gresham's law went into effect and gold coins disappeared from circulation. People tried to pay their debt in the legal tender—greenbacks—and hoarded or exported the artificially undervalued gold. An exception was California where social sanctions against greenback users emerged. People paying debts with greenbacks would be blacklisted. Later "specific contract law" was passed in California, which made contracts for specific kinds of money enforceable.[288] In any case gold did still have its market share. Thus, the Treasury used to pay interest on its debts in gold and duties had to be paid in specie. Banks managed deposits in greenbacks and gold. Therefore, in this regard, a double standard of greenbacks and gold existed in the U.S. at this time.[289]

The greenbacks began to depreciate in terms of specie right after the suspension of specie payment. When Secretary of the Treasury Salmon Chase closed the convertibility of greenbacks into interest-bearing bonds, greenbacks depreciated further. As a rule, the greenbacks would depreciate with Northern defeats and increase with Northern victories. The hope that if the war would be victorious for the North, then greenbacks would eventually be redeemed in gold is the obvious explanation for fluctuations related to military victories and losses. In June 1864 the greenback fell to a low of 40 cents equivalent in specie. At the same time prices of commodities in terms of the new paper money sharply increased.[290]

In regard to the monetary institutions of the time, it should be added, that officially the U.S. was on a bimetallic standard, setting a fixed exchange rate from silver to gold. However, for a long time silver had been undervalued in relation to gold and had already disappeared from circulation. Only fractional silver coins were being used. But as soon as greenbacks depreciated even these fractional silver coins became undervalued and disappeared from circulation as did eventually nickel coins.[291]

[287] The name "greenback" resulted from its printing, which was black on the front and green on the back. The name also refers to the backing of these notes by essentially green paper, in contrast to previous notes that were backed by gold.

[288] See Mitchell (1903. p. 143).

[289] See Shields (1977, p. 115).

[290] See Studenski and Kroos (1963, p. 147)

[291] See Studenski and Kroos (1963, p. 148)

Another institutional change that occurred during the Civil War was the passing of the National Banking Acts of 1863–1864 establishing a vigorous banking system. Under this system national banks could issue banknotes without taxation, whereas state banks had to pay taxes at a rate of 2 % in 1863, soon increased up to 10 %, making this endeavor unprofitable.[292] The state banks[293] had to have accounts with the national banks and could inflate demand deposits or bank notes on top of these accounts. Moreover, the note issue of banks was tied to the ownership of U.S. government bonds in order to create a large market for U.S. government debts. Banks could only issue bank notes if they deposited the equivalent of U.S. government bonds as collateral at the U.S. Treasury.[294] Thus banks would monetize the government debts. The issue of deposits was not restricted in such a way. Banks, therefore, tended to increase deposits rather than notes.[295]

5.1.2.2 Post Civil War Greenback Era: 1865–1879

Having accumulated a vast amount of public debt by the end of the Civil War, the United States was on a depreciated inconvertible greenback currency. The question was if and when to resume specie payments. The Republicans proved to be generally more opposed to resumption than the Democrats. The "Loan Bill" of March 1866 that prepared for resumption of specie payments by contracting greenbacks was passed in the House by a Democratic vote of 27 "yes" and 1 "no" and a Republican vote 56 "yes" and 52 "no".[296]

Advancements were made toward resumption of specie payment; however, setbacks also occurred. The credit expansion after the Civil War[297] lead to an artificial boom and inevitably a recession in 1873 set in: The Panic of 1873. In the wake of this panic and the cry of businesses for cheap credits the "Inflation Bill" was passed in April 1874 with the Democrats voting against it 35–37 and the Republicans voting in favor 105–164. The "Inflation Bill" provided for the expansion of greenbacks and national bank notes. However, the "Inflation Bill" was vetoed later by President Ulysses Grant.

As Democrats succeeded in 1874 congressional elections, Republicans united with them in monetary matters and the Resumption Act was passed in January 1875.[298] The Resumption Act provided for the Secretary of Treasury to buy gold

[292] See Studenski and Kroos (1963, pp. 154–155).

[293] State banks were only allowed to do business in the borders of the state that chartered them.

[294] Vera Smith calls this system a "bond deposit system," because in order to issue notes government bonds had to be issued (1990, p. 52).

[295] See Smith (1990, p. 149).

[296] See on this Rothbard (2002, pp. 151–152).

[297] See Rothbard (2002, p. 154).

[298] See on the Resumption Act, Dewey (1907, pp. 372–274).

with government bonds and prepare in this way for the resumption on January 1, 1879.[299] However, this was a compromise between hard money and soft money advocates, since it eliminated a $300 million limit on the issue of national bank notes, which was in law before. Specie payment was finally resumed as the Treasury John Sherman sold U.S. bonds for gold in Europe to provide for sufficient gold for redemption.

Another major change in the monetary affairs of the U.S. in this sub period deserves to be mentioned: the demonetization of silver. As mentioned before, the U.S. had been technically on a bimetallic standard with silver being undervalued since 1834. Therefore, silver had disappeared from circulation. In 1853, the bimetallic standard set a silver-gold ratio of 16-to-1 while the market value for silver was higher. As an effect, only subsidiary fractional silver coins remained in circulation. For all practical matters, the U.S. was on a gold standard. In 1872, as Rothbard argues,[300] it is possible that some knowledgeable men at the U.S. Treasury began to expect that the market price of silver was about to fall. A fall was to be expected as the amount of silver due to new mining in Nevada and other Western states was about to increase and European nations were shifting from a silver to a gold standard. This would have meant that with a 16-to-1 parity, gold gradually would have become undervalued and driven out of circulation. Instead, silver would have flown into the U.S. This development which would practically have set the U.S. on a silver standard was prevented by several laws. In February 1873, a bill provided the discontinuation of the minting of further silver dollars. This event became later known as the "Crime of 1873." And an act in June 1874, abolished the legal tender quality of all silver dollars above the sum of $5, which practically meant the demonetization of silver. Indeed, after this legislation was passed, the market value of silver fell to a ratio higher than 16-to-1. It went to nearly 18-to-1 in 1876 and as high as 32-to-1 in 1894. In 1878, the Bland-Allison Act was passed to appease the silver interests, which obliged the Treasury to buy $2 million to $4 million market value of silver per month. As the price of silver kept falling, more silver ounces had to be bought.

5.1.2.3 The Gold Standard Era Under Price Deflation: 1879–1896

The road to resumption in 1879 was long and burdensome. However, with the specie redemption in sight the gold premium to greenbacks steadily fell and returned to par when specie redemption occurred successfully. When the Grant administration decided for specie resumption in 1875, the premium was still 17 % against a gold dollar. With new confidence in the gold-backed greenbacks, gold flew into the U.S., increasing American exports. The gold inflow increased from $110.5 million in 1879 to $358.3 million in 1882. On top of this incoming gold the

[299] See Barrett (1931, p. 186).

[300] See Rothbard (2002, p. 157).

national banking system pyramided deposits that rose from \$2.149 billion in 1879 to \$2.777 billion in 1882. After the three boom years from 1879 to 1882, incited by monetary expansion, a recession hit in 1882 followed by a financial panic in 1884. The panic was triggered by an outflow of gold caused by falling confidence in the U.S. commitment to a gold standard as silver interests grew stronger.[301]

The silver forces grew stronger again in 1890 with the result of the passing of the Sherman Silver Purchase Act. The Sherman Silver Purchase act required the Treasury to acquire 4.5 million ounces of silver per month, an increase of about 100 % of the average purchase under the Bland-Allison act. However, the difference with the Bland-Allison act was that a certain weight of silver was to be bought. This implied that the amount of silver bought would not be increased as silver prices kept falling. In the long-run, this meant fewer silver purchases by the Treasury than would have occurred under the Bland-Alison Act. The payment for the silver was made in new redeemable greenback notes (1890 notes) that had full legal tender. These greenback notes were, at the discretion of the Treasury, redeemable into silver or gold. This meant a step back towards bimetallism which at the ratio 16-to-1 would have led to an inflationary silver monometallism. As a consequence, foreigners lost confidence in the U.S. commitment to the gold standard and gold flew out in the early 1890s. Other facts deepened this loss in confidence. Thus, in July 1892 the U.S. Senate passed a free-silver coinage bill. The bill did not proceed further but would have made silver legal tender and led in praxis to a silver monometalism. The Treasury's gold reserve declined as gold exports intensified in 1892. At the same time an economic boom spurred by credit expansion was under way. The recession was triggered in June 1893 when the distrust of the public led to massive bank runs and bank failures. These events became known as the Panic of 1893. Banks suspended specie payment. Deposits no longer being redeemable in cash sold at a discount in relation to currency in August of 1893. In November the Cleveland administration repealed the Sherman Silver Purchase Act and the Treasury bought gold from a group of bankers around J.P. Morgan and August Belmont, thereby winning back foreign confidence in the U.S. commitment to the gold standard. With the victory of pro-gold Republicans in 1896 and the defeat of Democratic candidate and free silver advocate William Jennings Bryan, finally the commitment to the gold standard was made convincing.

In sum, the period of 1865–1896 was a period of substantial institutional change in the U.S. The financial system of fractional reserve banks not backed by a central bank demonstrated instability, leading to several monetary expansions and contractions, to financial panics (1873, 1884, 1890 and 1893)[302] and suspension of cash payments. The instability and the malinvestments during the boom periods and the subsequent liquidation of them during the recession disturbed economic growth. However, as we will see below, while the construction of the financial system did repress economic growth, the remaining growth was still impressive.

[301] See Rothbard (2002, p. 160).

[302] See Smith (1990, p. 151).

5.1.3 Prices and Money from 1865 to 1896

5.1.3.1 Prices

After summarizing the history of the monetary institutions in the period, we will now consider the history of prices during the period of 1865–1896. Prices during the period of 1865–1896 generally fell. As caution must always prevail in dealing with economic statistics, we will try to make more qualitative than quantitative statements on prices. Nevertheless, we will illustrate our qualitative claims by different price statistics. According to George F. Warren and Frank A. Pearson the wholesale price (1910–1914 = 100)[303] developed as follows below (Chart 5.1).

In 1865 the index was at 185. It fell until 1871 to 130 or 30 % in only 6 years. This implies that prices fell on average 5.7 % during those 6 years. There was a slight increase in the credit fueled boom in 1872 to 136, followed by declining prices to 90 until 1879. This was followed by an increase during the expansionary boom year to 108 in 1882. Until 1890 prices fell to 82 according to Warren and Pearson whose index ends here. However, in 1890 the wholesale price index from the Bureau of Labor Statistics (BLS) begins (1913 = 100). It states 1890 as 76.1 falling until 1896 to 61.7, which is a decrease of 18.9 %. In the Warren and Pearson numbers this would be 66.5.[304] This means for the whole period an average annual fall in prices of about 3.5 % and a total fall in wholesale prices in four decades of 64 %. The prolongation of the Warren and Pearson numbers with the BLS statistics leads to the graph below (Chart 5.2).

An alternative consumer price index was constructed by Ethel D. Hoover and it covers the period from 1851 to 1880.[305] The Hoover index falls from 175 in 1865 to 108 in 1879 and increases to 110 in 1880 (Chart 5.3).

This index states a smaller fall in price from 1865 to 1880 than the Warren and Pearson index (37 % fall in the Hoover index vs. 46 % fall in the Warren and Pearson index during the same period). This might have been caused by a stronger weighting of sharper declining farm products and raw materials in the Warren and Pearson index than in the Hoover index.[306] Nevertheless, the Hoover Index still indicates a substantial and continuous fall in prices.

Another index is the cost-of-living index constructed by the Federal Reserve Bank of New York and Michael C. Burgess with 1913 = 100.[307](Chart 5.4)

These indexes show similar tendencies as the Warren and Pearson index or the Hoover index. The cost-of-living-index constructed by the Federal Reserve Bank of New York falls from 102 in 1865 to 74 in 1896 and the Burgess Index from 108.1 to 62.9 in the same period. These indexes do not fall as much as the whole sale

[303] Source: U.S. Department of Commerce, 1975, Series E 52–63, p. 201.

[304] See U.S. Department of Commerce, 1975, Series E 87–89, p. 203.

[305] See U.S. Department of Commerce, 1975, Series E 174–182, p. 212.

[306] See Friedman and Schwartz (1971, p. 33).

[307] See U.S. Department of Commerce (1875, p. 212).

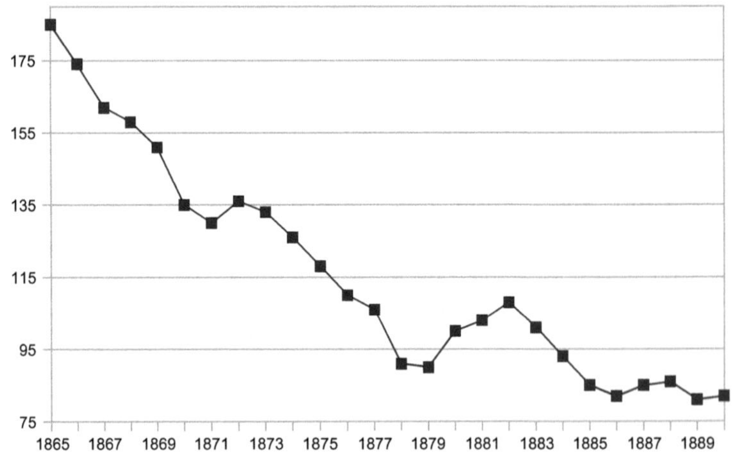

Chart 5.1 Wholesale price index (Warren and Pearson), 1865–1890

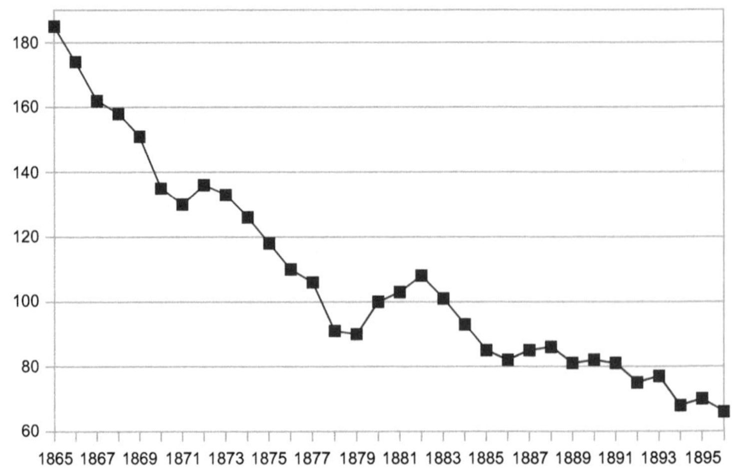

Chart 5.2 Wholesale price index (Warren and Pearson + BLS), 1865–1896

indexes, which shows that costs of living did not fall as much as wholesale prices. Nevertheless, both indexes demonstrate a substantial fall in prices.

One can also calculate an implicit price index from the gross national product statistics, setting 1958 = 100.[308] It starts with an average of the 1869–1878 decade at 32.1 and falls to the average of 26.5 in the 1879–1888 decade ending in 1896 at 21.7, thereby also indicating a substantial fall in prices during the period.

Basically, all of these price indexes imply the same insight, namely that prices over the period under consideration fell almost consistently with only a few

[308] See U.S. Department of Commerce (1875), Series F 1–5, p. 224.

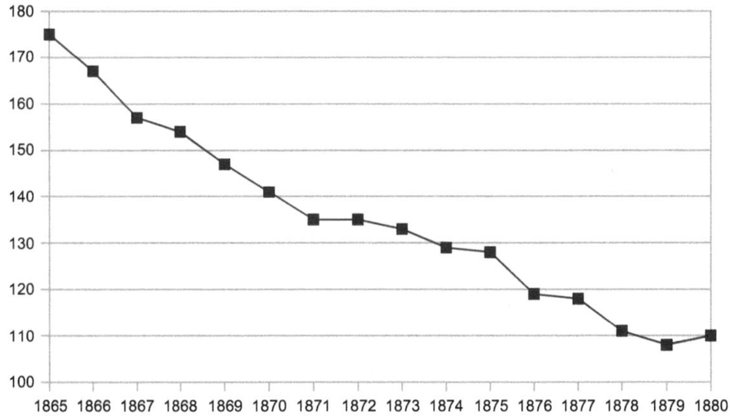

Chart 5.3 Consumer price index (Hoover), 1865–1880

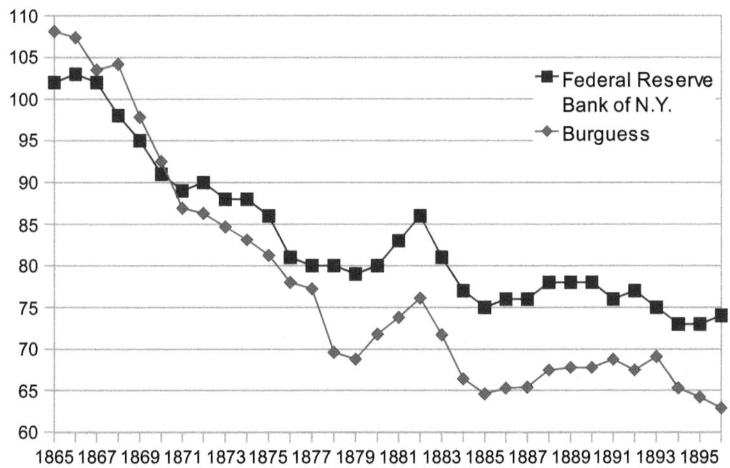

Chart 5.4 Cost-of-living indexes (Federal Reserve Bank of N.Y., Burguess), 1865–1896

exceptions during expansionary booms. Even though one should not take price indexes at face value, the evidence is conclusive and we can make one qualitative statement about the period under consideration: Generally speaking, prices fell considerably. It should be added, that 1896 was the last year of this period of price deflation and that from 1897 on prices started to increase almost every year as the world's gold production soared and banks increased deposits on top of this additional gold.

5.1.3.2 The Quantity of Money

As we have shown, prices generally decreased in the period of 1865–1896. Theoretically, this might have been caused by a reduction in the money supply and not by a growth deflation as is the thesis of this work. Hence, we have to look at the development of the money supply during those years. Friedman and Schwartz have provided us with estimates of monetary figures. Again we are faced with a dubious quality and also an incompleteness of the data. The figures start only in 1867 and do not distinguish between demand and time deposits at commercial banks. I will use the aggregate that Friedman and Schwartz provide, which includes currency[309] held by the public, demand and time deposits at commercial banks. I thereby exclude the deposits at mutual savings banks as they are not payable on demand. Unfortunately, time deposits cannot be excluded from the figure as Friedman and Schwartz provide only a total of demand and time deposits together.

According to Friedman and Schwartz' figures (Chart 5.5),[310] it must be stated that in both sub periods, the greenback era and the gold standard era, the money supply (currency held by the public plus demand and time deposits at commercial banks) increased. In the first period, the greenback era, the money supply rose 17 % from January 1867 to February 1879.[311] However, the money supply did not increase steadily. In the first year, from 1867 to 1868, the money figure decreased slightly from $1,314 million to $1,244 million. The money supply would then increase at a high rate until the Panic of 1873 to $1,622 million to fall back in the wake of the panic to $1,592 million in February 1874 and to increase again until August 1875 to $1,695 million. During the next 4 years the money supply would fall slightly back to $1,543 in February 1879. So here we are faced with a bank credit deflation occurring in a recession after an inflationary boom. There had been a strong increase in the money supply leading to malinvestments, for example in the railroad industry. The increased money supply was aided by capital imports. When the capital inflows declined and some railroads defaulted on their obligations, bank failures occurred.[312] This triggered the financial panic of 1873. Not only did it become obvious that malinvestments had to be liquidated, but there was also a gold outflow. A credit contraction sped up the liquidation of the malinvestments.

In sum, for the greenback era we are, therefore, faced with a increasing money supply, and also with years of recession in which the money supply actually slightly

[309] Currency includes gold coins, gold and silver certificates, U.S. notes, currency notes, treasury notes of 1890, standard silver dollars, subsidiary silver, fractional currency, other U.S. currency, state bank notes, national banknotes, minor coin, federal reserve notes and federal reserve bank notes.

[310] These figures are in million dollar. Source: Friedman and Schwartz (1971, pp. 704–705), Table A-1.

[311] It must be noted that these numbers cannot be taken at face value. 17 % presents an accuracy that is unrealistic. However, it is safe to state that there was an increase in the money supply over this period between 10 and 30 %.

[312] See Friedman and Schwartz (1971, pp. 77–78).

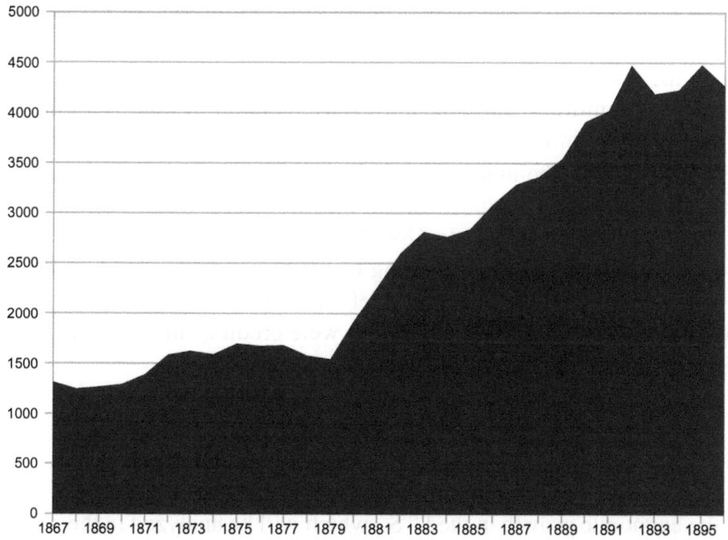

Chart 5.5 Currency held by the public and deposits at commercial banks, 1867–1896

decreased, which is rather unusual for modern history. As Friedman and Schwartz put it:

> This behavior is in one respect most unusual. There are 5 calendar years in which the money stock declined and 7 in which it rose. The rises were on the average larger than the declines, but even so the money stock in February 1879 was only 17 % above its level 12 years earlier in January 1867. By comparison with later experience, this is an extraordinarily high ratio of declines to rises and a small total rise. (1971, p. 31)

Nevertheless, there was after all still an increase in the money stock.

The resumption of specie payment in 1879 restored confidence in the dollar leading to an influx of gold. And in the following gold standard period the money supply increased in total 276 %. The growth of the money stock was especially fast from 1879 until 1883. There was a huge credit expansion and malinvestments. A loss of confidence in the U.S. commitment to the gold standard lead to a outflow of gold[313] which triggered the recession and a financial panic. A credit contraction ensued and the money supply fell slightly from 1883 to 1884.

After the recession, another cycle started. Again in 1892 a distrust in the U.S. commitment to the gold standard led to a outflow of gold and triggered the downturn. The failure of a stock market favorite triggered then in 1893 a financial panic. Malinvestment became obvious. After a short revival, in 1895 a new outflow of gold caused by the political upswing of silver forces caused another panic.[314]

[313] See Friedman and Schwartz (1971, pp. 106–107).

[314] See Friedman and Schwartz (1971, pp. 108–111).

Due to the Panic of 1895, the money supply fell slightly back to $4,266 million in 1896 the last year of the period of our analysis.

In sum, the gold standard era the money supply increased more steadily year for year from $1,543 million until reaching $4,477 million in June 1895. It should be noted, that the years of decline in the gold standard era were not as numerous as in the greenback era and the money supply increased at an accelerated pace.

It can, therefore, be concluded that the money supply did not fall during this period but increased from 1867 to 1896 from $1,314 million to $4,477 million or 340 % while wholesale prices according to Warren and Pearson were down about 60 % in the same period. The price deflation was, therefore, not caused by a shrinking money supply, even though there were credit contractions and temporary reductions of the money supply in recessionary periods.

5.1.3.3 The Quality of Money and Gold's Unusual High Demand

Beside the economic growth in the U. S., which will be analyzed in the next section, there were three other important reasons for an increase in the purchasing power of the gold currency. First, there was an unusual demand for gold in the 1870s when industrial nations like Germany, Spain, and those of the Latin Monetary Union (Belgium, Switzerland, France, Italy), as well as the Scandinavian countries installed a gold standard. In addition, as already mentioned, the United States bought gold in order to return to the gold standard.[315]

Second, there was a world wide increase of population and output. World population increased from 1.2 billion in 1850 to 1.65 billion in 1900. Furthermore, especially in Europe, the industrial revolution led to extraordinary economic growth. Gustav Cassel estimated the worldwide annual average rate of production growth between 1865 and 1896 to be 3 %.[316] Consequently, the world demand of the new world medium of exchange (gold) soared.

A third reason for the price decreases in the period from 1865 to 1879 were expectations about an improvement in the quality of money. When the Civil War ended there was the widespread expectation that the quality of money would recuperate and improve in the long-term. When the quality of money is expected to improve, the demand to hold it as cash balance increases and money prices fall.[317] During the greenback era, the quality of the inconvertible fiat currency could be improved in the eyes of economic agents by making this paper convertible into gold. And resumption was promised from the beginning of the suspension onward. As the expectations that this promise would be fulfilled gained certainty, the expected quality of the greenback notes increased. People valued the dollar higher than without this expected increase in the quality. As a result the demand for

[315] Austria would follow in 1892 and Russia and Japan in 1897.

[316] See Palyi (1972, p. 22), fn 19.

[317] See on the quality of money Anderson ([1917] 2000) and Bagus (2009).

holding money increased and prices fell. A qualitative cash building occurred. Therefore, the increase in the quality of money until resumption is one very important reason for the increase in the purchasing power of money.

It is difficult to say how much of the fall in prices was caused by an increased demand of gold by countries who intended to switch to a gold standard, and how much was caused by an increase in the quality of money, and how much was caused by world economic growth. However, one might suggest that after the resumption of specie payment an expected increase in the quality of money was not a very important issue anymore. And likewise, the effects of the switch of many industrial nations to the gold standard were not as strong anymore in the 1880s. Therefore, economic growth can be considered a main factor for the fall in prices, especially after 1879. In the next section we will look at U.S. growth during the period in detail.

5.1.4 Growth and Its Causes

5.1.4.1 Growth: A Rise in Output

The national income statistics for the period are not fully available. The statistics start only in 1869 and for the first two decades there are only averages available. Nevertheless, the evidence of impressive economic growth is clear.[318] Average annual gross national product (GNP) (in 1958 prices) nearly doubled from $23.1 billion in the decade 1869–1878 to $42.4 billion in the decade 1879–1888, which means an average annual increase of real GNP of 6.3 %. Until 1892 real GNP continued to rise at a very fast rate to $60.4 billion. In the wake of the panic of 1893 it would fall to $55.9 billion one year later to increase again to $61.3 billion in 1896. Over the whole period GNP rose from $23.1 billion in the 1869–1878 period to $61.3 billion in 1896. Taking as a very broad approximation of 1874 as $23.1 billion, this would imply an increase of 265 % of real GNP in 22 years and an impressing 4.5 % per year. Again the data is very questionable. But it seems to be safe to claim that there was economic growth and even strong economic growth in the period under consideration.

One might think that this economic growth was only caused by a population increase and per capita production did not increase. But this is an error. Per capita income increased from an average of $531 in 1869–1878 to $774 in 1879–1888. The growth per capita extended until the end of the period under consideration. In 1896 yearly per capita GNP was at $865.[319]

---

[318] See U.S. Department of Commerce (1975), Series F 1–5, p. 224.

[319] The purchasing power of wages increased from 32 (1910–1914 = 100) in 1865 to 104 in 1896. See Warren and Pearson (1933, p.197).

Furthermore, there are other indicators that physical output increased heavily in the period. A basic production index constructed by Warren and Pearson shows this, too.[320] The index increased from 10.81 in 1866 to 38.78 in 1895, thereby nearly quadrupling. An especially strong increase occurred between 1874 from 13.97 to 23.03 in 1879. This implies an increase of 64.8 % in only 5 years. Curiously, National Bureau of Economic Research (NBER) chronology states a recession in this period between 1873 and 1878 and more recently Lance Davis still declares 1873–1875 as a recessionary period (2006, p. 106).

There are even more statistics that show that physical output of commodities greatly increased.[321] For example, the production of wheat flour increased from 1865 at 42.5 mil. bbl. to 93.6 mil. bbl. in 1895. In the same period, the production of refined sugar soared from 733 mil. lb. to 3,961 mil. lb. From 1870 to 1895, fermented malt liquor increased from 6,600,000 bbl. to 33,600,000 bbl. beer. Cigar production in million increased from 1,183 in 1870 to 4,099 in 1896.

In sum, it must be stated that even though GNP figures nor indexes nor physical output figures of manufactured commodities are accurate at all and should not be taken at face value, it is safe to say that there was tremendous growth in the U.S. from 1865 to 1896. This domestic economic growth was the main reason of the falling prices during the same period.

5.1.4.2 Reasons for Economic Growth

Introduction

Now we will consider reasons for the above shown economic growth. First of all the institutional freedom of the U.S. must be pointed out. The entrepreneurial function was not inhibited by many interventions. Taxes were low, regulations scarce and the legal framework was, in general, friendly to business. In the next section, following my theoretical analysis of growth deflation, I will look at innovations that made the increase in growth possible, at an increase in population, the division of labor/knowledge, and also capital accumulation. The increase in the division of labor/knowledge is hard to prove with economic data. However, one must keep in mind that an increase in population allows for a higher division of knowledge. In addition, innovations or capital accumulation often make necessary or imply an increase in the division of labor.

[320] See Warren and Pearson (1933, p. 44), Table 5.

[321] See U.S. Department of Commerce (1875, pp. 231–300, 689–697).

Innovations

There is some evidence that enables us to grasp the relevance of innovations for economic growth in the period of 1865–1896. Even though quantity is not nearly as important as the quality of innovations, it is important to note that the number of patents (of inventions) issued soared from war levels at 6,088 in 1865 to 12,277 2 years later, remaining on this high level until 1880. In 1880, another increase in patents (of inventions) issued towards about 20,000 per year set in.[322]

A few innovations deserve special mentioning due to their importance. An important invention for agriculture was the twine binder in 1878 which increased the harvesting speed 80 times.[323] As well, other new machinery in agriculture was responsible for an increase in output. Furthermore, important innovations emerged around the railroad industry, for instance, the double box car, refrigerated cars and special livestock cars, the automatic coupler, and the Westinghouse air brake and the steel rail.[324] The improvement in transportation enlarged the market and provided opportunities for economics of scale. The Bessemer process greatly increased the productivity of steel production. Moreover, the McKay sewing-machine was improved, the electric telegrapher and new steamships invented.[325]

Another important form of innovation was the growth of industrial concentration, that allowed making use of economies of scale. Without any need of capital accumulation the existing capital was combined in a more efficient manner by concentration.[326] Entrepreneurs like Andrew Carnegie in the steel industry and John D. Rockefeller in the petroleum sector might be named as examples of entrepreneurs who by the implementation of innovations and entrepreneurial genius created highly efficient concentrated companies. Davis and North summarize the effect of these innovations:

> Developments in transport turned the region east of the Mississippi into a single market for most commodities and integrated at least a portion of the trans-Mississippi West (Minnesota, Iowa, and eastern Kansas and Nebraska) into this now near-national market. At the same time, major technical breakthroughs were achieved in several important industries, and the new techniques were subject to increasing returns over wide ranges of output. In steel, for example, the Bessemer process was widely innovated, in petroleum new sophisticated methods of fractional distillation were applied, and in milling, Hungarian reduction techniques were widely used in the new mills of the Upper Midwest. [footnote omitted] *All were subject to substantial scale economics. The average size of a firm grew substantially as new plants and mills, designed to realize these economics of scale and to serve the "national market", came into production.* [Italics added] (1971, pp. 170–171).

---

322 See US Department of Commerce, 1975, W 96–106, pp. 957–959.

323 See Faulkner (1924, pp. 426–428).

324 See Shields (1977, pp. 241–242)

325 See Laughlin (1887, pp. 336–338).

326 See on the industrial concentration Davis et al. (1965), p. 368. See also Shields (1977, p. 12). The possibility of economies of scale is implied in Mises' Law of Returns (1998, pp. 127–130).

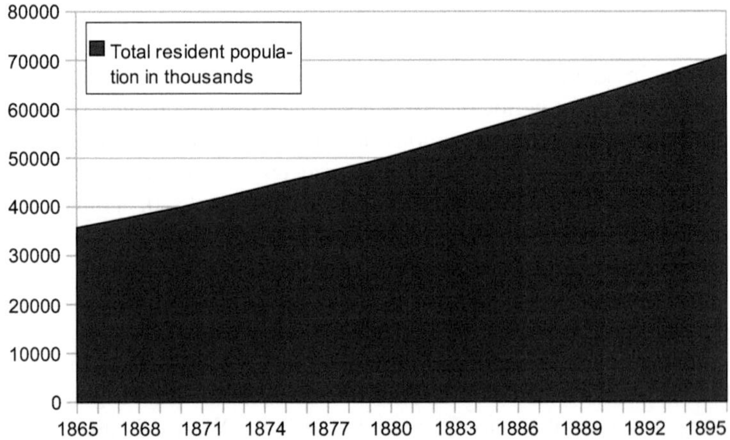

Chart 5.6 Population estimates for the U.S., 1865–1896

Population Increase and the Division of Knowledge

At some point in the development of humanity due to the limited capacity of the human brain, an increase in population becomes a necessary condition for the increase in the division of knowledge. The sufficient condition of an increase of the division of knowledge is an increase in specialization. An increase in population allows for an increase in specialization. In the period from 1865 to 1896 the population of the U.S. increased tremendously as can be seen in Chart 5.6.[327]

From 1865 to 1896 the population increased every year. Moreover, it was a rapid growth with the population almost precisely doubling from 35,701,000 in 1865 to 1870,885,000 in 1896. This population growth was to a great part result of "the vast international movement of people out of England and Europe to the empty lands of the world..." (North 1961, p. 198).

Indeed, a main reason for the tremendous increase in the population was immigration. In 1865, 248,120 people immigrated. Immigration reached a high in 1886 with 884,203 people and ended our period with 243,267 people in 1896.[328] Over the whole period almost 13 million people immigrated to the U.S.

One reason for this high immigration beside the political freedom might have been the fact that growth was high in this period. When production increases in a country, and more specifically the production per capita increases, this is an incentive to emigrate to this country. Thus, growth becomes a self-enforcing process, as it attracts more people thereby creating more growth. Also, a higher standard of living in the U.S. than in the countries of origin might have been a reason for the immigration. In short, as people expected a higher and increasing

---

327 Source: US Department of Commerce, 1975, Series A 6–8, p. 8.

328 See US Department of Commerce, 1975, Series C 89–119, pp. 105–106. Of course by counting every immigrant these data are pretending an accuracy which is absurd.

standard of living and more freedom in the U.S. than in their own countries, they chose to immigrate.

The tremendous growth in population lead to an increase in the production of goods and services as the additional individuals started producing them. In this respect, it is also important to emphasize that the immigrants were mostly in the working age between 15 and 40 years.[329] Furthermore, the population increase allowed for an intensification and extension of the division of labor. This increase in the division of labor or knowledge allowed for a more efficient production.

But the division of knowledge did not only increase inside the United States. It also increased on a world wide scale as trade barriers were eliminated and transportation costs fell. International trade increased strongly. Also the international trade of the United States increased. Thus, U.S. exports increased almost fourfold from $261 million in 1865 to $1.048 million in 1896 and imports from $256 million in 1865 to $1.048 million in 1896.[330]

Capital Accumulation

The period from 1865 to 1896 was a period of great capital accumulation. Simon Kuznets estimates that gross capital formation increased from an average of $3.49 billion in 1929 prices during 1869–1888 to $8.68 billion during 1889–1908 (1961, p. 56). Gross total capital stock increased from $45 billion in 1869 to $190 billion in 1890 (both figures in 1929) prices.[331] This implies a substantial rate of growth in the total capital stock of about 60 % per decade. This rate of growth would slow down after 1900.[332] The net capital formation was also extraordinarily high in percent of net national product. This implies that the savings rate was very high. In the period from 1869 till 1898 net capital formation was, as Kuznets estimates, around 15 % of the net national product. This number would fall in the following decades reaching 5.8 % in the decade from 1946 to 1955.[333]

One sector that portrays the capital accumulation from 1865 to 1896 very well is the railroad industry. The Atlantic and Pacific coasts were connected in 1869. The number of miles operated increased from 35,085 in 1865 to 166,703 in 1890.[334] The number of miles built soared.[335] The capital accumulation in form of railroads greatly reduced transportation costs thereby integrating markets, allowing for economies of scale and was a main reason for the price decreases.

---

[329] See US Department of Commerce, 1975, Series C 138–142, p. 112. For the increase in the work force see US Department of Commerce, 1975, Series D 67–181, p. 189.

[330] See US Department of Commerce, 1975, Series U 1–25, pp. 864–865.

[331] See Kuznets (1961, p. 64).

[332] See Kuznets (1961, p. 65).

[333] See Kuznets (1961, p. 92).

[334] See US Department of Commerce, 1975, Series Q 321–328, p. 731.

[335] See US Department of Commerce, 1975, Series Q 329, p. 732.

5.1.5 Falling Prices: The Interpretation

We are now in a better position to interpret the period between 1865 and 1896. But let us first review the traditional interpretations of the period in the U.S. from 1865 to 1896. They can roughly be divided in three broad groups. The first group consisting of monetarists like Friedman and Schwartz does not reach a clear judgment of the period because they contemplate two contradicting indicators: falling prices, which indicate for them a depressive effect, and economic growth. The second group, more Keynesian inclined, sees the period as one of continuous economic depressions leading to social unrest. This group also presents the still traditional interpretation of some contemporaries of the period. The third group while granting the instability of the financial system and business cycles regards the period as one that was coined by high economic growth. This is the view maintained by some contemporaries, as well as a perspective that an Austrian interpretation of the data suggests.[336]

Let us first consider some representatives of the uneasy view of the period. They often have contradicting views on the period and due to their theoretical framework fail to understand and grasp what happened. Such is the case of monetarists like Milton Friedman and Anna Schwartz.[337] They have to acknowledge the growth of GDP data and the simultaneously falling prices. This strikes against the popular and also under economists widespread view that falling prices and economic growth are incompatible, i.e. it strikes against their very own theory. Thus, the period was astonishing to Friedman and Schwartz who write that this occurrence "casts serious

[336] Thus, the Austrian economist Patrick Newman (2012) argues that there was no depression between 1873 and 1879. He maintains that falling prices were the reason for the misinterpretation of the period. Also new institutionalists seem to come to a largely positive assessment of the period similar to the Austrians. Douglass C. North states: "In the era between the Civil War and World War I, we emerged as the greatest industrial nation in the world, without at the same time forfeiting our preeminence as a world supplier of raw materials and foodstuffs... [the] United States industrial development was spectacular during this period..." (1961, p. 195) Even though North speaks of a longer period than we are considering he makes a very positive statement on it. Thus, it would seem strange to argue that he thinks that in this period a "Great Depression" occurred. Moreover, North mentions the falling prices and does not make them responsible for disruptions but on the contrary sees them as the result of economic growth: "Up until 1896 the international price level fell, reflecting the fact that output was increasing at a more rapid rate than the money supply, but after that date the reverse was true." (1961, p. 201)

[337] See also as positive accounts of the period in the works of Dickey (1977) and Shields (1977) that belong to this first group. Those authors that are not Austrian economists but more in the monetarist tradition. Another case is Coppock (1961). His paper has the title "The Causes of the Great Depression, 1873–1896," however, he argues that only the trend rate of growth was reduced in this period (p. 216). Interesting is also that Friedman and Schwartz themselves note that the price fall might have misled economists about the severity and length of the recession of the 1870s: "But the sharp decline in financial magnitude, so much more obvious and so much better documented than the behavior of a host of poorly measured physical magnitude, may well have led contemporary observers and later students to overestimate the severity of the contraction and perhaps even its lengths." (1971, pp. 87–88)

doubts on the validity of the now widely held view that secular serious price deflation and rapid economic growth are incompatible" (1971, p. 15). However, Friedman and Schwartz acknowledge the growth and are not so negative on the period as other authors. The only problem for them is, that it did not really fit into their monetary theory as indicated in the above quote.

Yet, there are other authors that come to a more negative view. Those authors belong to the second group which seems to stand in strong contrast to the data that falling prices did not suppress production or growth. Indeed many authors believed that strong depressions occurred in the 1870s and later. This belief seems to have become one of the most curious myths of economic history. For example, Weinstein speaks of a depression in the 1870s (1970, p. 360). Rendigs Fels in the same manner states: "The cyclical contraction that followed the panic of 1873 was the longest in the history of American business cycles, lasting until March 1879, a span of 5 years and 5 months" (1959, p. 107).

This assessment bewilders a historian who is aware of the fact that the Warren and Pearson production index, as stated above, rises between 1874 from 13.97 to 23.03 in 1879! Fels, furthermore, speaks of the depression of the 1870s as "outstanding" in the history of business cycles (1959, p. 73).[338] The same author in another work speaks of a "long wave depression" from 1873 to 1897 (1949, p. 69). One factor indicating this depression would be falling wholesale prices! Thus it seems clear that falling prices mistakenly are considered as a synonym for depression. Also Asher Achinstein makes remarks in this direction and declares the years from 1873 to 1879 as the longest contraction in U.S. history and puts it in one class with the contraction of 1929–1933 as one of the severest depressions.[339] Unger states that economic historians "continue to debate the causes of the 'Great Depression' of 1873–1896" (1964, p. 338), fn. 71. Walter Nugent remarks about the 1870s: "The seventies were a depression decade everywhere, conditions varying from country to country only in the severity of their bleakness" (1967, p. 48).

Also Samuel Rezneck writes about the alleged severe depressions from 1873 to 1878, 1882–1886 and 1893–1897[340] and Charles Hoffman (1956) writes on the depression in the 1890s. Rezneck's main evidence for depressions seems to have been the social unrest in those periods. Furthermore, Earl J. Hamilton regards for the period 1873–1892 of declining prices in Europe[341] and the U.S. as

[338] See also Fels (1951, p. 325).

[339] Achinstein (1961, p. 166, 170)

[340] See Rezneck (1950), (1953), and (1956).

[341] In Britain the people living at the time and later academics regarded conditions as bad despite the fact that the "average consumer appears to have been considerably better off at the end of the 'depression' than before" (Selgin 1997, p. 50). Selgin (1997, pp. 51–52) declares it, thus, as a myth that there was a depression in Britain between 1873 and 1896. He makes out four causes for the myth that can also be found for the case of the U.S. First, some sectors of the economy were depressed indeed, like in the U.S. agriculture. Second, there were cyclical upturns and downturns. Third, there existed wrong theories, namely that falling prices would disturb production. Those

depressionary and he seems to give as his main proof the social unrest and revolutionary writing in this period:

> To the extent that prices fell because of a deficient money supply, profits were restricted and business depressed. In most countries of the Western world, business was very bad for considerably more than half this time, and the depression that began in 1873 was one of the most severe the world has ever known. [footnote omitted] Henry George, Edward Belamy, Henry Demarest Lloyd, and Karl Marx were pouring out protest literature; and some of their works were best sellers. The United States had the Granger Movement, Populism, and Coxey's Army. England had her famous Royal Commission on the Depression of Trade and Industry, before which Alfred Marshall was proud of having testified; and in English economic history the Great Depression means the quarter century, 1873–1897. (1952, pp. 345–346)

It is of course true, that the period was marked by social unrest and enunciations of the old age ideas of socialism and communism. However, the causality was probably not in the direction that Hamilton indicates. It were rather the new ideas, new philosophical writings that spurred the social unrest and not the social unrest that caused the new ideas.

Besides falling prices and social unrest, another though not independent reason for this widespread myth about the period from 1865 to 1896 stems from the standpoint and data of the NBER, maybe the most important institution for business cycle research. Indeed, the NBER chronology names 16 years out of 31 as recessionary.[342] This is the highest concentration of recessionary years in the NBER history and indeed impressive. Probably NBER historians were misled in their analysis by the persistent price deflation in this period.

However, the aforementioned judgments of economists are still surprising considering that even though between 1873 and 1879 prices fell continuously, even the money supply fell in some years, and there was social unrest, it was a time of a rapid economic growth.

An interpretation based on an Austrian analysis comes to quite a different result. Considering the data, apparently, it was a period of price deflation. The price deflation was mainly caused by economic growth in the U.S. and the rest of the world. Another reason for the decrease in prices, important at least in the greenback era, was an expectation of an increase in the quality of money. This increase was expected as redemption in specie of the paper greenback was considered more

theories existed also in the U.S. Fourth, sympathy for negatively affected groups. In the U.S. such a group would be farmers. See on this myth also Musson (1959).

[342] See Davis (2006, p. 106). Davis criticizes the NBER chronology. He uses his own data set, consisting of 43 annual components in the manufacturing and mining industries. He reduces the number of recessionary years in the period from 1865 to 1896 to seven eliminating three recessions completely. Davis argues convincingly that the persistent price deflation in the period made Willard Thorp (1926) in his Business Annals (on which NBER data, for example Wesley Mitchell's work (1927) is based) overestimate the duration and number of recessions (Davis 2006, p. 113). I regard Davis' data stemming from enterprises located in higher stages of production more adequate than GDP numbers to identify historical economic cycles because cycle movements are more pronounced in the higher stages of production.

probable. Furthermore, especially in the first subperiod many industrial countries changed from a silver standard to a gold standard, thereby increasing demand for gold and pushing prices dominated in gold down.

Of course, not everything in this period was perfect or wonderful. There were some severe defects in the financial system. The fractional reserve banking system, by expanding credits resulting in malinvestments, (as for example in the railroad industry) caused a continuous series of booms and busts. Further, the fractional reserve banking system, lacking a lender of last resort, experienced several financial panics. Of course, all this entailed severe personal tragedies. And in the financial panics and bankruptcies of the recessionary days during this period, the social movements and agitators grew strong.

However, despite the waste of resources due to malinvestments, the American economic growth was still tremendous and resulted from the combination of an increase in the division of labor, an increase in population, an increase in savings and capital accumulation, and innovations in a free market framework.

It is important to emphasize that falling prices did not suppress business or production, as can be seen by rising GNP. It seems to be the case that in retrospect the fall in prices, combined at times with a fall in the money supply as well as the social unrest was taken by economic historians as evidence of a recession instead of taking the declining prices as evidence for economic growth and prosperity. Thus, Rothbard states:

> It should be clear then, that the "great depression" of the 1870s is a great myth—a myth brought about by misinterpretation of the fact that prices in general fell sharply during the entire period [1865–1879]. (2002, pp. 154–155)

Indeed, falling prices did not cause a recession. Rather, in the recessions of the period, the bank credit deflation led to a stronger downward pressure on prices. In general, however, the increase in production was one of the causes of the falling prices. Output rose more strongly than the money stock and prices fell. This observation was also made by some contemporary economists who were able to witness the economic growth without being blinded by the price deflation. The blessing of the economic growth that caused prices to fall was recognized by the contemporary economist David Ames Wells, who wrote in 1891:

> ... if the fall of prices has been mainly due, as has been demonstrated, to natural and permanent causes, namely, the increased power of mankind in the work of production and distribution, then the result, by creating a greater abundance of all good things, and bringing a larger amount of the same within the reach of the masses for consumption and enjoyment, has been one of the greatest of blessings. (1891, p. 250)

In response to the bimetallist's argument that businesses are always in debt, and therefore deflation is a burden on the production, an economist of this time, Frank W. Taussig, makes the following observation on the American experience:

> Prosperity, activity, general industrial advance, have been so great and so obvious that the argument as to any check to industry could take serious hold only in occasional periods of depression or slackened advance. (1892, pp. 89–90)

Taussig also ingeniously points out that a falling price level must not lead to a business depression:

> If money became scarce, if its value rose and all prices fell, every producer, to be sure, would receive a smaller money income than before, and would have a smaller money capital. But he would be able to buy as many commodities and as much labor as before, and would be in reality just as rich and prosperous. (1892, p. 87)

In sum, the price deflation from 1865 to 1896 was mainly caused by a tremendous economic growth being supplemented by a switch of several industrial countries to a gold standard and before 1879 by an increase in the quality of money. That a great depression occurred is a myth.

5.1.6 Falling Prices: A Political Struggle

5.1.6.1 Social Unrest

As we have seen, the time period of 1865–1896 was a period of exceptionally high growth in the U.S.[343] However, it was also a time of social unrest. At first sight, it seems that the social unrest was caused by falling prices, as many individuals and groups opposed falling prices. As Roger E. Shields writes about some part of the period:

> The years of 1873–1896 in the United States were marked by labor strife, political agitation, and social unrest. The Greenbackers, the Populists, and the militant Knights of Labor all put their mark on the U. S. economy during these years. Although each of these groups had many complaints and made many demands which were unique to them, *the complaint of economic hardship caused by declining prices,* and the demand that the money supply be vigorously expanded to reverse the falling prices, formed a common bond of interest between them. [Italics added] (1977, p. 1)

Also Friedman and Schwartz find a "[...] slow but rather steady downward tendency in product prices that prolonged and exacerbated the political discontent initiated by the rapid decline in prices after the end of the Civil War" (1971, p. 8). How is it theoretically explainable that in a time of growing output and a fast growing income per capita, social unrest occurs?

As I have developed in Sects. 4.1.1 and 4.1.2.1, there are several reasons individuals have for opposing falling prices. There is a redistribution to the disadvantage of debtors. Thus, one expects debtors as a potential source for social unrest even in times of price deflation.

---

[343] See Kuznets (1961, p. 72). According to Rothbard (2002, p. 64), per capita income (in 1958 dollars) increased from $531 in the decade average 1869–1878 to $795 in the decade average 1889–1898, an increase of almost 50 %!

Another factor during this period contributing to the discontent of debtors was falling interest rates.[344] The fall in the interest rates made the present value of existing debts increase. If debtors wanted to pay back their debts before they were due or buy them back, they had to pay higher prices. The creditors, in contrast, could sell the debts at higher prices.

I also pointed out in Sect. 4.3.3. that the losing groups in a price deflation are usually well organized. During the period of the American growth deflation, i.e. 1865–1896, groups like indebted farmers, and businesses were in danger of suffering considerable losses due to falling prices. These groups had a greater political leverage. Particularly, the farmers managed to organize as a formidable group as their organization offered services that could be withheld from non--members.[345] Thus, the Grange was a social and educational organization. Also business interests could be organized easily in small groups with strong common interests. Businesses, indeed, had much to lose in a price deflation, as they were highly indebted.

Indeed, the injured interests of the debtor class and its pushing for the restoration of the old price level were already recognized at the time being. As David Ames Wells writes in 1891 about the period of falling prices:

> Probably the most signal feature of the recent economic transition has been the *extensive decline in the prices of most commodities; and as great material interests have been for a time thereby injuriously affected*—commodities at reduced valuation not paying the same amount of debt as before—the drift of popular sentiment seems to be to the effect that such a result has been in the nature of a calamity. Accordingly, a great variety of propositions and devices have been brought forward in recent years, and have largely occupied the attention of the public in all civilized countries, which, in reality, had for their object not merely the arrest of this decline, but even the restoration of prices to something like their former level. [Italics added] (1891, p. 447)

In the following section we will look on the movements that opposed falling prices in detail: namely, the greenback supporters and the silver advocates. We will also look at the motives of constituents of those groups as there are miners, business establishment and the farmers, who were the origin of the greatest social discontent. These groups will be discussed in their own section. Also we will consider the economic justifications that were made for the opposition to declining prices and how this was related to these interest groups. This might give us an understanding how the notion arose that swiftly declining prices and economic growth are somehow incompatible.[346]

---

[344] See Siegel (1998, p. 8).

[345] Olson, (1971, p. 132) explains that the free rider problem can be overcome in large groups if they offer as a "by-product" services from which non-members can be excluded.

[346] Friedman and Schwartz state that there is the "now [!] widely held view that secular price deflation and rapid economic growth are incompatible" (1971, p. 15). With the "now" it is suggested that this belief was not always so widespread.

5.1.6.2 Greenback Supporters

Between 1865 and 1878 there was a "political controversy about the greenbacks and about their role in the accompanying price decline" (Friedman and Schwartz 1971, pp. 24–25). Several groups called for immediate resumption, especially importers, eastern bankers, and some manufacturers, especially textile men, who as exporters were interested in a stable currency.[347] On the other side, there were several groups that supported the greenbacks and opposed redemption, for example farmers and some business groups. Friedman and Schwartz indicate a "[. . .] support for inconvertible currency by many business groups both during and after the war [the Civil War], and growing farm support after the war, as agricultural prices fell" (1971, p. 7). Later they add:

> Currency expansion was just as strongly advocated, to offset the baleful effects of deflation, by an even more mixed lot—agrarian groups that had initially been strong proponents of currency contraction, spokesmen for labor groups, western merchants and bankers, Pennsylvania ironmasters, and businessmen with interests in western real estate and transportation (pp. 45–46).

Rothbard supports Friedman and Schwartz' view that some industrialists supported the movement: "A powerful group of industrialists calling for continuation of greenbacks, opposing resumption and, of course, any contraction of money to prepare for specie resumption, was headed by the Pennsylvania iron and steel manufacturers." (2002, p. 147)

It is not difficult to find the reasons why these groups opposed resumption in order to avoid price deflation. Price deflation implied a redistribution of wealth from groups in favor of expansion to other groups of the population. The stand of the groups mentioned in the above citation by Friedman and Schwartz can be explained. Many farmers and industrialists were highly indebted.[348] Their real debt would increase in time of price deflation. Western real estate would be more attractive for farmers, the potential buyers, if farm product prices would not fall relatively to other prices and the burden of debt would not increase. Especially railroads were highly indebted as well and the ironmasters were their most important clients. The situation became even worse when the Panic of 1873 revealed that many businesses and railroads over-expanded their business.[349] The railroad promoters were most severely hit and one-eighth of the total national railroad debts were in default in November of 1873.[350] The intertemporal misallocation of resources had become obvious. Also indebted iron and steel industries were hit

[347] See Friedman and Schwartz (1971, p. 45).

[348] Taussig 1892, p. 90 states that farmers and railroads were mostly hurt by an increase in their long-term debt burden.

[349] For the Panic of 1873 see Dewey (1907, pp. 370–372). Fels (1959), claims that railroads had overestimated the amount of capital available.

[350] See Unger (1964, pp. 220–221).

by falling prices and the fact that they had to invest huge sums for new technologies.[351]

Not surprisingly, many businessmen and bankers opposed falling prices and were also in favor of a continuous issue of greenbacks. As Irwin Unger states: "Boot and shoe manufacturers, even merchants and bankers, joint the attack on the Contraction Act after 1866 (footnote omitted), and tipped the balance of forces that in these years normally immobilized Congress." (1964, p. 44)

Railroad speculator George Francis Train demanded a vast issue of new greenbacks: "Give us greenbacks we say, and we build cities, plant corn, open coal mines, control railways, launch ships, grow cotton, establish factories, open gold and silver mines, erect rolling mills. ... Carry my resolution and there is sunshine in the sky."[352]

Another businessman involved in life insurance, timber lands, railroads, coal and iron investments was Jay Cook. He was in favor of expansion, arguing that the growing west needed the new money to build railroads and improve farms.[353] After the collapse of the railroad boom in 1874, Richard Schell, another railroad speculator, argued for substantial increases in the money supply and a proto-Keynesian governmental spending program.[354]

There existed indirect and direct relations between politics and business. Due to the political leverage of businesses, many politicians were open to the complaints of business men. For example, the Republican majority leaders George S. Boutwell and Oliver P. Morton had close industrial contacts.[355] Often, there was also even a more direct relation between politics and economic interests. For instance, the cotton magnate William Sprague was Senator. Thomas Ewing Jr., who with his family members had interests in railroads as well as coal and iron lands, was at the head of the Ohio Democratic Party.[356]

All mentioned interest groups cried for additional credits and for an expansion of issue.[357] Many of them gathered in the Greenback Party. The Greenback Party had formed in the wake of the 1873 panic. Hence, the boom and the recession caused by the expansionary banking system, gave the munition of social discontent to the agitators. The discontent was not caused by falling prices per se, but rather by the bankruptcies and misery of the recession. On the discontent the Greenback Party was founded. The party had several goals that would help the interest groups that

[351] See Unger (1964, p. 49).

[352] Cincinnati Enquirer, Aug. 17, 1867, quoted in Unger (1964, p. 46).

[353] See Unger (1964, pp. 46–47).

[354] See Unger (1964, p. 47).

[355] See Unger (1964, p. 45).

[356] See Unger (1962, pp. 59–62). It should be added again that not all business men were opposed to resumption (Unger 1962, p. 69). Textile exporters were in favor while iron masters and business men with western interests were opposed.

[357] See Friedman and Schwartz (1971, p. 47). See also Unger (1964, p. 222), for the ironmasters and railroads asking for inflation.

were supporting the party. One goal was to prevent prices from falling further in order to foster business and solve farmers' problems.[358] One element to achieve this was the repeal of resumption and an increase in the supply of currency. Another goal was the reduction of the burden of debt.

Not surprisingly, the Greenback Party was founded by a group of farmers.[359] Farmers had been paid for supplies in greenbacks by the government during the Civil War and had indebted themselves during the greenback era. They regarded it as unfair that they had to pay their greenback debts with gold as they had been paid in greenbacks and consequently opposed resumption. One of their slogans reflecting this argument was: "the same currency for the bondholder as for the plowholder."[360]

Also, the idea that insufficient money would harm business can be found in the arguments of the Greenback Party. Representative George O. Jones, a greenback supporter who later ran for office independently backed by the Populist Party writes in a pamphlet titled *More Money and less misery!*:

> Twenty-three years of Republican rule has piled up mountains of debts, created and perpetuated Bank, Bond, Railroad, Land, and other monopolies and with an overflowing treasury at its command it has failed to provide American Citizens with sufficient money to transact their business, *until*, European capital now puts its own price on every pound of American produce and determines the value of every hour of American labor. That party is responsible for the universal bankruptcy caused by contracting the currency before 1873, and for bringing down to present prices, grain, manufactured goods, and day's wages, so that to-day American Farmers, Mechanics, Manufacturers and Merchants are threatened with universal ruin and enforced idleness. (1884, p. 4).

The reference to European capital by Jones indicates the different interests. European capital was in favor of a gold standard, because its investment would have decreased in value if the U.S. dollar would depreciate due to greenback expansion or by the U.S. turning to a silver standard.

At 1880, when specie resumption had been attained, a new program was adapted by the Greenback Party. The program demanded a government fiat paper currency and unlimited coinage of silver. This leads us to the second important political force opposing falling prices: the silver advocates.

5.1.6.3 Silver Advocates

Parallel with the greenback issue, there arose the silver question from about 1875 and onward. Silver proponents wanted silver to play a larger part in the U.S. monetary system.[361] The world silver price had declined after the

---

358 Often mortgages would not be renewed in the wake of the Panic of 1873. See Shannon (1957, p. 55).

359 See for the support of farmers for the greenback movement in the 1870s, Shannon (1957, p. 57).

360 See Shannon (1957, p. 59).

361 Hugh Rockoff (1990) argues that the children's book "The Wizard of Oz" is a monetary allegory about the free silver movement.

demonetization of silver in the Coinage Act of 1873, caused by the opening of new silver mines in the American West and the shift of several European countries (Germany, France and the Latin Union) from bimetallic or silver standards to a gold standard, which put pressure on the price of silver.[362] Of course, silver producers and people interested in inflation would have been better off without the legal demonetization of silver. They wanted to monetize silver again. With a bimetallist standard at the 16 to 1 ratio and free coinage at this rate, silver would have been overvalued and gold undervalued. Gold would have disappeared from circulation into hoards and foreign countries. On the other side, silver would have suddenly made its comeback into circulation. The monetary demand for silver would have increased, thereby providing windfall profits for silver miners. In addition, the silver of the world would have flown to the U.S.

As the silver supply increased at a faster rate than gold and silver would have flown into the U.S., the monetization of silver probably would have caused a slow down or even a reversal of the decline in prices.[363]

Therefore, the legal tender laws that set a legal ratio of silver to gold at 16 to 1 and the demonetization of silver lead to a legal tender deflation during the whole period from 1865 to 1896, in the sense that prices were lower than they would have been without these monetary policies. In the first part of the period before 1874 silver was not used as a medium of exchange as would probably have occurred in the absence of the legal tender laws of bimetallism that drove the undervalued silver out of circulation. The total amount of media of exchange or monies was reduced by the legal tender laws of bimetallism. Therefore, money prices were lower than they would have been in the absence of bimetallism. In 1873 and 1874, silver was then practically legally demonetized. It lost its legal-tender status over amounts of $5. In the competition with legal tender gold that was in circulation silver had a hard stand. By the legal demonetization of silver that prevented its use as a media of exchange, prices were kept by government fiat lower than they would have been in a free money market, where probably both gold and silver would have been in use. We are faced with a case of a legal tender deflation.

Of course, some groups became aware of the fact that without the legal tender deflation, and also with just keeping the old bimetallist legal tender ratio of gold to silver, prices would have been higher. Those groups of individuals that were opposed to falling prices agitated against the demonetization of silver. As a consequence silver miners were joined in their demand for free coinage by other interest groups that had opposed falling prices during the greenback era: farmers

---

[362] For the reasons for the fall in the price of silver see Laughlin (1968, pp. 109–206). The ratio of production of silver to production of gold increased from 6.0 in 1861–1865 to 12.5 in 1871–1875, the period of demonetization of silver. The ratio kept increase to its peak in 1890 of 23.4. See Warren and Pearson (1933, p. 145), Table 26.

[363] See Friedman (1990, pp. 1174–1175) for an hypothetical estimation of prices under free silver coinage.

and highly indebted business men. Thus, there were three main groups advocating silver.[364] The southern and western Agrarians, who were indebted,[365] over-indebted industrialists that would benefit by inflation, and the Western silver miners, who wanted a guaranteed government market for their products. It was a natural alliance of those who expected to benefit directly, by producing the money stuff, and indirectly, by higher prices than otherwise, from the monetization of silver.[366] Thus, most support for silver came from "politicians, publicists, business-men, and voters in the urban Midwest".[367]

Not surprisingly, remonetization of silver won the support of a number of industrialists, real estate brokers, and investors in railroads, iron and coal mines.[368] Indeed, bimetallism, i.e. a gold silver double standard, at the old ratio, appealed to businessmen who regarded the loss of legal tender of silver to be responsible for the business slump after 1873.[369] Thus, not only did the Greenback Party come about due to the discontent of the recession of 1873, but so did the silver movement. The business cycle recession with its liquidations and bankruptcies fed the discontent.

The reduction of the debt burden played a major role for the silver advocates as it did for the greenback supporters. Throughout the controversy the mid western business groups also remained favorable to silver as they wanted to reduce their burden of debt.[370] As Senator William B. Allison said in favor of legal bimetallism during a Senate debate in February 1878:

> Those who favor this measure do not propose to violate any promise, and least of all to tarnish or impair the public credit, but rather to establish it upon more enduring foundations by increasing our ability to pay according to promise the heavy public burdens which now weight us down.[371]

In this line, George M. Weston, business man and 1882 founder of a food company, interpreted the 1873 demonetization of silver as a defrauding of the American people in favor of creditors.[372]

---

[364] See Weinstein (1970, p. 6). Shannon states: "Indebted farmers were quick to pick up the chorus of the mine owners" (1957, p. 59). For an overview on the different argument reflecting the different interests also offered for free coinage of silver see Robert F. Hoxie: "(1) A lack of confidence and business enterprise. (2) A low range of prices. (3) Increasing indebtedness. (4) The depression of our great silver mining industry." (1893, p. 546)

[365] See Shannon (1945, p. 314). See also Friedman and Schwartz (1971, p. 48, 115) on debtor farmers in the Middle West and South allying with the Greenback Party.

[366] See on this alliance Dewey (1907, p. 406).

[367] (Weinstein 1970, p. 293). Weinstein adds that the south was only giving passive support.

[368] See Unger (1964, p. 335).

[369] See Weinstein (1970, p. 125).

[370] See Weinstein (1970, p. 128).

[371] See Cong. Record, 45th Cong. 2D see., vol. 7, pt. 2, p. 1,061, Feb. 15, 1878, quoted in Weinstein (1970, p. 302).

[372] See Unger (1964, p. 330).

There were also pseudo-economic arguments advanced in favor of free silver coinage at the old gold silver ratio in the name of bimetallism. The first bimetallist was Senator John Percival Jones.[373] He himself had interests in silver mines, as well as farming. He claimed that if silver would be remonetized this would be very stimulating for the economy:

> prices [will] rise; exchange or commerce is stimulated; new enterprises are set a foot; the products of agriculture, manufactures, and mining are increased; the commercial and industrial classes find abundant employment and earn remunerative profits and wages; bankruptcies and suicides rarely happen; marriages are promoted; the newly born survive in greater numbers; population increases in quicker ratio; education, intelligence and morality, and the observance of religion are promoted; and the general happiness of mankind becomes greatly enhanced.[374]

Senator Jones implicitly makes deflation responsible for many if not all economic problems of that time. He even regards monetary inflation as the solution to all educational, moral, and religious problems.

5.1.6.4 Gold Proponents

However, there is also the other side that was strongly in favor of the demonetization of silver and opposed its monetization. What was at stake here was the loss of the money standard of the major industrial countries. Gold would have been exported from the U.S. and the U.S. would have stayed on the silver standard while the rest of the world began using a gold standard. This would have meant a monetary isolation of the U.S. and the loss of the gold to foreign countries.

We do not know if bankers were conscious about the favorable consequences the demonetization of silver would have on the capacity of credit expansion of the banking system. However, some of the people who pressed for the demonetization of silver had links to the banking system. This seems to be intuitively indicated by the propagandistic silverite literature in which a conspiracy of the plutocracy was made responsible for the demonetization of silver.[375] The Coinage Act of 1873 was initiated in response to a report written in 1870 by H. R. Linderman and John Jay Knox that recommended dropping silver coinage. John Jay Knox had been in the banking business since 1849, and in 1872 he became President of the National Bank of the Republic in New York City. Support for the recommendation by Knox and Linderman was also given by the Secretary of the Treasury George Boutwell (Friedman 1990, p. 1166) and the chairman of the Committee on Finance: Senator Sherman (Rothbard 2002, p. 157). Sherman also did have ties with the banking industry, as his younger brother Hoyt Sherman was a successful banker.

---

[373] For John Percival Jones, see Weinstein (1970, pp. 53–81).

[374] See Jones, *Resumption and the Double Standard*, pp. 92–93, quoted in Weinstein (1970, p. 99).

[375] See Friedman and Schwartz (1971, p. 115), fn. 40.

But why did the demonetization of silver have favorable consequences for the bankers? This can be explained by considering three causes. First, price deflation increases the incentives to accept fiduciary media.[376] In order to maintain the expected income stream entrepreneurs are more likely to accept fiduciary media like bank notes. The use of money proper can thereby be reduced which increases the potential for the lucrative process of credit expansion. Second, by demonetizing silver bankers achieved another important aim. They directly increased the use of fiduciary media. For small purchases silver had been used.[377] Gold due to its high value per weight was not used in small purchases. Due to the legislation silver became artificially "underused." By eliminating silver from circulation a vacuum for the payment of small purchases emerged. In daily exchanges money substitutes like token coins and bank notes instead of silver began to be used.[378] Everyone had to have a bank account as with gold payments alone one could not fulfill the daily exchanges. Business had to resort to banks, as silver was "outlawed." Bankers, of course, were glad to satisfy the demand, filling the vacuum with the issue of bank notes and bank accounts. The use of bank notes, thus, became more accepted and widespread. The increased use of the banking system for payments and increased use of bank notes lead to an influx of money proper in the banks. This allowed for a greater issuance of fiduciary media.

Third, bankers represented foreign investors who feared that their investments would decrease in value were the U.S. to change to a factual silver standard. As new silver mines opened and the international sentiment began to favor a gold standard, it was likely that the price of silver would fall relative to gold and drive gold out of circulation. If silver would not have been demonetized, silver would have become the only money in circulation. As the major industrial countries shifted to a gold standard, the silver of the industrialized world would have flown into the U.S. There it would have been exchanged at the official rate against gold, and with this gold people would have bought foreign exchanges. The U.S. dollar would have been depreciated relative to gold currencies due to the import of silver, and new silver mine production. The foreign investors would have lost part of their investments. In great measure, bankers represented foreign investors and as such opposed a devaluation of dollar investments.

In addition to bankers, importers likewise opposed an international monetary isolation of the U.S. The U.S. would have had a silver currency, while other countries were already on or turning to a gold standard. This would have augmented foreign exchange risk in comparison to a situation where the whole world was on a gold standard. Furthermore, these importers favored a strong U.S. dollar and not a depreciating silver dollar, which would have made imports ever more expensive in terms of dollars.

---

[376] Concerning this point, see Hülsmann (2004, p. 40).

[377] Fekete argues that gold coins won out in a free market setting and pushed silver out of the market. Advances in metallurgy made it possible to mint small gold coins also (1996, p. 12–13). In fact, the two reasons together, the demonetization of silver and the new technologies might be responsible for the triumph of gold.

[378] See Hülsmann (2004, p. 38–39).

5.1.6.5 The Populist Party

During the 1880s, after the Greenback Party had disappeared in the wake of weak election results, new farmer's interest groups called the "Alliances" would form, joining the ranks of the silver advocates. A union of the Northwestern Alliance and a minority of the Southern Alliance would finally form an agrarian party, The People's Party or Populist Party in 1889–1990. The Populist Party had its main supporters in farmers. After 1891 many farmers had difficulties paying back their debts, and it came to another wave of foreclosure of city and farm mortgages in the West.[379] This made many in the agricultural West think that their future depended on the remonetization of silver and this demand was picked up by the Populist Party. Once, again a recession caused by the artificial credit expansion before, gave fuel to the agitators. And of course, in the wake of the panics of 1893 and 1895 the popularity of the People's Party soared. It is not surprising that top party representatives were also representatives of the silver interests.[380] The People's Party agitated for alleviating the farmer's debt burden by free and unlimited coinage of silver at the 16 to 1 ratio.[381] A common aim of the agitation was the allegedly unfair redistribution by declining prices from the people, i.e. farmers, to the mortgage holders, who were supposed to be from the East.[382] Not surprisingly, the main rhetoric was the problem of falling prices that the Populists wanted to combat with two suggestions: (1) free silver coinage, and (2) introduction of a legal tender paper money.[383] Thereby the Populist party appealed to several groups of people. As Michael Kazin writes about the opportunistic party policies of the populists who tried to appeal to silver interests, workers and farmers alike:

> For debt-ridden agrarians, they promised an increase in the money supply, a ban on alien land ownership, and a state takeover of the railroads that so often made small farmers pay whatever they could bear. For wage earners, they endorsed the ongoing push for a shorter working day, called for the abolition of the strike-breaking Pinkerton Agency, and declared that "the interests of rural and civil labor are the same." For currency reformers and residents of Western mining states, they demanded the unlimited coinage of both silver and gold. (1998, p. 38)

[379] See Dewey (1907, p. 460).

[380] See Goodwyn (1978, p. 239).

[381] A silver dollar containing 371.25 grains of fine silver. See Friedman and Schwartz (1971, p. 113).

[382] See Friedman and Schwartz (1971, p. 116). Faulkner states about the farmer: "He felt strongly that eastern capital was benefiting from his misfortune" (1924, p. 424). Also Shannons states that Eastern investors kept providing for the mortgages (1945, p. 306). See also Goodwyn who states that the bondholders and the Eastern financial community were almost identical (1978, p. 11).

[383] The Populists in addition demanded the end of the national banking system. See Nugent (1968, p. 106).

5.1.6.6 Explaining the Farmer's Discontent and Unrest

Let us return to the situation of farmers in the second half of the nineteenth century in the U.S. since much of the social unrest that was later taken as an evidence for a depressionary period was caused by dissatisfaction with economic conditions of agriculture.[384] Indeed, the position of the farmer was rather weak. This weak position was partly caused by government policies. For example, the government gave subsidies to railroads in the form of large land grants alongside the railroad tracks contingent upon the miles built. This lead to railroads sometimes being constructed in a zig-zag manner in order to collect subsidies.[385] This came in addition to other subsidies for the railroads, as tariff remission on rails or direct financial aid. The number of land grants was vast, amounting to 242,000 square miles, a region, larger than Germany or France.[386] That had negative consequences for farmers. Instead of being able to ordinary homestead the land which they could have done in the absence of the land grants, farmers had to buy the land from the railroads and indebted themselves with mortgages. Thus, many farmers entered a debtor-creditor relation because they had to buy the land from the railroads. He, who wanted to homestead land, had to locate many miles away from the crucial transportations lines.[387]

Another government policy partly responsible for the farmers' position was the Civil War, as the Civil War uprooted many families and let to inflation of farm prices that induced many people to become farmers. Farmers taking the high Civil War prices as long term prices, had indebted themselves to invest in their production capacities.[388] As Harold U. Faulkner states:

> Ex-soldiers, tradesmen, and mechanics, encouraged by the Homestead Act, hastened to take up land: but in all of these cases capital was usually lacking and the land was mortgaged to provide for the necessary equipment. All went well until the inflated war prices collapsed (1924, p. 24).

In a period of paper money inflation, and Civil War food prices, farmers over-expanded their farms, buying new machinery and malinvesting scarce resources in an artificial boom. This implies that it was not falling prices per se that brought difficulties for farmers but the malinvestments. The liquidation of those malinvestments in over-expanded farms would have to be done independent of the price level. The differences between buying and selling proceeds will occur independent of the movement of a general "price level" and indicate if an expansion was not beneficial. The fall in the price level only sped the liquidation up.

As prices for their products and their selling proceeds fell, the real burden of debt of those new farmers in the West increased. This of course, gave rise to discontent

[384] See Shields (1977, p. 201).

[385] See Folsom (2003, p. 18).

[386] See Faulkner (1924, p. 456).

[387] See Shannon (1945, p. 173).

[388] See Shannon (1957, p. 48).

among farmers. This discontent grew especially strong when business cycle recessions occurred as in the period after 1873 when the Grange flourished, and in the period after 1884 when the Alliances were at their high point, and in the 1890s with the success of the Populist Party. The farmers' claims were directed against banks, insurance companies, and land mortgage associations. They saw their "enemy" in the financial establishment of the East.

Indeed, the mortgage companies came mainly from the East, where thousands of private loan companies had evolved to collect money for mortgage loans.[389] These people anticipated the falling prices better than many farmers who continued to indebt themselves. As a consequence farms on several occasions changed ownership from bankrupt farmers to the private loan companies.[390] Moreover, as farmers took on credits coming from the city they lost more and more of their financial independence aggravating their discontent.[391] The demonetization of silver was another government intervention that harmed farmers. Without the demonetization of silver, prices would not have fallen as much and neither would real debt burden have increased as much. The monetary and institutional basis of debt contracts was changed by the government. From this perspective it seems understandable that many farmers considered this situation as unjust. It meant new burden to debtors.

As mentioned earlier, the fact that debtors become discontent in an unanticipated deflation, is something to be expected. What was adding to the farmers' discontent in the second half of the nineteenth century in the U.S. was, that great numbers of the farmers went into debt, a fact related to the specific circumstances after the Civil War, with ex-soldiers without capital seeking their luck in the West. Southern farmers were not doing any better than the indebted West due to declining cotton prices. And for the farmers in the northeast, competition of Western farms located on a more fertile soil made life hard. As a consequence, farmers abandoned their farms leaving for the cities.[392]

However, falling prices were not the only reason for farmer's discontent in those years and it would not be accurate to make price deflation solely responsible for the social unrest on part of farmers in those years. For example, the Grange, a social and educational organization for farmers, complained about both a shortage of money and high railroad rates.[393] Farmers regarded railroad freight rates too high and thought that middlemen would take too much profit and speculators on the exchanges would reap unjustified gains.[394] Other reasons for the farmers' unrest

[389] See Shannon (1945, p. 189). See also Ritter (1997, pp. 196–198), for the farm debt problem and the Eastern mortgage companies.

[390] See Shannon (1945, p. 189).

[391] See Elliot (1890, pp. 36–52).

[392] See Faulkner (1924, p. 424).

[393] See Stock (1996, p. 65). According to Mancur Olson's group theory it is easier to organize a group when services like the educational services can be withheld from non-members. Thus, even large groups can organize and as a additional service start lobbying for the interests of the group as a "by product". See Olson (1971, p. 132).

[394] See Faulkner (1924, p. 424). Also Shannon (1957, pp. 51–52).

were that many talented young men and women left the country for the city and that the political representation of farmers was rare.[395] Davis and North assert that a drought that hit the Western States in the late 1880s was partially responsible for the difficult financial situation of farmers (1971, p. 123). Moreover, farmers' political power was waning as they were increasingly outnumbered by industrial workers.[396] Kendrick estimates that the percentage of people working in agriculture dropped from 48.3 % in 1869 to 36.9 % in 1899.[397]

The situation and problems of the farmer is summarized by Shannon's words:

> Low prices for crops and livestock and the high cost of purchased necessities combines with scarce money, tight credit, towering interest rates, burdensome transportation charges, and the exactions of the middlemen—particularly the produce exchanges, grain elevator operators, and meat packers—to make agriculture a doubtful commercial venture and hardly even a way of life.[398]

However, maybe the most important reason for the farmers' unrest consisted in something else. Farmers felt their significance fading as the U.S. became industrialized. The significance of farming to overall production was steadily reduced in the period under consideration as a result of huge structural changes in the U.S. economy. While non-farm gross private domestic (in 1,929 prices) product soared from the decade 1869–1878, from an average of $6.8 billion to $21.7 billion in 1892–1896 or 219 %, farm gross private domestic product only increased from $4.1 billion to $6.8 billion or 66 %.[399] That means that non-farm gross private product rose more than three times faster than farm gross private product. Farmers lost in wealth relative to other groups of the population. Social life in the city was becoming ever richer. The agricultural part of national income fell from 20.5 % in the decade 1869–1878 to 17.1 % in the decade 1889–1898.[400] The "Martin estimate" states an even greater fall. Those estimates show that the percentage of national income obtained by agriculture fell from 22.2 % in 1869 to 14.2 % in 1889.[401] The economic gap was widening.[402] However, it seems that farmers did not lose absolutely, but only relatively as farm productivity, farm land, the number

---

[395] See Unger (1964, pp. 201–202).

[396] See Elliot (1890. pp. 175–186). Shannon (1945, p. 349) states that the changes in the industrial structure challenged the old supremacy of agriculture.

[397] See US Department of Commerce, 1975, Series F 250-261, p. 240.

[398] Shannon (1957, p. 50); Shannon's statement has to be qualified in one point. Namely, the necessities of farmers fell also in price. Actually, as U.S. Department of Commerce (1975), Series E 52–63, p. 201, indicates that farm prices did not fall faster than other commodity prices. See on this point also Bemis (1893, p. 208).

[399] US Department of Commerce, 1975, Series F 125–129, p. 232.

[400] US Department of Commerce, 1975, Series F 216–225, p. 238. Emerick writes that the rural wealth fall from 49 % in 1860 to 25 % in 1890 while urban wealth increased from 51 % to 75 % (1896, p. 493).

[401] US Department of Commerce, 1975, Series F 250–261, p. 240.

[402] See Unger (1964, p. 202). Shannon states that farmers felt a "lack of parity with other economic groups." (1957, p. 49)

of farms, the value of farm gross output and product were on the rise.[403] As Edward W. Bemis states:

> The one fact above all others complained of by farmers and wage-earners alike is relative, not absolute, decline in the share of national income secured. The city grows faster than the country. The income of capitalists, or monopolist, or speculator, or man of large affairs grows faster than that of the farmer or wage-earner. (1893, p. 193)

This relative loss, also caused by the relatively high indebtedness of farmers stirred social unrest.

5.1.7 Interest Groups and Economic "Theories"

Unfortunately, the lobbying of the pressure groups also had adverse effects for economic theory. As always in deflationary recessions or deflationary periods in general, discontent by those who suffered under large redistribution led to theories dealing with the deflation. Thus, with the experiences in the U.S. between 1865 and 1896 economic theories emerged that presented growth deflation as problematic.[404] The interest groups were, therefore, backed by economists who provided arguments against falling prices.

For example, the moral argument for free silver as a means against "artificial" changes induced by a price deflation was very popular at the time. Indeed, the bimetallists argued in favor of both gold and silver as a money. Francis A. Walker is one of the bimetallists making a moral argument in favor of remonetizing silver and against an artificial demonetizing of silver by government intervention. He states:

> The object of the Bi-metallists—at least of the European Bi-metallists [footnote omitted]—is not so much to favor the debtor class by diminishing the weight of debt, as to prevent

[403] See Rothbard (2002, p. 166). Also Shields states "that income in agriculture in real terms increased at a relatively rapid rate during these years of falling prices, and farm unrest, although not as rapidly as economy-wide income" (1977, p. 219). See also on the absolute increase in farmers' wealth Emerick (1897, p. 109).

[404] However, these theories are not completely new. Rather old theories were used to make the argument that seemed to fit one's course. The old idea that the amount of money could be insufficient was vindicated by making the quantity theory of money popular. The declining prices thereby indirectly helped the quantity theory to its popularity. As McClean Hardy indicates: "The *Quantitäts-Theorie* is not a new one, but several circumstances have combined recently to give to it exceptional prominence. In the first place, it forms the basis of the demand for the free coinage of silver: There is not enough silver in the country to supply the needs of business and trade; it is impossible for one metal alone to fulfill all the demands made upon it; and since prosperity can neither be restored nor maintained while there is a scarcity of the circulating medium, silver must be remonetized, if low prices and consequent hard times are not to continue" [Italics in the original] (1895, pp. 145–146). It is also interesting to see the undifferentiated reasoning that equates low prices with hard times as it happens in this quote, not taking into account that price differentials are the relevant factor for the entrepreneur.

> those debts being artificially increased by a diminution in the stock of money, through the demonetization of one of the precious metals. (1883, p. 268)

Indeed, the demonetization of silver in 1873, seems to be unfair for debtors, since debtors probably expected that the government monetary institutions would remain unchanged and the ratio of 16 to 1 with free coinage would be upheld. As the government demonetized silver their burden of debt suddenly increased, in the sense that they were not allowed to use silver anymore to pay them. The demonetization modified contracts already incurred. Debtors would have had the right to pay back in silver, and possibly that had been their plan if they were expecting falling silver prices. Those debtors failed to anticipate correctly the interventions of government into monetary affairs. This is one example that shows that government and its possible interventions make anticipation of the future more difficult.

There are other economists who developed theories that claimed price deflation to be something to be prevented. Thus, Henry C. Carey created some respectability for the soft money philosophy, thereby founding the so called American school with representatives such as E. Peshine Smith, William Elder, Stephen Colwell, and Henry Carey Baird.[405] Carey was very famous and influential. Walter Nugent writes of Carey that he was probably "America's greatest political economist in the nineteenth century" (1967, p. 61). Not only did he favor protective tariffs allegedly benefiting workers, farmers and manufacturers, he also attacked the "money lender." He became the foremost apologist of the American heavy industry, who was highly indebted and suffered from declining prices. Interesting is that Carey and Colwell themselves were iron manufacturers and promoted their own cause. Carey's theories fell on fertile ground with iron master Joseph Wharton, railroad promoter Thomas A. Scott, the manufacturers Robert Patterson and William Sellers, as well as publisher Henry C. Lea. The popularity of Carey's neo-mercantilism was fed by falling prices and financed by interest groups. For instance, the president of the Iron and Steel Association in the late 1860s, Eber B. Ward, made financial contributions to Carey's monetary writings.

The American Industrial League, the Pennsylvania Industrial League and the publications *Iron Age*, edited by Carey disciple John Williams, and *National American*, the paper of the American Industrial league, served as a forum for Carey's doctrines. Carey and his group, of course, opposed contraction and resumption of specie payment. They favored greenback issue and were sponsored by the interest groups that would lose in times of falling prices. Carey and his followers were even partly members of these interest groups.

Another economist who wrote against price deflation was Benjamin Andrews. His writings show many of the common arguments against deflation. He argues, that deflation leads to an unfair redistribution: "Appreciation money is occasioning injustice in case of every one of these obligations" (1895, p. 302). He also mentions the problems for debtors: "[the] increase in the value of money robs debtors" (1895, p. 302). Moreover, Andrews offers the popular argument that deflation would

[405] See Unger (1964, pp. 50–60) or Nugent (1967, pp. 61–63) for information on Carey.

provide disincentive for business activity: "Falling prices (appreciating money) set up a special, positive motive for abstaining from productive industry. This is the impulsive to hoard" (1895, p. 306). Andrews wanted to have both silver and gold as money to forestall a fall in prices (1895, p. 321). He resigned as President of Brown University in Rhode Island in 1897 over that issue as the University lost its hard money supporters. He had also been a teacher at Cornell University, a university that was more open to his monetary views. Cornell University had a strong department of agriculture and is still today considered by many as the top school of agriculture-related sciences in the world. Someone who was open to the concerns of farmers was apparently welcome at Cornell University.[406] Indeed, Andrews writes about the situation of the mortgaged farmers, who have the least capital and are hurt by falling prices: "Hence the agrarian distress in every farming country and section of the gold using world." (1895, p. 309)

5.1.8 Conclusion

We have shown that from 1865 to 1896 there was a price deflation in the U.S. caused by economic growth. The price deflation did not pose any problems for fast economic growth.[407] On the contrary, price deflation was caused by economic growth mainly, and in the greenback era supported by increases in the expected quality of money and the switch to a gold standard by some countries. Furthermore, a legal tender fiat deflation prevented the use of silver that would have led to higher prices. There was a bond deflation in order to prepare for the resumption of specie payment. There was a legal tender deflation as silver was demonetized. There were punctual credit contractions, i.e., bank credit deflations. They led to temporary reductions of the money supply. Nor could the booms and busts and malinvestments in this period curb the economic growth very much, but

[406] It happens that the co-founder of the University and agriculture enthusiast Ezra Cornell entered the railroad business, getting into trouble during the Panic (and credit contraction) of 1873. The anti-deflation stand of Cornell University personell would last longer. Later in the 1930s George F. Warren and Frank A. Pearson from Cornell University would attack deflation, complaining about the injustice it allegedly does to the traditionally long-term indebted farmers (1983, p. 274, 431). Palyi named them "agricultural economists." (1972, p. 281)

In the midst of the controversy about his monetary stand in the summer of 1897, Andrews had also accepted the offer received from John Brisben Walker, editor of *Cosmopolitan Magazine* to take part in his proposed "Cosmopolitan University." This project was never realized. Walker, who was an automobile and railroad entrepreneur and owner of 1,600 acres in North Denver, was apparently more sympathetic with the monetary views of Andrews. All this is not to say that Andrews became corrupted in his monetary opinion. But it indicates that there were naturally forming alliances between interest groups gaining from a reversal in the price fall and economists that provided theories that seemed to support those interests.

[407] One of the most widespread monetary fallacies is that economic growth is only possible if accompanied by a growth of the money supply.

they did incite social discontent and unrest. This historical case also serves as an illustration that price deflation does not necessarily stop economic growth. The economic growth itself was caused by innovations, population growth, increases in the division of knowledge/labor and capital accumulation. Despite the economic growth there were interest groups who favored greenback issues, free silver coinage, and bimetallism in order to forestall a decline in prices. These people were mainly indebted business men and farmers. Also silver miners naturally favored free silver coinage adopting anti-deflationary arguments. The most unrest though stemmed from farmers who in addition to the rise in their real debt burden saw their economic and political significance fading.

In times of bank credit deflation and recession, social unrest grew stronger due to the necessary restructuring of the economy and the additional downward pressure on prices. In the surroundings of those crises and the aforementioned groups emerged political parties, newspapers and economists who made arguments and developed economic theories that justified inflation to avoid price deflation.

5.2 The German Bank Credit Deflation of the 1930s

5.2.1 Introduction

One of the sharpest price deflations in history occurred during the Great Depression. This was particularly the case in Germany at the time. Due to the severity of the price deflation there in the 1930s and due to the fact that Germany was, next to the U.S., the country hit hardest, by the Great Depression, the German case is especially interesting.[408] I will, therefore, deal with the question why there was such a big downturn in Germany. Furthermore, the German deflation is a good example for a bank credit deflation, as the main factor in the price decreases was a bank credit deflation. Thus, the analysis of this period illustrates the theoretical case of bank credit deflation.

I will also turn to the question of whether the bank credit deflation or the price deflation added to the severity of the Great Depression in Germany. It is often maintained that the bank credit deflation and Chancelor Heinrich Brüning's deflationary policies made the Great Depression more severe. Theoretical analysis, however, shows that this hypothesis is not necessarily true. The deflation might have led to harsh changes in ownership, but disturbed neither production nor the adjustment of the structure of production. Thus, I will show the reasons that made the depression so harsh. Not surprisingly after our analysis of the consequences of a price deflation, there was opposition to falling prices by special interests who called for inflation.

---

[408] See Born (1967, p. 34).

I will proceed as follows: As for a bank credit deflation to occur, there must be a bank credit inflation first, I begin with analyzing the bank credit inflation of the 1920s. Then, I will show what triggered the bank credit deflation and how the crisis grew stronger. Third, I will examine the reasons for the severity of the depression. Fourth, I will analyze which role price deflation played in the depression. Last, I will present the opposition to the deflation and the interest groups pushing for inflation.

5.2.2 *Bank Credit Inflation*

5.2.2.1 From Versailles to the Dawes Plan

The Significance of Versailles

In May 1919, the Treaty of Versailles was signed.[409] Its significance for the depression of the 1930s does not lie so much in the stipulated reparations but rather in its psychological and political implications. Germany was declared guilty of World War I. She lost 10 % of her population and 13 % of her territory. Besides other military restrictions, the German army was not to have over 100,000 soldiers. Germany had to pay monetary and physical reparations in the form of animals or ships or vehicles. The reparations were a ready scapegoat for German politicians for reckless behavior.[410] They could always say that the reparations were the cause if anything went wrong.

International Credit Structure After World War I

The problematic international credit structure can be traced back to its disastrous origins in World War I. In order to win the war, governments of belligerent countries indebted themselves, intending to pay back the loans with reparations from defeated countries. However, the war lasted longer and was more destructive than was thought in the beginning. During the war, the United States became the production machine of Europe. It shipped goods, machines, weapons, and food to Europe. Europe bought against credit. This procedure was facilitated by the expansionary monetary policies of the Federal Reserve that made it possible that European bonds could be sold in the U.S.

After the war, the structure of production had to be adapted to peace time demands. Moreover, it became obvious that due to the credit expansion and easy

---

[409] See Aldcroft (1978, pp. 36–37) and Bartsch and Eismann (2005, pp. 11–12) for the Treaty of Versailles.

[410] Borchardt (1979, p. 121), fn. 43 points out that many people regarded the reparations as the cause of the depression. Thus, the real causes were not seen.

credit of the Federal Reserve, many U.S. industries and farmers had malinvested their scarce resources. Therefore, their ventures had to be liquidated. Of course, many interests were against this process and pushed for monetary inflation to make the adjustment more "smooth."

Europe had to adopt its structure of production to peace time conditions, as well. However, when the U.S. government stopped providing loans to the Allies in March 1919, private creditors took its place. American exporters that depended completely on the European demand, started to sell on credit.[411] Again, this was made possible by the credit expansion of the Federal Reserve. The Federal Reserve discounted credits below the market interest rate, thereby giving commercial banks additional reserves, which they used to expand their credits to exporters. The exporters used the credit to sell their exports on credit to Europe.

Developments in the U.S.

As stated above, the international credit structure of the war continued. America produced and sent goods to Europe on credit hoping to be paid one day. An artificially high standard of living could continue in Europe which in the end made the payment of the loans more difficult.[412] The underlying credit structure was of course, very fragile. It collapsed in the recession of 1920–1921. Because it was using gold to pay for its increasing imports, the U.S. began to lose its gold reserves. This induced a credit contraction and higher interest rates. It was no longer profitable for exporters to sell on credit to Europe.[413] The European demand collapsed. Many projects were liquidated and the resources invested in other industries. The adaption of the structure of production finally took course.

However, the Federal Reserve embarked on a new credit expansion starting in 1922 with its first open market operation.[414] The artificially low interest rate lead to malinvestments at home. The idea was to help business men to finance investment projects. The credit expansion also made it possible for Europeans to buy American products with credit and thus sustain artificially high prices.

Another important incident of these years is the introduction of the Fordney-McCumber Tariff in the U.S. Due to the Fordney-McCumber Tariff, installed in September 1922, it became more difficult for Europeans to export to the U.S. and get dollars to pay their imports and repay their debts. The solution was the U.S. credit expansion to finance the imports and debt payment via more credits. As Anderson explains:

[411] See Anderson (1979, pp. 61–69).

[412] See Rallo (2006, p. 11).

[413] See Rallo (2006, p. 12).

[414] See Anderson (1979, pp. 144–150) for the extent of U.S. credit expansion 1922–1928.

> Our tariffs would not allow the Europeans to earn dollars here in adequate amounts to buy our farm products and to meet service on the past debts, so we proceeded to lend them the dollars they needed for theses purposes! But we did not consider how they would ever repay the sums we were lending them if they could not sell goods here. (1979, p. 128)

German Hyperinflation

After World War I, while gold payments were still suspended, the German government embarked on high expenditures for health care, education, etc.[415] The 8-h working day was enacted and the labor unions were given privileges. At the same time demobilization expenses, reparations, and deficits of nationalized industries put a heavy pressure on the treasury. Tax revenues continued to decline. Government expenses were financed through the German central bank, the Reichsbank, by literally printing bank notes for the government. The result was the famous German hyperinflation that reached its height in 1923. In 1923, the French and Belgium occupation of the German industrial zone Ruhr in response to delays of reparation payments put even more pressure on the treasury. Germany stood before a total collapse and asked for a renegotiation of the reparation question.

5.2.2.2 The Dawes Plan

At this point the Dawes commission searched for ways to stabilize the Mark and stabilize Germany's budget. It came up with the Dawes Plan that sought to put reparations at a reasonable and payable level.[416] Naturally, the Allies were very interested for the plan to work. In particular, Great Britain and France were interested that Germany was able to pay the reparations. France had to stabilize its own budget. If Germany would pay the reparation, France would also be able to pay its war debt to Great Britain, and Great Britain its war debts to the U.S.

There are five basic points in the Dawes Plan. First, the Reichsmark was stabilized definitely at its old prewar parity (RM 4.20 = $1). This was possible as France reduced its reparation claims, which had threatened Germany's monetary stability.

Second, the Reichsbank was made independent from the government in order to prevent a financing of government deficit by the central bank. The Reichsbank was given a control council with Allied representatives. All circulating bank notes had to be covered 40 % with gold or foreign exchanges that were redeemable in gold.[417] The possibility of central bank credits to the government were strictly limited.

---

[415] For accounts on the German hyperinflation see Bresciani-Turroni (2007) or Ferguson (2010).

[416] Concerning the Dawes Plan, see Anderson (1979, pp. 115–121); Stucken (1953, pp. 61–76) and Palyi (1972, pp. 160–169). See in general on German post-war monetary history Ahamed (2009).

[417] The U.S. wanted the Mark 100 % backed by gold but the British, French and Italian did not want Germany to have a 100 % gold standard while their own redemption was still suspended. Furthermore, Great Britain wanted a sterling-based gold exchange standard. See Rallo (2006, p. 14).

Third, the reparations question was settled once again. Reparations had to be paid in cash, increasing from $60 million to about $250 million. The Dawes Plan never settled when these reparations would end. There was also a "welfare clause" in the Dawes Plan. If Germany's capacity to pay would increase, the reparations would also increase.

Fourth, a transfer agent was installed. He supervised the transfer and could invoke the so-called "transfer clause." The transfer clause stated that transfers would be suspended, if the reparation transfer would endanger the German mark.

Fifth, a substantial loan of $110 million was raised to help the payment of reparations—the Dawes Loan. The bonds were nominated in foreign currencies and sold abroad, largely in the U.S. Moreover, a great quantity of small short term loans were attracted by the high interest rates.[418] This was what was to happen during the next 5 years: foreign loans would be used to finance the German reparations payments.

The Dawes Plan measure was thought to bring back confidence in Germany's capability to repay the reparations and stabilize its currency. In this way it should bring back foreign capital into Germany. Germany was to be integrated in Western society again. The acceptance of the plan also terminated the occupation of the Ruhr.

5.2.2.3 From the Dawes to the Young Plan

From the Great Inflation to the German Black Friday

After the Great Inflation, Germany was left with manufacturers that were overextended and their malinvestments had to be liquidated. The inflow of new credit from abroad helped to maintain these malinvestments for a while. As long as credits were renewed the adaption of the structure of production could be stopped or at least slowed down. Of course, the Reichsbank did not try to stop this capital inflow, as important pressure groups, like the Federal Association of German Industry, the trade unions, and the German Agrarian Association were dependent upon it or in favor of it.[419]

After the Dawes-Boom of 1924/1925 there was a short recession in Germany in 1926. Several marginal enterprises went bankrupt, and their resources were freed for more profitable investment projects. After the recession, world economy thrived from 1927 to 1929. However, Germany stayed behind the world boom due to higher union wages.[420]

In Germany, as in the U.S., there was also a stock market boom that had been financed by credit expansion. On "Black Friday" of May 13th 1927, though, the

[418] See Rallo (2006, p. 28).

[419] See Palyi (1972, p. 177).

[420] See Schumpeter (1929, p. 849).

stock market collapsed. The main reason was that the Reichsbank had imposed a 25 % margin requirement on old and new security loans. Another possible reason was, as Ritschl indicates, that the unsustainable credit expansion worried investors and led to the selling of securities (2002, p. 13). The impetus for the Great Depression would then have originated in Germany. Due to the stock market collapse, the German industry started to finance itself abroad.[421]

German Balance of Payment

From the time of the Dawes Plan in 1924 until 1929, the German balance of payment was maintained by credits from the West, and especially from the United States. Germany's net capital imports estimated by the German official *Untersuchung des Bankwesens* of $4,420 million were enough to pay the less than $2,000 million reparations, the German trade deficit plus an increase in the Reichsbank's gold reserve by $550 million.[422]

As was its aim, the Dawes Plan had restored confidence in Germany's future and led to a capital inflow from overseas to Europe. Indeed, Germany was constantly importing more capital than she paid out in reparations. As a consequence of the higher debts, the interest payments on foreign loans continually increased, as can be seen in Table 5.1.

The Role of the Federal Reserve Credit Expansion for Germany

The Federal Reserve assumed the role of the leading central bank holding two-fifths of the world's gold reserve.[423] It changed its policies in the 1920s. As Benjamin Anderson remarks:

> The Federal Reserve System was created to finance a crisis and to finance seasonal needs for pocket cash. It was not created for the purpose of financing a boom, least of all financing a stock market boom. But from early 1924 down to the spring of 1928 it was used to finance a boom and used to finance a stock market boom. (1979, pp. 146–147)

For the credit expansion of the Federal Reserve see Table 5.2.

Besides the speculation and malinvestments at home, the Federal Reserve monetary expansion also financed malinvestment abroad, including in Germany. German imports, the welfare state, and reparations were paid by foreign loans.[424]

---

[421] See Stucken (1953, p. 75) and Palyi 1972, p. 174.

[422] See Palyi (1972, p. 162).

[423] See Palyi (1972, pp. 46–47).

[424] It does not matter whether they were government loans or commercial bank loans. Also the government loans were financed in the end via the expansionary banking system.

Table 5.1 Germany's balance of payments, 1924–1932

Year	Exports	Imports	Balance	Reparations	Interest and dividends	Other services	Total current balance	Net capital flow, in (+) or out (−)	Flow of gold and for. exch. into (−) or out of (+) central bank reserves
1924	7,816	9,664	−1,848	−281	+159	+269	−1,701	+2,913	−1,212
1925	9,572	11,934	−2,362	−1,057	−6	+421	−3,004	+3,240	−236
1926	10,700	9,883	+817	−1,191	−173	+449	−98	+679	−581
1927	11,126	14,016	−2,890	−1,584	−345	+566	−4,253	+4,777	−524
1928	12,644	13,868	−1,224	−1,999	−563	+676	−3,110	+3,172	−62
1929	13,655	13,624	+31	−2,501	−800	+871	−2,399	+2,307	+91
1930	12,192	10,548	+1,664	−1,694	−1,000	+521	−529	+494	+35
1931	9,637	6,779	+2,858	−988	−1,200	+445	+1,115	−2,722	+1,607
1932	5,778	4,724	+1,054	−160	−900	+258	+252	−489	+237

In millions of Reichsmarks. Source: League of Nations, *International Currency Experience* (Princeton, 1944, p. 103) as quoted in Palyi (1972, p. 165)

Table 5.2 Money supply in the U.S., 1921–1929

Date	Total deposits adjusted and currency outside banks (in billions of dollars)
1921 June 30	37.79
1922 June 30	39.00
1923 June 30	42.75
1923 December 31	43.50
1924 June 30	44.51
1924 December 31	47.08
1925 June 30	48.32
1925 December 31	50.30
1926 June 30	50.57
1926 December 31	51.12
1927 June 30	52.23
1927 December 31	54.08
1928 June 30	54.68
1928 December 31	55.64
1929 June 30	55.17

Source: Rothbard (2000, p. 92).

As Anderson writes:

This immense expansion of bank credit, added to the ordinary sources of capital, created the illusion of unlimited capital and made it easy for our markets to absorb gigantic quantities of foreign securities as well as a greatly increased volume of American security issues. The combination of the Dawes Plan, restoring confidence in the *quality* of European credit, and the cheap money policy of the Federal Reserve banks creating a vast *quantity* of available funds, enabled us to purchase in 1924 approximately $1 billion of foreign securities (refunding excluded). [Italics in original] (1979, p. 128).

The malinvestment by German states and municipalities worried Reichsbank President Hjalmar Schacht, who "personally appeared in New York to urge the American banking community to make no further state and municipal loans to Germany. Schacht made a tremendous effort then, and in the years that followed, to hold down Germany's borrowings from foreign countries" (Anderson 1979, p. 161).[425] The challenge was the overly-abundant liquidity and artificially low interest rates made possible by the Federal Reserve's credit expansion:

But under the impact of the gigantic flood of bank money generated by the policy of the Federal Reserve System in 1924, money was superabundant in New York and the illusion of unlimited capital was growing. The market for high-yield bonds in the United States seemed insatiable, and the American investment bankers were trying to supply the market. In late 1925 the agents of fourteen different American investment banking houses were in Germany soliciting loans from German states and municipalities. (Anderson 1979, p. 161)

[425] See also Stucken (1953, p. 70).

Despite Schacht's efforts, German state and municipalities increased their public investments tremendously from 458 million RM in 1924 to 1,426 million RM in 1928.[426] It was an irresistible temptation for German politicians to finance the welfare state with these loans. For foreign investors it seemed to be very attractive, too, to invest in Germany. Due to the U.S. credit expansion long-term interest rates were lower in the U.S. than the short-term interest rates in Germany. Thus, it was attractive to take on long-term credits in the U.S. and invest short term in Germany.[427]

It should be pointed out that German industrial companies also financed themselves via Wall Street loans. The U.S. credit expansion spilled overseas and distorted the German structure of production or helped existing distortions to survive. For example, in 1924 the Stinnes Loan, a $20 million bond was issued in the U.S. It saved the overextended Stinnes industrial conglomerate that was built during the German hyperinflation by Hugo Stinnes.[428] American credit could prevent the necessary liquidation and reorganization.

In the course of this process, the American financial system became ever more dependent upon the solvency of Germany. The U.S. itself had an expanded credit structure, that Germany's difficulties in remaining solvent would only endanger. In fact, these difficulties with Germany's solvency would place the American banking system into severe difficulties. Thus, the Federal Reserve continued pumping more credits into Germany. The endless inflow of gold and foreign exchanges financed industrial and public projects, of which many were malinvestments and unsustainable in the long run.

The Credit Expansion in Germany

Not only did German industrial companies and municipalities borrow short-term loans from abroad, but German banks did also. Thus, parallel to the U.S. credit expansion there was another problem, namely the credit expansion by German banks who themselves expanded on basis of the gold and gold exchanges that they had borrowed short-term. In other words, they were pyramiding credits on top of those loans: Credit expansion on a short-term borrowed gold base. As a consequence of their credit expansion they became highly illiquid. The cash-to-deposits ratio fell in 1930 to 1.7 % although it had been 7.4 % in 1913.[429] German companies received large volumes of credits, maintaining insufficient equity.

Chart 5.7 shows the debts of the Reichsbank and German banks to foreigners in million RM.[430]

In only 4 years, from 1925 to 1929 liabilities increased more than sevenfold, a remarkable increase.

---

[426] See Keiser and Benning (1931, p. 154).

[427] See Born (1967, p. 19).

[428] See Palyi (1972, pp. 206–207).

[429] See Palyi (1972, p. 229).

[430] Source: Deutsche Bundesbank (1976, p. 4).

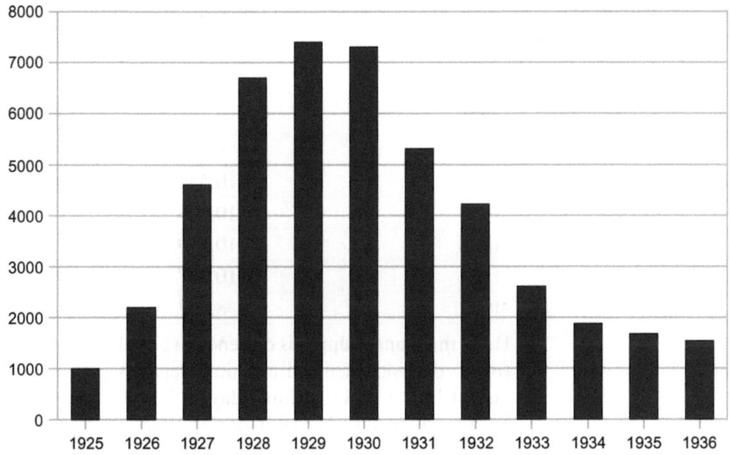

Chart 5.7 Liabilities of German banks to foreigners

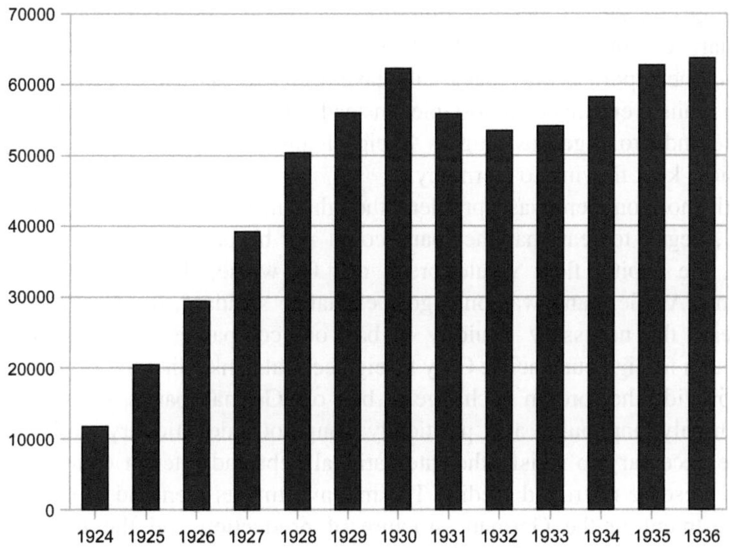

Chart 5.8 Loans by German credit institutions, 1924–1936

The credit expansion of German banks was spectacular as can be seen in Chart 5.8 which shows loans by credit institutions in million RM.[431]

One can also see a great increase in the German money supply from 1924 to 1928. It increased between 7.4 and 23.6 % annually as can be seen in Table 5.3.

[431] Source: Deutsche Bundesbank (1976, p. 4).

Table 5.3 German money supply, 1924–1928

Year	German money supply (millions)
1924	5,715
1925	7,061
1926	8,403
1927	9,027
1928	10,544
1929	10,893
1930	10,539
1931	10,007
1932	8,652

Here, the money supply is currency in circulation plus short-term (bank) deposits (demand and time deposits payable by the five largest Berlin banks within 7 days). Source: League of Nations, *Statistical Yearbooks*, 1931–1932, 1935–1936 (Geneva, 1932, 1936); League of Nations, *Commercial Banks*, 1925–1933 (Geneva, 1934) as quoted in Palyi (1972, p. 176).

The influx of foreign capital and credit expansion helped to keep the German prices high. Backed by the high liquidity and imposed by labor unions, wages, in particular, rose quite substantially. This, in turn, dampened exports and spurred imports. The export surplus that would have been necessary to effectively pay back foreign loans were made impossible. Instead, the import surplus continued to be financed and prolonged as long as foreign loans, the basis for an internal credit expansion, kept flowing to Germany.

On the horizon there was a problem, though. Once the U.S. and foreign banks, in general, began to fear that the loans could not be paid and therefore, contract credits, the capital flow would break off. Or worse, the credits would leave Germany. As Germany was on a gold exchange standard, the Reichsbank could not create the necessary liquidity to bail out companies and state authorities indebted in foreign currencies. Only foreign central banks, like the Federal Reserve could provide the foreign exchange to bail out German banks and corporations. Thus, highly unpopular and politically dangerous deflationary policies would become necessary to satisfy the international debt and interest charges once the Federal Reserve restricted credits. The malinvestments then had to be liquidated. Malinvestment in the German structure of production and the municipalities' malinvestments could not be sustained.

The Situation of Germany's Foreign Debts in 1929

Let us return to the issue of the war debt. At the end of the war, France and Great Britain were indebted to the United States. Germany had to pay reparations to France and Great Britain as stipulated in the peace treaties. In order to pay the reparations Germany would have to export more than it imported or to pay out of the citizens' savings, i.e. to lower its standard of living. The German government did not want reduce its citizens to this lowered standard of living. Actually, imports were higher than exports. The government and local authorities indebted themselves also in the U.S. to pay reparations and to pay for the import surplus. The international credit flow was then as follows: Germany took on loans in the U.S., which was made possible by the credit expansion of the Federal Reserve, to pay reparations to France and Great Britain. With these funds, France and Great Britain paid their debts to the U.S. The U.S. was thereby indirectly financing its own credit payment. This can not go on forever, of course. At some point Germany had to pay down its loans to the U.S. Yet, Germany's debts kept increasing and Germany became the largest debtor in the world. In 1931, her net liabilities to foreigners were $4.1 billion.[432]

The basic problem concerning the debts was that the loans were to a great extent, not invested in productive facilities that could have produced the goods and increased the profits necessary to pay back the debts. In contrast, funds were used for other purposes. They were used to pay for public deficits, be it municipal, state or federal. They were used to enlarge the welfare state and boost public expenditures. They built sport arenas, parks or other recreational infrastructures, etc. The use of the loans to pay reparations was not a productive investment either. Funds also maintained overextended and unprofitable business projects and helped pay for higher wages and social benefits. Instead of reducing consumption and increase savings to pay for investments, foreign credits were used.[433] See Table 5.4 for the rise in German investment from 1924 to 1928.

As the foreign credits were mainly made possible by the credit expansion of the Federal Reserve System, and were, therefore, not backed by real savings, we are faced with an example of an artificial boom, as described by the Austrian business cycle theory. The German structure of production was heavily distorted and the necessary liquidation was inhibited by further American credits. Relative to the consumer goods industry, the capital goods industry boomed.[434] At the same time, capital was consumed in Germany, as German industry was not competitive particularly due to exorbitant wages. The productive capacity of Germany was reduced, while at the same time its debts were increasing. It became ever more difficult to pay back the loans.

The first problems occurred, when U.S. short-term credits were withdrawn from Germany to be re-invested in the booming U.S. stock exchange, which had a higher yield.[435] Then problems grew when in 1929 the Federal Reserve tightened credit and U.S. interest rates rose.[436] This made investment in the U.S. more attractive. After the U.S. stock market collapsed even more credit was withdrawn, in order to secure liquidity in the U.S. American capital exports dried out.

---

[432] See Palyi (1972, p. 200).

[433] See Stucken (1953, p. 76).

[434] See Aldcroft (1978, p. 240).

[435] See Nussbaum (1978, pp. 270–271).

[436] See Anderson (1979, p. 205).

Table 5.4 German investment, 1924–1928

Year	Investments in million RM
1924	2,701
1925	4,552
1926	5,156
1927	7,168
1928	7,273

Source: Keiser and Benning (1931, *p. 17).*

5.2.2.4 The Young Plan

In 1928 and near the end of the five-year term of the Dawes Plan, it became apparent that the plan's reparation schedule, which was increasing, would place the German government into severe difficulties. The "limitless" reparation stirred up resistance in the German population. As stated above, the easy credit influx from the U.S. began to trickle. Requesting to invoke the transfer clause, the German government pushed for a renegotiation of the reparation issue, which was settled in the Young Plan in the summer of 1929.[437] The amount to be paid for 1930/1931 was 1.6 billion Gold Marks, a sum that was to be raised until 1965/1966 to 2.3 billion with reparations ending in 1988. The welfare clause was abolished, disappointing France. Germany was disappointed, as well, as the "unconditional" parts of reparations and the Dawes and Young loans were exempted from the transfer clause.[438] The new, limited transfer clause lowered the confidence of German creditors. When Reichsbank president Schacht seemed to endanger the success of the Young Plan conference because of his reluctance to sign the agreement for the plan, a run on the mark began to develop, a run which ended when he finally decided to signed it. The Young Loan brought the Reichsbank about $300 million.[439] Confidence was regained for the last time and international creditors calmed down.

5.2.3 *Bank Credit Deflation*

5.2.3.1 The Situation in 1930

At the beginning of the crisis, Germany was already in a very problematic situation. The stock exchange had been falling since April 1927, the economy was shrinking slightly in 1929[440] and unemployment was continuously high. The most important problem, though, was the unsustainable credit structure of the German economy. The German government did not want its people to make sacrifices to pay

[437] See Bartsch and Eismann (2005, p. 14).

[438] See Palyi (1972, p. 166).

[439] See Palyi (1972, p. 167).

[440] See Deutsche Bundesbank (1976, p. 7).

reparations. Instead of reducing its spending, it erected a welfare state to buy votes. Imports were higher than exports. Short-term credits were used to finance imports, government expenditures, reparations, and public companies that practically burned money. Moreover, on basis of this foreign capital, banks had expanded credits to finance long-term investment projects. In this case, once the foreign capital would leave, the whole credit structure would break down.

In 1930, it became more and more apparent that German companies had to go through a liquidation process. By 1929, inventories were already at a huge surplus in relation to customary sales-inventory ratios and continued to rise. Prices started to fall. Prices would have fallen sooner, but the accumulation of excess inventories had been made possible by credit practices. In other words, banks, via "current account" loans financed excess inventories.[441]

The farming sector was in an especially difficult condition. During the 1920s there had been a rapid expansion of its production capacities. Also financed by credit expansion, a commodity speculation kept prices high. The increase in commodity production became visible in 1928 when prices started to fall. By mid-1929 the prices index of nine world commodities (1923–1925 = 100) had fallen below 80. Wheat prices fell 12.9 % from 1929 to 1930.[442] Farmers reacted to the falling prices and dwindling demand with an increase of production in order to meet mortgage payments, thus putting more downward pressure on prices. The Junkers, Prussian aristocracy who owned land, had amassed an enormous amount of farm-related debt. *Osthilfe*, subsidies made available to the Junkers, prevented an adjustment of production to falling prices.[443]

The export sector was not doing any better. Exporters were negatively affected by the beginning depression in the U.S. in the wake of the 1929 stock market crash. This was especially the case for exporters of capital goods who had profited most from the credit financed American boom.[444]

Due to the consequences of the credit expansion, the situation of the banking system became alarming. The banking system was terribly illiquid. About 50 % of the commercial bank deposits belonged to foreigners who could withdraw them immediately. Commercial banks deposits rose from RM 7.6 billion in 1913 to RM 11.4 billion in 1929. Savings banks deposits rose from RM 1.6 billion in 1925 to 10.4 billion in 1930. Bank assets were invested long-term.[445] Thus, Melchior Palyi writes: "It would be difficult to find a situation of such illiquidity of a whole financial system as that of Germany on July 13, 1931" (Palyi 1972, p. 261). The position of the banks was further weakened by the fact that during the hyperinflation these banks had lost much of their equity. The relation between equity and

[441] See Palyi (1972, p. 219).

[442] See Palyi (1972, p. 223).

[443] See Palyi (1972, pp. 220–228).

[444] See Stucken (1953, p. 79).

[445] See Palyi (1972, p. 254, 259).

outside capital, mainly foreign and short-term, was 1:15.5 for the big Berlin banks.[446]

On the political front, matters did not look much better. The reparations were a heavy burden on the treasury and politically problematic. Nationalists bitterly opposed reparations and the hated Versailles Treaty. The National Socialist German Workers Party (NSDAP) promised radical domestic and foreign policies, thus frightening away foreign investors. Successful in the elections for the Reichstag on September 14th, the NSDAP increased its number of seats from 12 to 110. Chancellor Heinrich Brüning's government was in danger. The NSDAP success in the September election led to a capital flight, but the Reichsbank, after raising its discount rate could still defend the gold parity.[447]

Despite all these problems, it seemed that the crisis could be over soon. After some liquidations, industrial production began to rise again from January to April 1931.[448] But then the Credit-Anstalt in Austria collapsed.

5.2.3.2 The Collapse of the Credit-Anstalt

In May 1931, the largest commercial Austrian bank, the Credit-Anstalt became insolvent, after having expanded credits substantially and absorbing two illiquid competitors. It had given credits to companies who had malinvested the capital and could not pay back their loans. Moreover, the Credit-Anstalt had a huge security portfolio which had suffered severe losses. As the assets of the bank began to shrink and the losses were published, a run on Austrian banks began.[449]

A complete failure of the Credit-Anstalt would have had severe consequences for the Austrian industry as 70 % of Austria's major industrial enterprises depended upon it. Thus, the bank was bailed out by Baron Alphonse von Rothschild, the Austrian government, and the Austrian National Bank.[450] The repercussions of the collapse of the Credit-Anstalt and other Austrian banks were felt in Germany, triggering increased suspicion by foreign investors of Germany's capacity to pay back her loans. German banks had a similar capital structure to that of Austrian

[446] See Born (1967, p. 14, 20).

[447] See Stucken (1953, p. 82).

[448] See Borchardt (1979, p. 91).

[449] See Born (1967, p. 65); It is often maintained, that the Credit-Anstalt became insolvent due to another problem. In the spring of 1931 the plan of a German-Austrian customs union aroused the suspicion of the French that Germany tried to circumvent the prohibition of an "Anschluss" by the Versailles Treaty. The French government threatened consequences were the plan to be put through. Then, it is often stated, French banks withdrew short-term capital from Germany and Austria, with other foreign banks following suit. Karl E. Born, however, shows that until April 1931, Austria enjoyed an influx of foreign exchanges. Thus, the collapse of the Credit-Anstalt was not politically caused but rather caused by the economic losses the bank suffered. Charles Kindleberger shares Born's assessment (1987, p. 146).

[450] See Palyi (1972, p. 252).

banks, with a large portion of outside capital, losses in their security portfolio, and with industrial loans.[451]

Moreover, political incidents lowered foreign confidence in the stability of Germany and its capacity or willingness to pay back debts. In June the Brüning government was in crisis and nearly fell. Brüning also declared that he wanted to renegotiate the reparation question as the economic condition of Germany was so weak.[452] As a consequence, the withdrawal of short-term foreign credit accelerated. Foreign depositors converted their mark balances and domestic depositors started hoarding marks and foreign currencies (i.e., cash building ensued).

Furthermore, some large German companies either went bankrupt or were on the verge of it.[453] Profits plummeted and losses surged. In 1931, according to the German *Institut für Konjunkturforschung*, some 2,000 industrial concerns suffered a net loss of 5 billion Reichsmarks.[454] On June 25, the Danatbank (Darmstädter und Nationalbank), Berlin's second largest bank became insolvent. Financed by short-term American credits, the bank had given credits to finance long-term investment projects. It suffered a loss of 250 million marks, four times its own capital due to the collapse of the Nordwolle and Ultramare concern, a cotton producing conglomerate that suffered losses due to over-expansion and speculations. The Commerzbank reported its insolvency shortly thereafter. All this intensified the run on German banks and the Reichsbank lost much of its gold reserve. Banks restricted credits in order to secure liquidity. An internal run threatened the whole banking system.[455] A cash building deflation ensued as people tried to secure and enlarge their cash holdings and prices continued to fall.[456] On July 13th banks had to close and the German government suspended the redemption promise of Reichsmark into gold and gold currencies.[457] Two bank holidays were declared and in the following weeks only parts of deposits could be withdrawn.[458] Thus, there was a confiscatory deflation for some time.

5.2.3.3 A Bank Credit Deflation on Its Way

Besides the cash building and confiscatory deflation, this crisis clearly illustrates the case of a bank credit deflation. After a credit expansion, an event usually occurs, shaking confidence in the banks. This time several factors came together: (1) the

[451] See Born (1967, p. 65).

[452] See Born (1967, p. 71).

[453] See Born (1967, p. 67). See Nussbaum (1978, pp. 324–325) for the corporations and companies that went bankrupt.

[454] See League of Nations (1935, p. 41). In 1932, the net loss would fall to 3 billion Reichsmarks.

[455] See Stucken (1953, p. 85).

[456] Concerning "hoarding," see Born (1967, p. 108, 114–115).

[457] See Borchardt (1979, p. 92).

[458] See Nussbaum (1978, p. 318) and Born (1967, p. 108).

Chart 5.9 Price index of German net social product, 1925–1936

internal political crisis; (2) the external political crisis with France about reparations and the Anschluss-question; and most importantly (3) the bankruptcies or financial difficulties of German companies that had malinvested capital; as well as (4) the resulting losses in the banks' assets. Then a cumulative process ensued. As foreign capital and deposits were withdrawn, banks tried to restrict credit. Restriction of credits and falling prices brought more companies into difficulties. It caused bankruptcies and unemployment in a regulated labor market.[459] Bank runs lead to the closure of banks and more foreign capital was withdrawn. The whole banking system collapsed. The money supply shrank as can be seen in Table 5.3. Credits were contracted as Chart 5.8 shows. Also prices fell after the boom years, as is indicated by Chart 5.9.[460]

We see that there was substantial price deflation from 1929 to 1933. The same is indicated by the whole sale price and consumers price indexes, which are shown in Charts 5.10 and 5.11.[461]

Wholesale prices fall more than consumer prices. From 1929 to 1933 consumers prices fall 23 % and wholesale prices fall 32 %. The reason is the excessive speculation on inventories and commodities in the 1920s. This also conforms completely with the Austrian business cycle theory. In a recession, consumer prices rise relatively to prices in higher stages of production.

[459] See Anderson (1979, p. 241) and Stucken (1953, p. 83).

[460] 1936 = 100. Source: Deutsche Bundesbank (1976, p. 7).

[461] Chart 10: 1913 = 100 and Chart 11: 1913/14 = 100. Source: Deutsche Bundesbank (1976, p. 7).

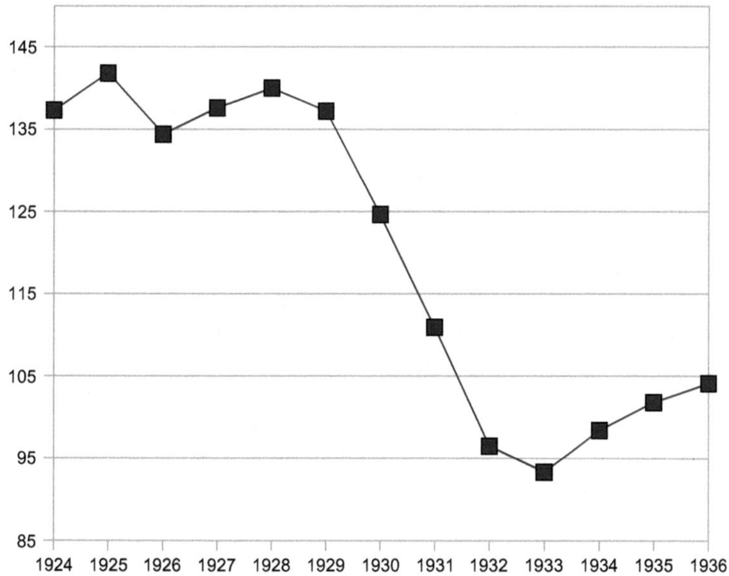

Chart 5.10 German wholesale prices, 1924–1936

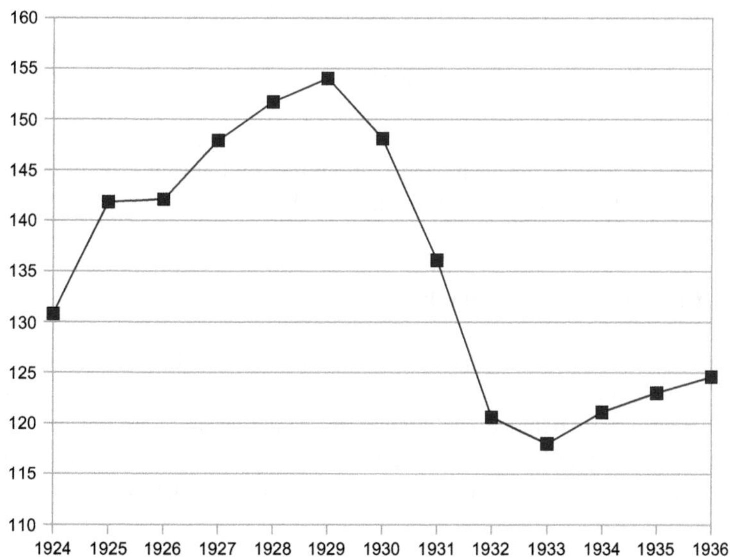

Chart 5.11 German consumer prices, 1924–1936

5.2.3.4 Government Bail-Out

When the financial and banking system threatened to break down, the Brüning Government intervened and bailed out the banking system.[462] Defaulting banks were recapitalized and merged. There were guarantees and subsidies. The Reichsbank was given more freedom to expand the money supply by the possibility of discounting a wider range of bills of exchange.[463] As stated above, the Reichsbank stopped redemption of marks into gold. A foreign exchange control was introduced. Officially, the old parity was maintained. The foreign exchange control was basically a substitute for a classical moratorium. German residents could not buy and spend freely on foreign goods or exchanges anymore, but had to offer foreign exchanges at the official rate to the Reichsbank. Moreover, they needed an authorization to buy foreign exchange.[464] Shortly after the German break down, the Bank of England went off the gold standard following attacks on its reserves. The gold exchange standard had broken down and malinvestments continued to be liquidated.

On June 20th 1931, President Herbert Hoover announced a 1-year moratorium on all intergovernmental debts other than the service of the Dawes and Young Loans. However, France protested and only after week-long negotiations, in which France insisted on the payment of the unconditional portion of the Young Plan, was it put through. The crisis deepened. Germany's incapacity to pay back the governmental debts, further increased private creditors' suspicions of her capability to pay back private loans. Short-term capital continued to leave Germany. It only stopped when a standstill agreement for private short-term foreign credits became possible. Negotiated in August 1931, the standstill agreement was for the duration of 6 months, requiring only interests and a quota to be paid. This agreement was renewed several times.[465] During the Conference of Lausanne in July 1932, the reparations were finally postponed indeterminedly.

5.2.3.5 Brüning's Deflationary Policies

On March 30th 1930, Brüning had become German chancellor. Chancelor Brüning pursued very unpopular deflationary policies in 1930 and the first 7 months of 1931.[466] He tried to balance the budget by reducing government expenditures (except on military) and increasing taxes on wages, income, and sales, as well as on sugar, beer, and tobacco. As the free market prices began to fall, he lowered

---

[462] See for instance, Patch for the bail out of the Danatbank (1998, pp. 174–175); or Nussbaum for the bail out of the Dresdner Bank (1978, p. 318).

[463] See Patch (1998, p. 176).

[464] See Palyi (1972, pp. 254–256).

[465] See Born (1967, pp. 141–149). See on the standstill agreement also Lüke (1958, pp. 328–333).

[466] See Palyi (1972, p. 168).

salaries of government employees.[467] He reduced pensions of war invalids and government employees. Unemployment benefits were also cut.

By emergency decree, Brüning also empowered state governments to do anything necessary to balance state and municipal budgets. As a result, in the fall of 1931, local governments were forced to reduce spendings. Public theaters, libraries, and museums were closed, construction projects stopped, and some public health programs terminated.[468] Interest rates on existing long-term credit contracts were also reduced.

Despite all these measures, the relative size of government in the economy was not reduced, because the expenditures in the private economy were shrinking faster than government expenditures.[469] Brüning also tried to lower costs of companies. Through government wage arbitration (Schlichtung), wages were lowered, and in an emergency measure all wages were lowered. Wages were cut by government decree in December 1931 to the height of January 1927, i.e. 10–15 %.[470] As Gustav Stolper comments on the cutting of prices by government decree: "The aim of the deflationary polices was, to lower the political price to the level, that they would have attained in a flexible price system automatically".[471]

Through his deflationary policies, Brüning tried to maintain Germany's reputation as an "honest debtor" (Palyi 1972, p. 168). He knew that a loss of this reputation would have caused an immediate run on the mark and the flight of foreign capital. Germany would have been condemned to autarky. Brüning was partly successful, as imports reduced and exports increased in a shrinking world market as can be seen in Table 5.1. Germany finally had a trade surplus and started paying back its debts with exports. In 1930, 1931, and 1932 there were trade balances surpluses of 1.644, 2.858, and 1.054 billion Reichsmark. The net capital influx was reduced to 494 million Reichsmark in 1930, and in 1931 and 1932 there was respectively 2.772 billion RM and 0.489 billion RM net capital outflow.

5.2.4 The Severity of the Depression and Its Causes

5.2.4.1 Severity of the Depression

The Great Depression is called "Great" because it was so harsh. In Germany, it was harsher than in most other countries. Germany's portion in world production fell

---

[467] See Borchardt (1979, p. 99).

[468] See Patch (1998, p. 182).

[469] See Nussbaum (1978, p. 295).

[470] See Stucken (1953, pp. 90–91) and Nussbaum (1978, p. 305).

[471] (Stolper 1966, p. 136). The original text is as follows: "Ziel der Deflationspolitik war es, die politischen Preise auf den Stand herabzudrücken, den sie in einem anpassungsfähigen System von selbst eingenommen hätten".

Chart 5.12 German gross social product, 1925–1936

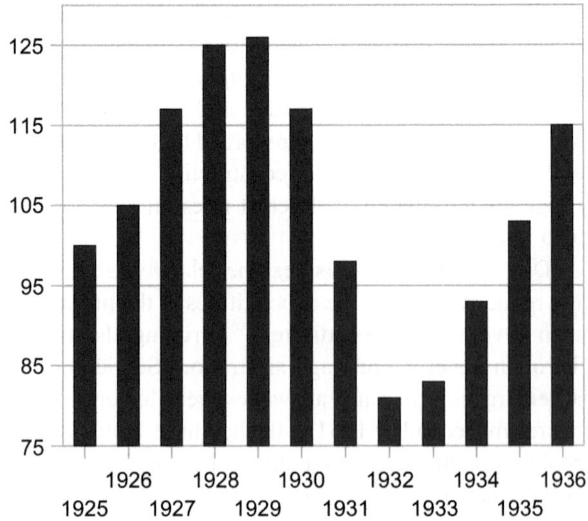

from 11.6 % in 1928 to 8.9 % in mid 1932.[472] Gross social product[473] fell 35.7 % from 1929 to 1932. In the liquidation process, many unprofitable investment projects were eliminated, thereby releasing resources for profitable projects. From 1932 to 1933, there was already a small increase in the gross social product, and the recovery occurred more quickly in the following year as shown by Chart 5.12.[474] Germany was recovering relatively fast and strong from the harsh bust.[475]

Industrial production figures describe even more strongly the course of the depression. From 1929 on there is a sharp decline a 41.5 % decline until 1932 when the recovery starts as Chart 5.13 shows.[476]

There are several reasons why the depression was more severe than others, most significantly, the enormous credit expansion initiated in the U.S. and expanded further by German banks building credits on top of it. I have outlined this process in detail above. However, there are additional reasons for why this depression was so particularly harsh. These reasons I will discuss in the following section.

---

472 See Wagenführ (1933, p. 42). Born states that the Great Depression was harshest in Germany and the U.S. (1967, p. 34).

473 Gross social product is an insufficient measure of economic activity. It would be better to have a gross measure of production including all stages of production. Nevertheless, the gross social product can indicate the trend of a depression.

474 1925 = 100. Source: Statistisches Bundesamt (1972, p. 260).

475 See Hülsmann (2013, p. 104).

476 1928 = 100. Source: Deutsche Bundesbank (1976, p. 7).

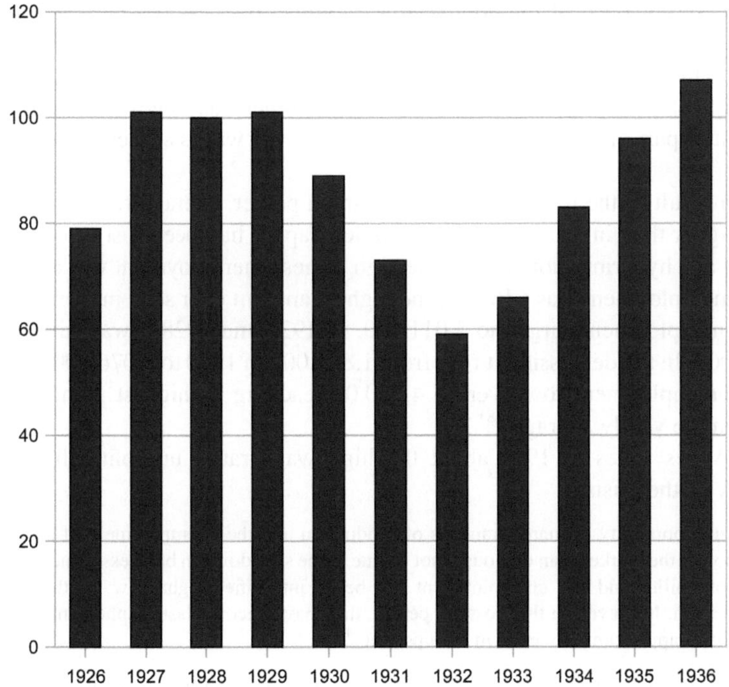

Chart 5.13 German industrial production, 1926–1936

5.2.4.2 Reasons for the Severity

Restrictions of the Labor Market

After the Revolution of 1918, German labor unions used the chaotic circumstances to push for privileges. In order to forestall a revolution, entrepreneurs gave in to old labor union demands, such as the 8-h day and wage determination by mutually acknowledging collective bargaining parties. After the stabilization of 1923, entrepreneurs unsuccessfully tried to correct these developments and dampen the wage increases.

When collective bargaining parties, i.e. labor unions and employers associations, did not reach an agreement, the government was to arbitrate the conflict and settle standard wages. As politicians did not want to lose workers' votes, they settled for ever higher wages. Entrepreneurs called this procedure of government-dictated higher wages "Lohndiktat."[477] These wage rates, which were too high, reduced savings and investment on part of entrepreneurs. Many companies could no longer remain competitive.

[477] See Borchardt (1979, p. 107).

One consequence of the compromised competitiveness of German companies due to high wages was the attempts by entrepreneurs to substitute workers with capital. This further increased the demand for credits.[478] Another consequence was, that some product prices did not fall as much as others, as wages (and taxes) were a substantial part of the costs.[479] Thus, the rigidity of wages spilled over onto other prices.

As a result of the new legislation and union power, average real wages in 1924 were higher than in 1914 even though much capital had been lost or consumed in the war and hyperinflation. Due to the high wages, unemployment was also high. In 1925 unemployment was 646,000, the highest amount ever seen in Germany.[480] In 1926 unemployment surged to 2,011,000. In 1927 and 1928 it was still high with 1,353,000. In the depression it rose from 1,892,000 in 1930 to 3,076,000 in 1931. In 1932, unemployment rose even to 4,520,00 reaching its highest point in 1933 at 5,575 in the yearly average.[481]

As Mises states in 1931 about the high wage rates, unprofitability, and the severity of the crisis:

> The unprofitability of many branches of production and the unemployment of a sizeable portion of the workers can obviously not be due to the slowdown in business alone. Both the unprofitability and the unemployment are being intensified right now by the general depression. However, in this postwar period, they have become lasting phenomena which do not disappear entirely even in the upswing.[482]

One reason for the severity of the depression was, thus, the inflexibility of the labor market. Wage rates were not free to fall as labor unions could almost dictate them. They were sticky. It was, therefore, very difficult for workers who became unemployed in the recession to find a new job. They were not allowed to offer low enough wage rates for potential employers.

Welfare State

The foundation of a democracy in Germany, the Weimar Republic, brought with it the rise of a modern welfare state. The ideological weak state needed the support of

---

[478] See Stucken (1953, p. 74). See also Schumpeter (1929) for the effects of the excessively high wages.

[479] See Mises (1931, p. 21).

[480] See Borchardt (1979, p. 104).

[481] See Wagemann (1935, p. 16).

[482] Mises (1978, p. 185); The original text is as follows: "Es ist nicht zu verkennen, daß die Unrentabilität vieler Produktionszweige und die Arbeitslosigkeit eines nicht unbeträchtlichen Teiles der Arbeitnehmer nicht nur Folge des Abstieges der Konjunktur ist. Unrentabilität und Arbeitslosigkeit werden im Augenblick durch die allgemeine Depression verstärkt, sie sind aber in der Nachkriegszeit zu dauernden Erscheinungen geworden, die auch im Aufschwung nicht ganz verschwunden sind." (1931, pp. 14–15)

the population. Politicians tried to buy votes to win elections or stay in power. The means to buy votes consisted in economic and social policies.

As a result, the state began to grow, playing a larger role in the economy. Stolper estimates that the share of government expenditures in GDP, including public enterprises, would be close to 50 % (1966, p. 144). The gold value of government expenditures per person rose from 107.2 RM in 1913 to 161.7 RM in 1925, and 213.6 RM in 1928.[483] New taxes on production were continually introduced,[484] thereby discouraging production. And as James Angell writes about the height of this burden: "... the German tax burden will be found to be one of the heaviest in the world today, and possibly the heaviest of all" (1929, p. 318). When it came to the crisis, caused by a lack of savings in relation to the undertaken investment projects, the tax burden disrupted a fast recovery.

Furthermore, there were other features of the welfare state that deepened the crisis. For instance, unemployment insurance and unemployment benefits were installed. This sustained the union policy of coercively increasing wages and causing long lasting unemployment.[485] Without the subsidies for the unemployed, the union policy and the rise of the welfare state would have faced much more resistance.

Reichsbank President Schacht describes the consequences of the welfare state and unemployment insurance:

> The biggest mistake of this system is obvious. It substitutes the responsibility of the individual with a supposed collective responsibility.... The duty to work and to help oneself with one's own power, i.e., that what makes a nation great and that is in every healthy human being, is killed: the desire to save is reduced and the declination for lavish consumption is increased.[486]

Also, fiscal redistribution and subsidies increased, with subsidies for agriculture being the largest. These agricultural subsidies often saved highly inefficient farms from bankruptcy. Therefore, scarce resources were bound up in agriculture and other subsidized industries, and not available to the rest of the economy, which would have otherwise allowed for a more speedy recovery.

As if this were not enough, the new welfare state engaged in deficits as its expenditures could not be financed completely via taxes. The deficits were partly motivated by the fear that a healthy budget would incite the French and other war

[483] See *DWI-Forschungshefte*, Nr. 3/1968, p. 10 quoted in Nussbaum (1978, p. 166).

[484] See Mises (1931, p. 27).

[485] See Mises (1931, p. 18).

[486] Schacht (1931, p. 181, 184); The original text is as follows: "Der größte Fehler dieses ganzen Systems liegt auf der Hand, es ersetzt die Verantwortung des einzelnen Individuums durch eine angebliche Kollektivverantwortung .... Das Gefühl der Arbeitspflicht und der Antrieb zur Selbsthilfe aus eigener Kraft, kurz das, was ein Volk groß macht und was in jedem gesunden Menschen drin steckt, wird durch die Überspannung und den Mißbrauch der Sozialversicherung getötet: der Wille zum Sparen wird geschwächt, die Neigung zum verschwenderischen Konsum gesteigert."

victors to demand higher reparations.[487] Thus, part of the new welfare state was financed via foreign loans. The Weimar Republic lived beyond its means.[488]

International Division of Labor Severely Harmed

The 1930s brought a severe disruption of the international division of labor.[489] International trade collapsed.[490] There are two main reasons for this. First, many countries directly controlled foreign exchanges. In Germany, a Devisenzwangskontrolle (foreign exchange control) was introduced in order to prevent the transfer of funds out of Germany. The old parity was officially maintained. Foreign exchanges had to be offered to the Reichsbank.[491] The Reichsbank decided who was to be given foreign exchange and for what purpose.[492] Imports were restricted. Exports, in consequence, also collapsed. This is so, because there were two ways for foreigners to pay for German exports. The first way to pay was via credit. This was of course, not done as Germans could not give credits to foreigners, as they could not export capital. The second way to pay was via the foreign exchanges or gold obtained by exporting to Germany.[493] However, German imports were restricted. Exports (or capital imports) pay for imports. As imports shrank, exports also shrank. Germany was on its way to autarky. The productivity advantages of international trade were forgone, deepening the crisis.

Second, new tariffs were erected. The U.S. installed the Hawley-Smoot Tariff in June 1930 on 20,000 products.[494] This made it more difficult for Europeans to sell their products in the U.S. in order to earn the funds necessary to repay their debts. The tariff also incited retaliatory tariffs by other states. Thus, in Germany agricultural imports were penalized in order to subsidize large inefficient agrarian estates. Great Britain also installed tariffs and tried to improve competitiveness of its exporters by the devaluation of the pound.[495] The tariffs also made it possible to keep the prices of protected products from falling.[496]

---

[487] See Palyi (1972, p. 166).

[488] See Borchardt (1979, p. 106).

[489] The decade of the 1920s was already a very protectionist phase. Christoph Buchheim sees the "lack of a liberal trade system" as the root for the problems (2002, p. 113).

[490] See League of Nations (1935, p. 92).

[491] See Stucken (1953, p. 93).

[492] See Stucken (1953, p. 94).

[493] Another possibility would be to use accumulated gold balances to pay for imports. But this possibility is limited by gold balances and cannot go on forever.

[494] Concerning the Hawley-Smoot Tariff, see Anderson (1979, p. 229). The tariff probably caused the stock exchange crash of 1929 (James 2002, p. xi).

[495] See Stucken (1953, p. 89).

[496] See Mises (1931, p. 21).

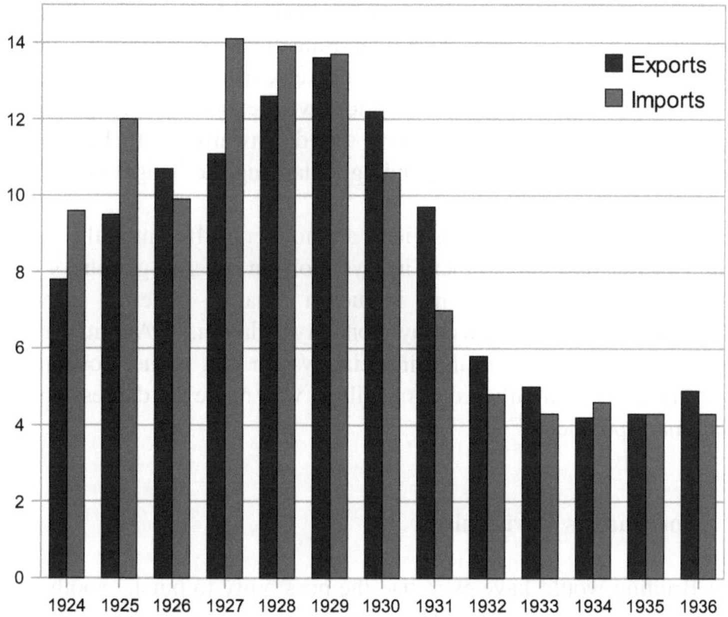

Chart 5.14 German foreign trade, 1924–1936

The decline of international trade reduced productivity and nearly led to autarky. Many exporters either had to release employees or went bankrupt. Germany, dependent on a level of high exports and imports, was especially harmed by this situation. The country's obligation to pay the annuities of the Young Plan required exports. So it seems like an absurdity that 3 days after the Young loan was offered in the United States, the Hawley-Smoot Tariff was passed.[497] German foreign trade can be seen in Chart 5.14.[498]

5.2.5 *Falling Prices: The Interpretation*

5.2.5.1 Traditional Interpretation

The traditional interpretation of the Great German Depression is either a Keynesian or monetarist one.[499] For Keynesians it is a collapse in effective demand that caused the Great Depression. For Monetarists it is a collapse in the money supply that

[497] See Anderson (1979, p. 230).

[498] In billion RM. Source: Deutsche Bundesbank (1976, p. 7).

[499] See Borchardt (1979, p. 88) for a critique of traditional interpretations and Korsch (1981) for a traditional interpretation of the German depression. Friedman and Schwartz (1971) criticise the failure of central banks and especially the Federal Reserve to inflate the money supply. Aldcroft

caused the Great Depression. It is also sometimes stated that there was an overproduction in the 1920s.[500] This overproduction combined with the hoarding of frightened consumers after the stock market crash led to a downward spiral. Consumers and investors spent less as prices were expected to keep falling. Thus, Brüning is criticized for not preventing this downward spiral. In particular, his policies of reducing government spending, balancing the budget and not inflating the money supply are attacked.

The Keynesian and Monetarists views are not very different at the root. In fact, they both call for more government interventions in order to get out of or prevent the crisis.[501] The Keynesian recipe in such a situation is deficit spending. This deficit spending could be financed by monetary inflation.[502] And it is exactly this monetary inflation to prop up the financial system that is the monetarist recipe. Hence, Brüning is commonly seen as a failure, who made the depression worse, by his deflationary policies.[503]

5.2.5.2 Borchardt's Revisionism

Whether Brüning would have even had the possibility to pursue another policy is the locus of another debate. This debate has been coined the Borchard-Controvery.[504] Knut Borchardt argues as follows[505]: Until 1931/1932, the recession did not seem to be different from others. Hence, the government did not consider new emergency measures such as a substantial increase in public expenditures to finance public work, etc. Borchardt goes on to claim that even in 1931/1932, when it became clear that the recession had worsened, the means for an increase in public

(1978, pp. 229–331) agrees stating that the restrictive monetary policies of the Federal Reserve were responsible for the severity of the crisis.

500 See, for instance, the Keynesian interpretation by Korsch (1981, p. 16).

501 In fact, Keynes himself recommended both monetary expansion and expansionary fiscal policy to get out of the depression. See Skidelsky (2002, p. 99).

502 Keynesian economist Andreas Korsch, in his discussion of the economic policies during the German depression, argues that it would be the task of the government to engage in expansionary monetary policies when credits are restricted (1981, p. 35). Also Kindleberger states that the Reichsbank should have acted as lender of last resort and bailed out the Danatbank (1987, pp. 294–295).

503 See Bombach (1976); Gottfried Bombach writes: "Man ist sich einig in Brünings Versagen." (1976, p. 6) [Translation: There is unanimity about Brüning's failure.] Korsch writes that it would be known that the economic policies of Brüning made the depression more severe (1981, p. 13). Werner Jochmann claims that the effects of the deflationary policies were ravaging (1978, p. 111). Kindleberger writes: "The deflationary policy was followed for two fateful years, though its inadequacy should have been immediately clear" (1987, pp. 131–132), adding that "the verdict is unanimous that Brüning failed" (p. 174).

504 Concerning the Borchard-Controversy, see Borchardt (1979 and 1982, pp. 165–224) or Bartsch and Eismann (2005).

505 See Borchardt (1979).

expenditure by deficit spending were not available. There were three basic ways to finance a deficit: financing by the Reichsbank, financing by selling bonds to citizens, or by selling bonds to foreigners. First of all, a higher government deficit could not be financed by the Reichsbank if it did not want to, as the Reichsbank was to be independent according to the Young Plan. Breaking with the Young Plan would have had an adverse effect on foreign creditors and foreign capital would have left the country. Moreover, it was thought that by showing that Germany was incapable of paying the reparations, the reparations might finally be abolished. However, using loans to finance government programs which the Allies themselves could not afford, of course, would defeat this plan. Furthermore, it was feared that the financing through the printing press would lead to another price inflation. The hyperinflation of 1923, was still in the minds of the people. Thus, the labor unions, the Social Democratic Party (SPD), and trade associations were against this option.

The second option was to finance the deficit spending by selling bonds at home. Selling bonds in Germany would have driven up interest rates and would have crowded out private investors searching for loans. The last option was to get a loan from the Allies. This was problematic for several reasons. First, the Allies had also economic problems and did not spend their money on public work programs, etc. Why would they then lend money to Germany to finance such programs? Second, there were political tensions between Germany and the Allies. There was the proposed customs unions with Austria that had upset France. There was also the reparation controversy, as well as the open question on the eastern German border that Germany wanted to be revised. France, nevertheless, offered help, but only on the condition of political concessions and guarantees that were impossible for Brüning to accept, such as a rejection of the plans of a German-Austrian customs union and armament restrictions. As the military, the opposition, and the public were against such accommodations, and as Reichspräsident Paul von Hindenburg threatened to step down if France's conditions were accepted, this option was illusionary.

Last but not least, Borchardt questions the effectiveness of such an increase in government spending. The proposed spending programs were, in his opinion, not enough to change the course of the recession and thus avoid Adolf Hitler's rise to power.[506]

---

[506] See Borchardt (1979, p. 99). There were two chancelor's in between Brüning and Hitler. Franz von Papen and Kurt von Schleicher did not change economic policies drastically. Franz von Papen, though, after July 1932, introduced some measure for credit expansion. See Nussbaum (1978, p. 375). He introduced a small public works program and a *Steuergutschein* program. The *Steuergutscheine* were tax deductibles for future tax payments and were given when taxes were paid. They were anticipating a reduction of future tax revenues. Kurt von Schleicher introduced another small public work program.

5.2.5.3 Interpretation on Basis of this Work

In the 1920s, there had been an artificial reduction of the interest rates by the Federal Reserve banks, also the relevant central bank for Germany, as German banks, companies, and public entities took on loans in the U.S. German banks pyramided a second level of credit on top of U.S. loans. Thus, we are faced with a typical Austrian business cycle. There is a boom in the 1920s and there is a recession beginning in 1930, triggered by distrust in banks due to their security and loan losses.[507]

The factors that made the depression so harsh have already been explained. Credit expansion and malinvestments were substantial. The restriction of credit by not renewing the foreign credits was also considerable. The unions and state imposed wages, leading to enormous unemployment rates. New unemployment insurance and benefits made unemployment long-lasting. Furthermore, the welfare state had been expanded in the 1920s to a hitherto unseen degree. The role of the state had increased, thus making it more difficult for the strangled private economy to cushion the effects of the necessary liquidations. In fact, the private economy had been in a continuous crisis during the 1920s and many companies only stayed in business, because they were propped up by home-made or foreign credit expansion. Also the international division of labor was inhibited by rising tariff walls. Thus, international trade shrank and production became less efficient.

Moreover, some government policies in response to the crisis made the recession more severe. Instead of a laissez-faire policy that reduced the weight of the public sector upon the private economy the German government partly followed other policies.[508] Thus, we come to an assessment of the policies of the Brüning government. Brüning policies, indeed can be criticized in many ways. There is the increase in taxes, the foreign exchange control, the reduction of interest rates for long-term contracts, an agricultural tariff, the bail-out of the banking system, and later on, also the subsidies for farms and companies, etc.

However, the Keynesian and monetarist critique of Brüning fails. His "deflationary" policies mostly worked to speed up the recovery. Of course, it would have been better to get rid of union privileges all together than to dictate lower wages by an emergency decree, i.e., a price decree deflation. A free-wage setting would have reduced wage rates and unemployment automatically on the free market.[509] Probably, the cost reduction by government decree was not large enough to improve competitiveness and reduce unemployment quickly, as indicated by the *Reichsreform*, a reform plan proposed by business men. Business men saw the *Versorgungsstaat* (welfare state) as the reason of the crisis and demanded "lower adminstrative costs, the abolition of unemployment insurance, central control over

---

[507] See Mises (1931), for this interpretation.

[508] See Rothbard (2000, pp. 23–29) for appropriate government policies in a depression.

[509] See Mises (1931, p. 20).

municipal spending, and above all freedom for employers facing bankruptcy to undercut the wage levels guaranteed in collective labor contracts."[510]

Yet, the deflationary policies certainly helped to speed up recovery. As Palyi states: "Most economists agree that 'sticky' wages and prices were the depression's major aggravating circumstances. In fact, eliminating such obstacles to cost adaptation was helpful in sparking Germany's boom in the late 1930s."[511]

Due to Brüning's policies, from 1930 on there were surpluses in Germany's balance of trade that allowed to pay for reparations and reduce its foreign debt. Brüning's plan of balancing the budget was indispensable to restore Germany's creditworthiness.[512] The plan of a customs union with Austria would also have revived industry in both countries.

Furthermore, Brüning let the price deflation and liquidation of malinvestments happen, at least, until October 1931.[513] He argued that contraction would go on until world market prices would increase again.[514] Until July 1931, the Reichsbank tightened the money supply more than any other central bank.[515] Marginal companies went bankrupt, thus giving breathing space to their competitors. Without the bankruptcies, the competitors would have stayed in continuous trouble. Now, they could expand their market share and thrive again. Capital was withdrawn from some industries to others where the demand was higher. The structure of production could adapt itself. In this way, the purging of the malinvestment incurred during the boom and the cost reduction was hastened to some extent by Brüning's deflationary policies. And in 1932 the recovery started.[516] The heir of this purge in Germany was

---

[510] (Patch 1998, p. 177); See also Kurt Gossweiler concerning the German industry and for the argument that the crisis was caused by too high nominal wages, too high taxes, and social insurance contributions (1971, p. 356).

[511] Palyi (1972, p. 293); In relation with the recovery and the next artificial boom in Germany, Palyi comments on Brüning's deflationary policy: "Actually behind foreign exchange restrictions and a host of petty regulations, Germany, well prepared for an upturn by Brüning's policy of cost deflation, was the one and only country that managed to establish full employment in the late 1930s—by 'contra-cyclical' policies, i.e., resource mobilization for war" (1972, p. 34). Palyi later states: "Brüning's heroic efforts to save the mark were largely futile, since he was unable to carry the deflation to its logical conclusion" (p. 339). At least, Brüning's deflationary policies, paved the way for the recovery as Palyi indicated. Also Nussbaum states that when the Brüning government dismissed on May 30th 1932, the end of the crisis was near (1978, p. 373).

[512] Hülsmann (2013, p. 105) argues that due to Brüning's deflationary policies and a lack of similar policies in France, France fell far behind Germany economically in the 1930s. Hitler used the German economic advantage gained thanks to Brüning's policies to overrun France in 6 weeks in 1940.

[513] Later, the government bailed out companies and thus the public sector of the economy increased. See Nussbaum (1978, p. 329).

[514] See Patch (1998, p. 176).

[515] See Palyi (1972, p. 259). From the fall of 1931 on, the money supply was expanded slightly and the discount rate was reduced from 10 % in the beginning of September to 6 % in March 1932. See Patch (1998, p. 205).

[516] See Fischer (1968, p. 46). Stolper remarks that there is unanimity that the crisis had its climax in the summer 1932 (1966, p. 139).

Hitler.[517] Hitler engaged in a vast expansion of public expenditures. With the help of public works programs and rearmament, unemployment was considerably reduced.

In sum, the Keynesians and Monetarists argue that Brüning's deflationary policies were wrong and Borchardt basically argues that his policies were not good, but that there was no alternative. However, Brüning's deflationary policies were, in fact, not strong enough and his fault was to add interventions into the economy. His deflationary policies did not endure long enough.[518] From the end of August 1931 on the Reichsbank lowered its credit constraints. Credit expansion in favor of big businesses became the policy and interest rates were reduced.[519]

5.2.6 *The Opposition to Price Deflation*

During every inflation a class of profiteers develops, heavily opposed to deflation. The same is true for the class of inflation profiteers that developed in the inflationary 1920s in Germany. However, due to the experience with the hyperinflation and fear of its repetition, the majority of the population did not oppose price deflation in the beginning. The *Reichsverband der Deutschen Industrie* (Federal Association of German Industry) still opposed inflation in 1931, as did the most influential German economic weekly publication, the *Deutsche Volkswirt* published by Gustav Stolper. Small and medium-sized businesses feared and opposed it very strongly.[520] The 1920s' inflation had destroyed their savings.[521]

The main opposition to the price deflation came from big business and the Junkers. Big business wanted to be bailed out by credit expansion as well as the farmers (Junkers) who were highly indebted. As William Patch writes about the suggestion of industrialists to overcome the crisis in July 1931:

> Some industrialists did advance innovative suggestions to ameliorate the process of deflation by creating a form of supplemental currency to compensate for the withdrawal of foreign credits. Hermann Warmbold, an expert on chemical fertilizers and I.G. Farben

---

[517] See Borchardt (1979, p. 109). Also Palyi writes: "The 'deflation' carried out until late July 1931 by Brüning and Luther [President of the Reichsbank] has been blamed for Hitler's rise to power. This is one of the most pernicious myths which has grown out of the interwar monetary and political confusion" (1972, p. 262). Palyi argues that there was no alternative to Brüning's policy. The political circumstances and German public opinion did not allow him to agree upon the French conditions for help. He also argues that it was General Schleicher's mistake to turn to the left, thereby irritating Hindenburg who replaced Schleicher on January 30, 1933 with an anti-labor coalition led by Hitler, whose party was almost bankrupt and falling apart. (p. 264). For a similar assessment see Hülsmann (2013, p. 105).

[518] Thus, the capital goods industry was still overextended in 1932. See Zumpe (1980).

[519] See Palyi (1972, p. 263).

[520] See Born (1967, p. 44).

[521] See Aldcroft (1978, p. 167).

> executive, suggested a new issue of 'stockpile note' (*Lagerscheine*) to grant framers and other small producers cash advances based on the value of the unsold products. Paul Silverberg [a coal and steel industrialist and lobbyist] supported him by declaring that 'one can combat a serious deflation only with measures that look like inflation,' but this would be a temporary and controlled inflation. [italics in original] (1998, p. 176).

Paul Silverberg would again in September 1931 propose a bolder plan to expand the money supply by 2 billion RM.[522] It is not surprising that industrialists wanted to be bailed out by inflationary measures. Industrialists were indebted and had often incurred malinvestments. Instead of liquidating malinvestments, industrialists asked to be bailed out via measures whose inflationary policies were not acknowledged. They wanted to prevent a change of ownership in the means of production. Especially, the steel industry had problems, having increased their capacity in the 1920s with bank loans to an such extent that their capacity utilization sank to 36 % in 1931.[523]

Academics also began to support inflationary policies. Thus, the industrialist and economist Heinrich Dräger argued for public works financed by credit expansion.[524] Albert Hahn, board member of the *Deutsche Effekten- und Wechselbank*, demanded that public expenditures be financed directly or indirectly by the Reichsbank.[525] Thus, he demanded expansionary monetary policies that certainly would have helped also the *Deutsche Effekten- und Wechselbank*. In order to help corporations, economist Gerhard Colm proposed a forced conversion of debts into shares to save companies. He argued, in accordance with the explanations of Sect. 4.3.3.3, that this was politically feasible as the debtors and interested workers were better organized than creditors. Indeed later on, debtors were helped by the government when interest rates of existing credit contracts were reduced by government decree.[526]

However, the special interests also were bitterly opposed. The Center Party (Deutsche Zentrumspartei), the party of small business men, usually not as highly indebted as the big business establishment, opposed those inflationary plans. Also labor organizations opposed the measures as inflationary. The memory of the great inflation, in which workers suffered losses, was still close. The only party that was in favor of a "supplemental currency" was the NSDAP. As a consequence, the centrist press launched a campaign denouncing the strategy of the big industrialists to get rid of their debts in a second hyper-inflation approved by the Nazis.[527]

---

[522] See Patch (1998, p. 207). Also Nussbaum states that the highly indebted coal and steel industries were in favor of inflationary policies (1978, p. 321).

[523] See Patch (1998, p. 179).

[524] See Korsch (1981, p. 31). Dräger was also engaged in the founding of the "Studiengesellschaft für Geld- und Kreditwirtschaft" [Research society for the economics of money and credit] in which politicians, state employees, scientists, entrepreneurs and members of labor unions gathered.

[525] See Jochmann (1978, p. 103).

[526] See Borchardt (1991, p. 37).

[527] See Patch (1998, p. 177).

Indeed, some members of the heavy industry pushed for inflation to get rid of their debts and found an ally in Hitler. Furthermore, the financial sector increasingly saw a credit expansion as a way out of its crisis.[528]

Beside the Center Party, the Social Democratic Party (SPD) denounced the inflationary plans of the NSDAP intended to bail out big farmers and big business. The SPD saw the interest groups lobbying for those plans and their consequences quite clearly. In a party newspaper an anonymous author writes on October 12th, 1931:

> Fascism is inflation. Its aim is to pay workers inflation wages, for which they can merely buy bread, so that bankrupt heavy industrialists and big farmers get healthy at the cost of workers. Fascism is a political means to enslave workers and inflation is its economic weapon against workers.[529]

Let us now turn to the Junkers, another group, beside industrialists and bankers, that opposed Brüning's deflationary policies. Farmers harshly attacked Brüning's policies and incited political unrest to destabilize the government. Palyi describes the year 1930 and the first 7 months of 1931 as "[n]ear chaotic conditions obtained in Germany, promoted by agrarian and industrial 'conservative' interests." (1972, p. 168). Farmers had been in a continual crisis after World War I and were heavily indebted. This was partly caused by the government, which did not allow unprofitable and indebted farms to go bankrupt but bailed them out. From the end of the hyperinflation to the end of 1929, the government gave 2,582 million RM credits to farmers and guaranteed private loans to farmers for 144 million RM.[530] But farmers wanted more. They wanted higher subsidies and inflation.

Eventually, the Junkers became partially responsible for Brüning's fall.[531] In spring 1932, Brüning's cabinet was working on an emergency decree. The idea was to reduce or stop the *Osthilfe*,[532] subsidies to the large, over-indebted farms in the eastern parts of the Reich, in Pommern, and in East and West Prussia. In the

---

[528] See Nussbaum (1978, pp. 333–335). The marxist author Lotte Zumpe argues that the majority of the financial sector, the coal and steel industries, the over-sea trade and the Junkers wanted Hitler to take power (1978, p. 11). She sees the rearmament as a reason for Hitler's support by for example the Keppler-Kreis, a circle of bankers, heavy industrialists and Junkers who supported Hitler (p. 35). However, it is also possible that the support for Hitler was partially motivated by Hitler's support of inflationary measures. Those measures would have benefited the economic establishment of bankers, heavy industrialists and Junkers who were threatened by price deflation.

[529] As quoted in Borchardt (1979, p. 123), fn. 51; The original text is as follows: "... Der Faschismus bedeutet Inflation! Sein Ziel ist es, den Arbeitern Inflationslöhne zu zahlen, für die sie kaum Brot kaufen können, damit die bankrotten Schwerindustriellen und Großagrarier auf Kosten der Arbeiterschaft gesund gemacht werden können. Der Faschismus ist das Mittel zur politischen Knechtung der Arbeiterschaft, die Inflation ist seine wirtschaftliche Waffe gegen die Arbeiterschaft."

[530] See Nussbaum (1978, p. 224).

[531] See Palyi (1972, p. 260).

[532] The aim of the *Osthilfe* was to maintain the structure of ownership in times of price deflation and farm debts. The agricultural establishment did not want to lose its property and opposed the looming redistribution. See Nussbaum (1978, p. 365).

foreclosure sale, the government would buy the lands and allow the still vast number of unemployed settle there. The Junkers had a significant influence on President Hindenburg. In fact, his son Oskar was also a Junker, and Hindenburg, himself, was the owner of Gut Neudeck, an estate, given to him by the Junkers. Therefore, Hindenburg also enjoyed the benefits of the *Osthilfe*. Influenced by the Junkers, Hindenburg declared he would not sign any further emergency decrees and Brüning stepped down on May 30th, 1932.

Indeed, the National Socialists would fulfill the hopes of both the heavy industry and the Junkers. They started to engage in credit expansion to finance public work programs and rearmament.[533] German public debts exploded.[534]

5.2.7 Conclusion

During the 1920s a bank credit inflation occurred. Foreign credits had come to Germany, on top of which German banks inflated the money supply. In 1931, doubts in the solvency of banks due to losses in securities and industrial loans triggered bank runs in Austria and Germany. Credits were restricted. Therefore, between 1930 and 1932, the bank credit deflation caused the price deflation in Germany. In addition to the substantial bank credit deflation other factors contributed to the severe price deflation. There was a cash building deflation, as people tried to increase their cash holdings in face of bank failures. The government decreed lower wage rates which constitutes a price decree deflation. For some time, bank deposits were frozen, which implies that there was also a confiscatory deflation.

In contrast to the traditional interpretations, Brüning's deflationary policies did not make the depression worse. Some of his other interventionary policies did inhibit the recovery, though. These were bail-outs of banks and corporations, increases in taxes, an agricultural tariff, subsidies and reduction in interest rates. Moreover, he did not go far enough in this deflationary policies. What made the depression so harsh, was the amount of the bank credit inflation, the high wage rates obtained through union privileges, the welfare state, and the barriers to the international division of labor. As during the American growth deflation, the opposition against price deflation in Germany was the strongest among debtors and unprofitable businesses that wanted to be bailed out. Junkers and big industrialists were, thus, the strongest opponents of price deflation.

---

[533] For the financial policies of the Third Reich, see Fischer (1968, pp. 66–71). For the Nazi public work programs and its financial policies, also see Stolper (1966, pp. 154–156, 169–173).

[534] See Stolper (1966, p. 172).

Chapter 6
Conclusion

In this work, I have dealt with the question of whether price deflation could scientifically be judged as harmful for the economy.

It was shown that price deflation became a theoretical issue in times of declining prices, like the Swedish experience in the eighteenth century, from the beginning of the suspension of specie payment in Great Britain in 1797 until the 1830s, and during the deflationary monetary policies after World War I and during the Great Depression. After World War II deflation was not discussed very much in the literature any more until Japan experienced a price deflation in the 1990s and fears of deflation arose in the U.S. and Europe.

Furthermore, those theories of deflation often were influenced by the misery of the people who suffered losses in these specific historical cases. Moreover, some of the theorists were even connected to the interest groups that suffered such losses in the price deflation and otherwise would have profited by a monetary expansion. This can explain some of the deflation phobia that has developed over the centuries. This phobia, as the analysis has demonstrated, has grown over the centuries, reaching a high point in the decades following World War II when Keynesian theories reigned in academia and in politics. Maybe the main goal of Keynesian policies is to prevent price deflation at any cost.

Today's economists view deflation less negatively than those of the Keynesian heydays. Yet, the fear of the liquidity trap remains, while economists undertake substantial efforts to find ways out of or means to prevent this alleged "nightmare." Due to the fear of a liquidity trap, price deflation is seen as more dangerous than price inflation by some economists. There are, though also economists, who aim at price stability and regard both price inflation and price deflation as harmful. Growth deflations are even regarded and named as good deflations. However, cash building deflations or bank credit deflations are, still widely seen today as harmful for an economy. The Austrian economists, like Murray Rothbard, see fewer problems in a price deflation. Only monetary deflation do they try to prevent in certain instances, for example, in a monetary reform.

P. Bagus, *In Defense of Deflation*, Financial and Monetary Policy Studies 41,
DOI 10.1007/978-3-319-13428-4_6

In Chap. 3, I presented the different causes or kinds of price deflation. One possible cause of a price deflation is economic growth. In a growing economy more goods and services are produced. When the increased production is exchanged against a slower growing money supply, prices tend to fall. In this respect, it does not matter if the economic growth is caused by innovations, an increase in the division of labor, an increase in net savings or a combination of them.

A second cause for a price deflation is cash building. People increase their demand for money. They want to hold higher cash balances, (i.e. they are willing to pay higher prices for money.) As a consequence, the purchasing power of money tends to increase. There are several reasons why the demand for money is increased. The industrial demand for uses, apart from the monetary uses of the money stuff, can rise. Also the exchange demand can rise, as people regard their future as more uncertain and try to increase their real cash balances to be prepared for the future. As prices tend to fall, individuals achieve an increase in their real cash balances without a change in the money supply. It is, furthermore, possible that people want to store a larger amount of their wealth in the liquid asset of money. Lastly, people who expect the purchasing power of money to increase, demand money. In this case the speculative demand for money increases and speeds up the price decline to the expected level.

A third reason for a price deflation is a bank credit deflation. In a recession after an artificial boom caused by credit expansion, credits are usually restricted. They might be restricted because banks become more cautious, or because the central bank changes to a more restrictive monetary policy, or because depositors try to increase their cash holdings. When, during a recession, the first credits turn bad, a cumulative process can set in. Credits are restricted even more. Companies dependent on further credits go bankrupt. Asset prices fall due to bankruptcies and credit contraction. Balance sheets of companies and banks deteriorate due to bankruptcies and bad loans. The credit contraction or reduction in the money supply implies a tendency for prices to fall. As prices fall the real debt burden increases. Highly indebted companies become bankrupt. Depositors, at some point, begin to doubt the solvency of the banking system and withdraw their deposits. This forces banks to restrict credits further. Prices fall even further and the real debt burden increases even more. This process, at the latest, ends following a bank panic when the banking system has broken down and the malinvestments of the boom, as well as marginal companies have been liquidated. Of course, at any point in this cumulative process in a fiat money system, the central bank can try to stop the price decline by inflating the money supply.

A last cause for declining prices is the state. When the government directly causes a price deflation this is considered a fiat deflation. There are three types of fiat deflation. In a price decree deflation, the government simply decrees prices to fall. It, thus, installs maximum prices. In a coercive monetary deflation, the government coercively reduces the money supply in three possible ways . It can just destroy collected taxes in a fiscal deflation. It can issue government bonds and destroy the collected money in a bond deflation, or it can block and confiscate money funds in a confiscatory deflation. A legal tender deflation, by setting a legal tender, leads to a demonetization of at least one other medium of exchange and thereby to lower prices than would have been otherwise.

In Chap. 4, I analyzed the consequences of a price deflation. A price deflation means that prices fall. Buyers gain from falling prices and sellers lose when prices decline. Everyone is a buyer and a seller. Companies also buy factors of production and sell the products they produce. When prices fall, which companies will thrive and which will suffer, which individuals will profit and which will suffer losses, depends on the relative strength of the price fall. The most important consequence of a price deflation, is simply that some individuals or companies make gains and others suffer losses. A change in the relative wealth positions occurs. For example there will be a redistribution in favor of fixed income groups. Moreover, creditors gain at the expense of debtors as the real burden of debts increases. These distributional effects of a price deflation are not anything peculiar. Any change in the economy has such effects and their outcome depends on the entrepreneurial skills of the involved individuals. Beside this main effect, there are some other consequences of a price deflation. In a recession, a price deflation can speed up the recovery by speeding up the credit contraction. Malinvestments are liquidated more quickly as credits are not renewed. As marginal companies go bankrupt more resources are available for other companies with viable investment projects. Furthermore, falling prices could lead to accounting losses and falling asset prices. This could spur savings to make up for these losses or because people feel poorer. Another possible effect of a price deflation is the breaking of institutional price rigidities. Individuals, who would profit from removing the barriers in order to allow prices to fall—for example, wages—will advocate policies for breaking those price rigidities.

Moreover, a price deflation can bring down a fractional reserve banking system. As prices fall, the real debt burden of companies increases. If this was not expected by companies, they might become bankrupt. This deteriorates the balance sheets of banks and triggers the cumulative process that was described in the case of a bank credit contraction. When one bank run occurs and sets off a domino effect of further bank runs, the stability of the fractional reserve banking system is endangerd. A bank panic can develop, if the central bank fails to intervene. The system may break down, giving place for a new monetary system to arise.

I have also pointed out that the government will be opposed to price deflation as it reduces the state's power. The real burden of government debt increases in a price deflation and governments are usually highly indebted. Moreover, a monetary deflation causes problems for the government's finances. This is so, because government expenditures are financed, to a substantial part, by monetary inflation.

Last, a continuous price deflation changes people's habits. They will be less dependent on the financial industry and financial markets to preserve their wealth, because their wealth is automatically increasing by just holding cash.

Furthermore, there are widespread myths concerning deflation in the literature and in the general public, as well. These myths have led to a strong anti-deflationary bias and the five most important myths are also discussed in Chap. 4. First, there is nothing arbitrary about the redistribution that occurs in a price deflation.

The outcome depends on the entrepreneurial skills of the market participants. If the price deflation is caused by government intervention, one might argue, though, that the government intervention was arbitrary and unfair.

Second, price deflation does not necessarily disturb production. By the purge of the financial system, and the birth of a sounder system, production might actually be spurred. Furthermore, bankruptcies imply a change of ownership and the getting rid of debts. Bankruptcies do not necessarily imply a disruption of production. If the investment project is sound, production will be carried on. In addition, entrepreneurs can anticipate falling prices, and bid their buying prices down in order to prevent losses.

A third myth states that price deflation leads to chaos. Only price stability would be desirable. However, entrepreneurs can calculate their business plans successfully in times of stable, rising, or falling prices. They always try to anticipate the movement of the prices relevant for them. Of course, price deflation could be used by demagogues to push for political changes.

A fourth myth claims that price deflation leads to mass unemployment. This is not true, because only government interventions can prevent wages from adjusting downward and thereby, causing involuntary unemployment.

The last fallacy about price deflation concerns the liquidity trap. When nominal interest rates are close to zero, deflationary expectations would lead to a high real interest rate increasing the real cost of borrowing. Investments would stop. Yet, deflationary expectations speed up the price deflation. Indeed, entrepreneurs stop investing until prices fall. They bid down prices. As a result, prices fall immediately to the expected level. Moreover, the price differentials between buying costs and selling proceeds (or the natural interest rate) are essential for investment decisions. Investments are, thus, not necessarily harmed by deflationary expectations.

The five common myths discussed do not hold as proof that price deflation should be prevented. These five arguments do not prove that there is something inherently bad in deflation. Rather, this depends on the cause of the price deflation. The ethical assessment of a price deflation caused by government intervention can be very different than that of a price deflation which is the result of actions of individuals on the free market.

Chapter 4 concludes with an explanation of the widespread opposition to price deflation. I argue that the fallacious theories about deflation themselves have caused widespread opposition. Those theories are often spread by those who suffer losses in a price deflation. The common opposition to deflation that today is harsher than the opposition to inflation must be explained by its distributional effects. The redistribution is more apparent than in a price inflation. Moreover, the losses are spread over fewer shoulders than the losses in a price inflation. Also the people suffering losses in a price deflation are normally better organized than the people who suffer losses in a price inflation. It is the economic establishment, especially the government, banks and big business that are overindebted and have to lose most in a price deflation. These elites usually have the power to prevent a price deflation, at least in a fiat money system.

Many of these theoretical insights have been illustrated in the historical case studies of Chap. 5. Thus, several of the types of price deflation previously outlined were illustrated. In the American growth deflation, there was not only a growth deflation, but also bank credit deflations, a legal tender deflation, and a bond deflation. In the German bank credit deflation, there was a bank credit deflation with its cumulative effects, along with a cash building deflation, a confiscatory deflation and a price decree deflation. Thus, the majority of the causes of deflation have been illustrated historically. The consequences of price deflation were demonstrated as well. Redistributions occurred, while a strong opposition to falling prices and social unrest, as well as a demand for expansionary monetary policies increased. This occurred even in the U.S. where there was tremendous economic growth. This has been explained by the well-organized interest groups that would have gained much from a monetary inflation. During the German bank credit deflation, there were many bankruptcies and a restructuring of the structure of production. The price deflation speeded up the recovery. Again the suspicious interest groups, especially indebted farmers, businesses, and banks, pressured for a monetary inflation.

In sum, that deflation cannot be regarded as something harmful for the economy is a conclusion that makes much sense. Falling prices are not harmful. When prices of personal computers fall, for instance, consumers regard that as positive. They do not see a problem with that, but welcome the lower prices. The main effect is a redistribution of wealth and income, but not a disruption of production. One could argue, though, that fiat deflation is harmful as the government forces people to act in a way they do not want to act, thereby reducing their welfare by force. However, price deflation *per se* is not harmful, but instead, can have some beneficial effects like purging malinvestments, as well as liquidating an unsound financial system.

After pointing out that price deflation per se cannot be regarded as something harmful, one also has to take in mind the recommendations offered to prevent price deflation. Economists who regard price deflation as harmful, implicitly or explicitly call for inflation, i.e., expansionary monetary policy. Even assuming for the sake of the argument that price deflation would be harmful, one would have to analyze the question if inflation would not be even more evil. This inflation would also bring about a redistribution of wealth and would distort the price system depending on where the new money enters the economy. If the new money enters the loan market and the interest rate is artificially reduced, the expansionary monetary policy will lead to malinvestments and a waste of the scarce resources of society. Stable consumer prices might deceive policy makers and economists concerning the distortion of the structure of production. Monetary inflation distorts the structure of production independent from the fact that consumer prices might remain more or less stable. Therefore, sooner or later, social hardships are involved in a readjustment of the structure of production during a recession.

Moreover, the anti-deflationary inflation can result in asset price bubbles and financial instability. Thus, the recommendation of fighting price deflation with monetary inflation has tragic consequences. In sum, even if price deflation could be proven to be harmful, which according to this study is not possible, it would be difficult to prove it to be more harmful than its prescribed medicine: inflation.

References

Achinstein A (1961) Economic fluctuations. In: Harris SE (ed) American economic history. McGraw-Hill, New York, pp 162–180

Ahamed L (2009) Lords of finance—The bankers who broke the world. Penguin Press, New York

Ahearne AG, Gagnon JE, Haltmaier J, Kamin SB, Erceg CJ, Faust J, Guerrieri L, Roush JE, Rogers JH, Sheets N, Wright JH (2002) Preventing deflation: lessons from Japan's experience in the 1990s. International finance discussion paper 729, Research paper series—FEDS papers. Board of Governors of the Federal Reserve System, Washington, DC

Aldcroft DH (1978) Die zwanziger Jahre—Von Versailles zur Wall Street 1919-1929 (trans: Bauer HW, Quenzer G, Seip G). Deutscher Taschenbuchverlag, Munich

Anderson BM (1979) Economics and the public welfare—a financial and economic history of the United States, 1924-46, 2nd edn. Liberty Press, Indianapolis, IN

Anderson BM [1917] (2000) The value of money. Libertarian Press, Grove City, PA (reprint).

Andrews B (1895) The fall of prices—the cause and the cure. In: White T (ed) Silver and gold: or, Both sides of the shield; A symposium of the view of all parties on the currency question as expressed by their leading advocates, thoroughly expounding the doctrines of free silver, monometalism and bi-metalism, with all arguments, pro. and con. From the pens of John Sherman, Wm. B. Allison, John G. Carlisle. . .and others. Publisher's Union, Philadelphia, pp 301–30

Angell JW (1929) The recovery of Germany. Published for the Council on Foreign Affairs. Yale University Press, New Haven

Attwood T [1819] (1964) A letter to the earl of liverpool on the reports of the committies of the two houses of parliament on the questions of the bank restriction act. In: Fetter FW (ed) Selected economic writings of Thomas Attwood. The London School of Economic and Political Science, London

Bagus P (2003) Deflation—when Austrians become interventionists. Quart J Aust Econ 6(4): 19–35

Bagus P (2009) The quality of money. Quart J Aust Econ 12(4):22–45

Bagus P, Howden D (2009) The legitimacy of loan maturity mismatching: a risky, but not fraudulent, undertaking. J Bus Ethics 90(3):399–406

Bagus P, Howden D (2011) Monetary equilibrium and price stickiness: causes, consequences and remedies. Rev Aust Econ 24(4):383–402

Bagus P, Howden D (2012a) The continuing continuum problem of deposits and loans. J Bus Ethics 106(3):295–300

Bagus P, Howden D (2012b) Monetary equilibrium and price stickiness: a rejoinder. Rev Aust Econ 25(3):271–77

P. Bagus, *In Defense of Deflation*, Financial and Monetary Policy Studies 41,
DOI 10.1007/978-3-319-13428-4

Bagus P, Howden D (2013) Some ethical dilemmas of modern banking. Bus Ethics Eur Rev 22(3): 235–245

Bagus P, Howden D, Block W (2013) Deposits, loans and banking: clarifying the debate. Am J Econ Sociol 72(3):627–644

Barrett DC (1931) The Greenbacks and resumption of specie payments, 1862-1879. Harvard University Press, Cambridge, MA

Bartsch M, Henry E (2005) Brünings Wirtschaftspolitik: Maßnahmen—Handlungsspielräume—Alternativen; Eine Retrospektive zur Borchardt-Kontroverse -. Dresden: Sächsische Landesbibliothek—Staats- und Universitätsbibliothek Dresden. http://nbn-resolving.de/urn:nbn:de:swb:14-1139911732466-76552. Accessed 1 Aug 2007.

Bemis EW (1893) The discontent of the farmer. J Polit Econ 1(2):193–213

Bernanke BS (1981) Bankruptcy, liquidity, and recession. The American Economic Review, papers and proceedings of the ninety-third annual meeting of the American Economic Society, 71(2): 155–159

Bernanke BS (2002) Deflation: making sure 'It' Doesn't Happen Here, speech before the National Economists Club, November 21. Washington, DC

Boianovsky M (1998) Wicksell on deflation in the early 1920s. Hist Polit Econ 30(2):219–275

Boianovsky M (2004) The IS-LM model and the liquidity trap concept: from Hicks to Krugman. Hist Polit Econ 36(Annual Suppl): 92–126.

Bombach G (1976) Einleitung. In: Bombach G, Ramser H-J, Timmermann M, Wittmann W (eds) Der Keynesianismus II—Die beschäftigungspolitische Diskussion vor Keynes in Deutschland, Dokumente und Kommentare. Springer, Berlin, pp 1–8

Borchardt K (1979) Zwangslagen und Handlungsspielräume in der großen Weltwirtschaftskrise der frühen dreißiger Jahre: Zur Revision des überlieferten Geschichtsbildes. Jahrbuch der Bayerischen Akademie der Wissenschaften: 85–132

Borchardt K (1982) Wachstum, Krisen, Handlungsspielräume der Wirtschaftspolitik: Studien zur Wirtschaftsgeschichte d. 19. u. 20. Jh. Vandenhoek und Ruprecht, Göttingen

Borchardt K (1991) Einleitung. In: Borchardt K, Schötz O (eds) Wirtschaftspolitik in der Krise—die (Geheim-)Konferenz der Friedrich List-Gesellschaft im September 1931 über Möglichkeiten und Folgen einer Kreditausweitung. Nomos Verlag, Baden-Baden, pp 17–50

Bordo MD, Filardo AJ (2005) Deflation and monetary policy in a historical perspective: remembering the past or being condemned to repeat it? Econ Policy 20(44):799–844

Bordo MD, Redish A (2004) Is deflation depressing? Evidence from the classical gold standard. In: Burdekin RCK, Siklos PL (eds, 2004a) Deflation: current and historical perspectives. Cambridge University Press, Cambridge, pp 197–217

Bordo MD, Lane JL, Redish A (2004) Good versus bad deflation: lesson from the gold standard era. NBER working paper no. 10329.

Borio C, Filardo AJ (2004) "Back to the future? Assessing the deflation record." BIS working papers no. 152

Born KE (1967) Die deutsche Bankenkrise 1931—Finanzen und Politik. R. Piper, Munich

Bresciani-Turroni C (2007) The economics of inflation: a study of currency depreciation in post-war Germany. Ludwig von Mises Institute, Auburn, AL

Bryan MF (1997) On the origin and evolution of the word inflation. Cleveland, Federal Reserve Bank of

Buchheim C (2002) The 'Crisis Before the Crisis'—the export engine out of gear. In: James H (ed) The interwar depression in an international context. Oldenbourg Verlag, Munich, pp 113–122

Burdekin RCK, Siklos PL (2004a) Deflation: current and historical perspectives. Cambridge University Press, Cambridge

Burdekin RCK, Siklos PL (2004b) Fears of deflation and the role of monetary policy: some lessons and an overview. In: Burdekin RCK, Siklos PL (eds, 2004a) Deflation: current and historical perspectives. Cambridge: Cambridge University Press, Cambridge, pp 1–27

Bye RT (1944) Principles of economics, 4th edn. F.S.Crofts & Co., New York

Cantillon R [1755] (1959) Essai sur la nature du commerce en général (trans. and ed: Higgs H). Frank Cass & Company, London
Cargill TF (1979) Clark Warburton and the development of monetarism since the great depression. Hist Polit Econ 11(3):425–449
Cargill TF (2001) Monetary policy, deflation, and economic history: lessons for the bank of Japan. Monetary Econ Stud 19(Special Issue): 113–134.
Carlson A (2003) What has government done to our families? Mises.org Daily Article, January 5. http://www.mises.org/story/1406/. Accessed 21 Nov 2006
Christiernin PN [1761] (1971) Lectures on the high price of foreign exchange in Sweden (trans. and ed: Eagly RV). American Philosophical Society, Philadelphia
Colander DC (1995) Economics, 2nd edn. Irwin, Chicago
Coppock DJ (1961) The causes of the great depression, 1873-96. Manchest School Econ Soc Stud 29:205–232
Davis JH (2006) An improved annual chronology of U.S. business cycles since the 1790s. J Econ Hist 66(1):103–121
Davis LE, North DC (1971) Institutional change and American economic growth. Cambridge University Press, Cambridge
Davis LE, Hughes JRT, McDougall DM (1965) American economic history. R.D. Irwin, Homewood, IL
DeLong BJ (1999) Why we should fear deflation. Brook Pap Econ Act 30(1):225–241
Deutsche Bundesbank (1976) Deutsches Geld- und Bankwesen in Zahlen 1876-1975. Knapp, Frankfurt am Main
Dewey DR (1907) Financial history of The United States, 3rd edn. Longmans, Green, and Co., New York
Dickey GE (1977) Money, prices and growth: the American experience. Arno Press, New York
Dowd K (1995) Deflating the productivity norm. J Macroecon 17(4):717–732
Eatwell J, Milgate M, Newman P (eds) (1987) The New Palgrave: a dictionary of economics. Macmillan Press, London
Ekelund RB Jr, Tollison RD (2001) The interest-group theory of government. In: Shughart WF II, Razzolini L (eds) The Elgar companion to public choice. Edward Elgar, Cheltenham, UK
Elliot JR (1890) American farms: their condition and future. Putnam's Sons, New York
Emerick CF (1896) An analysis of agricultural discontent in the United States I. Polit Sci Quart 11(3):433–463
Emerick CF (1897) An analysis of agricultural discontent in the United States III. Polit Sci Quart 12(1):93–127
Faulkner HU (1924) American economic history. Harper & Brothers Publishers, New York and London
Fekete AE (1986) Deflation: retrospect and prospect. Monograph #45, April. Committee for Monetary Research and Education. http://www.shoemakerconsulting.com/GoldisFreedom/Archives/deflationretropro.htm. Accessed 20 Aug 2007
Fekete AE (1996) Whither gold? Foundation for the advancement of monetary education, New York. http://www.fame.org/HTM/Fekete_Anatal_Whither_Gold_AF-001-B.HTM. Accessed 5 Oct 2007.
Fels R (1949) The long-wave depression, 1873-97. Rev Econ Stat 31(1):69–73
Fels R (1951) American business cycles, 1865-79. Am Econ Rev 41(3):325–349
Fels R (1959) American business cycles 1865-1897. The University of North Carolina Press, Chapel Hill, NC
Ferguson A (2010) When money dies. The nightmare of deficit spending, devaluation, and hyperinflation in Weimar Germany. PublicAffairs, New York
Fetter FW (1942) The life and writings of John Wheatley. J Polit Econ 50(3):357–376
Fetter FW (ed) (1964) Selected economic writings of Thomas Attwood. The London School of Economics and Political Science, London
Fischer W (1968) Deutsche Wirtschaftspolitik 1918-1945, 3rd exp. edn. C.W. Leske Verlag, Opladen

Fisher I (1928) The money illusion. Adelphi, New York
Fisher I (1933) The debt-deflation theory of great depressions. Econometrica 1(4):337–357
Fisher I (1945) 100% money, 3rd edn. City Printing Co., New Haven, CT
Folsom BW Jr (2003) The myth of the robber barons—a new look at the rise of big business in America, 4th edn. Young America's Foundation, Herndon, VA
Friedman M (1968) The role of monetary policy. Am Econ Rev 58(1):1–17
Friedman M (1969) The optimum quantity of money. In: Friedman M (ed) The optimum quantity of money and other essays. Aldine, Chicago, pp 1–50
Friedman M (1990) The crime of 1873. J Polit Econ 98(6):1159–1194
Friedman M, Schwartz AJ (1971) A monetary history of the United States 1867-1960. Princeton University Press, Princeton, NJ
Garrison R (2001) Time and money. the macroeconomics of capital structure. Routledge, London
Gesell S (2003) Die natürliche Wirtschaftsordnung, Online ed. of 9th edn. (differently formatted). Rudolf Zitzmann Verlag, Verlauf. http://userpage.fu-berlin.de/~roehrigw/gesell/nwo/nwo.pdf. Accessed 17 Apr 2007
Giffen RS (1971) Economic inquiries and studies, vol I. Irish University Press, Shannon
Goodfriend M (2000) Overcoming the zero bound on interest rate policy. J Money Credit Bank 32(4):1007–1035
Goodfriend M (2001) Financial stability, deflation, and monetary policy. Working paper 01-01. Federal Reserve Bank of Richmond
Goodwyn L (1978) The populist movement, a short hisotry of the agrarian revolt in America. Oxford University Press, New York
Gossweiler K (1971) Großbanken, Industriemonopole, Staat—Ökonomie und Politik des staatsmonopolistischen Kapitalismus in Deutschland 1914-1932. VEB Deutscher Verlag der Wissenschaften, Berlin
Hahn AL (1956) Common sense economics. Abelard-Schumann, New York
Hamburger M (1933) Deflation und rechtsordnung. J. Bensheimer, Mannheim
Hamilton EJ (1952) Prices as a factor in business growth: prices and progress. J Econ Hist 12(4): 325–349
Hayek FA von (1937) Economics and knowledge. Economica 4:33–54
Hayek FA von (1939) Prices and production, 2nd edn. Routledge, London
Hayek FA von (1945) The use of knowledge in society. Am Econ Rev 35(4):519–530
Hayek FA von (1979) Unemployment and monetary policy. Cato Institute, San Francisco
Hayek FA von [1931] (1966) Prices and production. Augustus M. Kelley, New York (reprint)
Hicks JR (1937) Mr. Keynes and the 'Classics': a suggested interpretation. Econometrica 5(2): 147–59
Hicks JR (1946) Value and capital, 2nd edn. Clarendon Press, Oxford
Higgs R (1997) Regime uncertainty—why the great depression lasted so long and why prosperty resumed after the war. Indepen Rev 1(4):561–590
Hoppe H-H (2001) Democracy the god that failed. Transaction Publisher, New York
Hoppe HH (2009) 'The yield from money held' reconsidered. N Perspect Polit Econ 5(2):129–136
Horwitz S (2000) Microfoundations and macroeconomics: an Austrian perspectives. Routledge, New York
Hoxie RF (1893) The silver debate of 1890. J Polit Econ 1(1):535–587
Huerta de Soto J (2001) Socialismo, Calculo Economico y Funcion Empresarial, 2nd edn. Unión Editorial, Madrid
Huerta de Soto J (2003) "The theory of dynamic efficiency". In: Backhaus JG, Heijmann W, Nentjes A, van Ophem J (eds) Economic policy in an orderly framework, Liber amicorum for Gerrit Meijer. Lit Verlag, Münster, pp 231–254
Huerta de Soto J (2006a) Money, bank credit, and economic cycles. Ludwig von Mises Institute, Auburn, AL
Huerta de Soto J (2006b) Dinero, Crédito Bancario Y Ciclos Económicos, 3rd edn. Unión Editorial, Madrid

Hülsmann JG (1998) Toward a general theory of error cycles. Q J Aust Econ 1(4):1–23
Hülsmann JG (1999) Discursive rationality and the division of labour: how cooperation emerges. Am J Econ Sociol 58(4):713–727
Hülsmann JG (2003a) Optimal monetary policy. Quart J Aust Econ 6(4):37–60
Hülsmann JG (2003b) Deflation and liberty. Working paper.
Hülsmann JG (2004) Legal tender laws, and fractional reserve banking. Quart J Aust Econ 18(3): 33–55
Hülsmann JG (2006) The ethics of money production. Ludwig von Mises Institute, Auburn, AL
Hülsmann JG (2008) Deflation and liberty. Ludwig von Mises Institute, Auburn, AL
Hülsmann JG (2009) "The Demand for Money and the Time-Structure of Production." In: Hülsmann JG, Kinsella S (eds) Property, freedom, society. Essays in honor of Hans-Hermann Hoppe. Ludwig von Mises Institute, Auburn, AL, pp 309–324
Hülsmann JG (2013) Krise der Inflationskultur. FinanzBuchVerlag, Munich
Hume D [1752] (1826a) Of money. In: The philosophical works of David Hume, including all the essays, and exhibiting the more important alterations and corrections in the successive editions published by the author, vol III. Adam Black, William Tait and Charles Tait, Edinburgh, pp 317–332
Hume D [1752] (1826b) Of the balance of trade. In: The philosophical works of David Hume, including all the essays, and exhibiting the more important alterations and corrections in the successive editions published by the author, vol III. Adam Black, William Tait and Charles Tait, Edinburgh, pp 348–367
Humphrey TM (2004) Classical deflation theory. Federal Res Bank Richmond Econ Quart 90(1): 11–32
Hutt WH (1956) The yield of money held. In: Sennholz M (ed) On freedom and free enterprise: essays in the honor of Ludwig von Mises presented on the occasion of the fiftieth anniversary of his doctorate February 20, 1956. Van Nostrand, Princeton, NJ, pp 196–216
Hutt WH (1977) The theory of idle resources, a study in definition, 2nd edn. Liberty Press, Indianapolis, IN
Hutt WH (1979) The Keynesian episode. Liberty Press, Indianapolis, IN
Hutt WH (1995) The significance of price flexibility. In: Hazlitt H (ed) The critics of Keynesian economics, 2nd edn. The Foundation for Economic Education, New York, pp 386–403
Issing O (2002) The Euro after four years: is there a risk of deflation? Speech at 16th European Finance Convention, London, December 2
James H (2002) Introduction. In: James H (ed) The interwar depression in an international context, VII–XV. Oldenbourg Verlag, Munich
Jochmann W (1978) Brünings Deflationspolitik and der Untergang der Weimarer Republik. In: Stegmann D (ed) Industrielle Gesellschaft und politisches System: Beiträge zur politischen Sozialgeschichte; Festschrift für Fritz Fischer zum 70. Geburtstag. Verlag Neue Gesellschaft, Bonn
Jones GO (1884) More money and less misery! Pamphlets in American history: Microfilming Corp. of America
Kazin M (1998) The populist persuasion. An American history. Cornell University Press, Ithaca, NY
Keiser G, Benning B (1931) Kapitalbildung und Investitionen in der deutschen Volkswirtschaft. Vierteljahreshefte zur Konjunkturforschung. Sonderheft 22, Berlin
Kent RP (1966) Money and banking. Holt, Rinehart and Winston Inc., New York
Keynes JM (1963) Essays in persuasion. W.W. Norton & Company, New York
Keynes JM [1923] (2000) A tract on monetary reform. Prometheus Books, Amherst, NY
Keynes JM [1925] (1963) The economic consequences of Mr. Churchill. Reprinted in Essays in persuasion. W.W. Norton & Company, New York, pp 244–270 (The original essay was printed in pamphlet form, with eds. Leonard Woolf and Virginia Woolf at the Hogarth Press)

Keynes JM [1930] (1971) A treatise on money. In Two Volumes. 1 The Pure Theory of Money. In The collected writings of John Maynard Keynes, vol 22. Cambridge University Press, New York

Keynes JM [1931] (1963) The consequences to the banks of the collapse of money values. In Essays in persuasion. W.W. Norton & Company, New York, pp 168–178

Keynes JM [1936] (1964) The general theory of employment, interest, and money. Harcourt, Brace & World, New York

Kindleberger CP (1987) The world in depression 1929-1939. Pelican Books, London

Kindleberger CP, Aliber RZ (2005) Manias, panics, and crashes. A history of financial crises. John Wiley, New Jersey

King M (1994) Presidential address: debt deflation: theory and evidence. Eur Econ Rev 38(3–4): 419–445

Korsch A (1981) Der Stand der beschäftigungspolitischen Diskussion zur Zeit der Weltwirtschaftskrise in Deutschland. In: Bombach G, Ramser H-J, Timmermann M, Wittmann W (eds) Der Keynesianismus I—Theorie und Praxis keynesianischer Wirtschaftspolitik, Entwicklung und Stand der Diskussion. Springer, Berlin, pp 9–132

Krugman PR (1998) It's Baaack: Japan's slump and the return of the liquidity trap. Brook Pap Econ Act 29(2):137–187

Krugman PR (1999) Can deflation be prevented. http://web.mit.edu/krugman/www/deflator.html. Accessed 1 Aug 2007

Kumar MS, Baig T, Decressin J, Faulkner-MacDanagh C, Feyziogulu T (2003) Deflation: determinants, risks, and policy options. Occasional paper 221. IMF

Kuznets S (1961) Capital in the American economy: its formation and financing. Princeton University Press, Princeton, NJ

Kuznets S [1960] (1965) Population change and aggregate ouput. In: Economic growth and structure. W.W. Norton & Company, New York, pp 123–131 (The essay was first printed in Demographic and economic change in developed countries. Princeton University Press, Princeton, NJ)

Laidler D (1992) Deflation. In: Eatwell J, Milgate M, Newman P (eds) The New Palgrave dictionary of money and finance, vol 1. Macmillan Press, New York

Laidler D (2000) Highlights of the bullionist controversy. Working paper 20002. University of Western Ontario

Laughlin LJ (1887) Gold and prices since 1873. Q J Econ 1(3):319–355

Laughlin LJ (1968) The history of bimetallism in the United States, 4th edn. Greenwood Press, New York

League of Nations (1935) World production and prices: 1925-1934. League of Nations, Economic Intelligence Service, Geneva

League of Nations (1944) International currency experience. League of Nations, Princeton, NJ

Leigh D (2004) Monetary policy and the dangers of deflation: lessons from Japan. Economics working paper archive 511. The Johns Hopkins University

Locke J [1691] (1824) Economic writings and two treatises of government (I). Vol. 4 of the works of John Locke, 12th edn. Rivington, London

Lüke RE (1958) Von der Stabilisierung zur Krise. Polygraphischer Verlag, Zurich

Manley T (1669) Usury at six per cent examined. London: Thomas Ratcliffe and Thomas Daniel.

Marshall A [1890] (1920) Principles of economy, 8th edn. Macmillan, London

McClean HS (1895) The quantity of money and prices, 1860-1891. J Polit Econ 3(2):145–168

Meltzer AH (2000) Monetary policy in the new global economy: the case of Japan. Cato J 20(1): 69–72

Menger C (1871) Grundsätze der Volkswirthschaftslehre. Wilhelm Braumüller, Vienna

Mill JS (1844) The currency question. Westminst Rev 41:579–98

Mill JS [1848] (1965) Principles of political economy with some of their applications to social philosophy, Bk. 1-5. University of Toronto Press, Toronto

Miller MH, Upton CW (1986) Macroeconomics a neoclassical introduction. University of Chicago Press, Chicago
Mises L von (1924) Theorie des Geldes und der Umlaufsmittel, 2nd edn. Duncker und Humblot, Munich
Mises L von (1931) Die Ursachen der Wirtschaftskrise: Ein Vortrag. J.C.B. Mohr (Paul Siebeck), Tübingen
Mises L von (1932) Die Gemeinwirtschaft—Untersuchungen über den Sozialismus, 2nd edn. Gustav Fischer, Jena
Mises L von (1933) Der Stand und die nächste Zukunft der Konjunkturforschung. In: Clausing G (ed) Festschrift für Arthur Spiethoff. Duncker & Humblodt, Munich, pp 175–180
Mises L von (1978) On the manipulation of money and credit (trans. and eds: Greaves BB, Greaves PL Jr). Freemarket Books, Dobbs Ferry, NY
Mises L von (1981) Theory of money and credit (trans: Batson HE). LibertyClassics, Indianapolis, IN
Mises L von (1990) In: Ebeling R (ed) Money, method and the market process: essays by Ludwig von Mises. Kluwer Academic Publishers, Norwell, MA
Mises L von (1998) Human action: a treatise on economics. Scholar's edition. Ludwig von Mises Institute, Auburn, AL
Mitchell WC (1903) A history of the greenbacks with special reference to the economics consequences of their issue: 1892-1895. The University of Chicago Press, Chicago
Mitchell WC (1927) Business cycles: the problem and its setting. NBER studies in business cycles, vol 1. NBER, New York
Musson AE (1959) The great depression in Britain, 1873-1896: a reappraisal. J Econ Hist 19(2): 199–228
Nevalainen A (2007) COINflation. http://www.coinflation.com/. Accessed 14 Oct 2007
Newman P (2012) The long depression of 1873-1879: an Austrian examination. Winning essay of society for the development of Austrian economics' 2012 Carl Menger Essay Contest
North DC (1961) The United States in the international economy. In: Harris SE (ed) American economic history. McGraw-Hill, New York, pp 1790–1950
Nugent WTK (1967) The money question during reconstruction. Norton & Company, New York
Nugent WTK (1968) The tolerant populists; Kansas, populism and nativism. The University of Chicago Press, Chicago
Nussbaum M (1978) Wirtschaft und Staat in Deutschland während der Weimarer Republik. Topos Verlag, Vaduz
Olson M (1971) The logic of collective action: public goods and the theory of groups. Harvard University Press, Cambridge
Palyi M (1972) The twilight of gold, 1914-1936, myths and realities. Henry Regnery, Chicago
Patch WL Jr (1998) Heinrich Brüning and the dissolution of the Weimar republic. Cambridge University Press, Cambridge
Pigou AC (1943) The classical stationary state. Econ J 53(212):343–351
Rallo JR (2005) Utilidad marginal y liquidez. Juan de Mariana Daily Article, September 2. http://www.juandemariana.org/comentario/254/utilidad/marginal/liquidez/. Accessed 16 Jun 2006
Rallo JR (2006) La Gran Depresión. Paper presented at the Juan de Mariana Institute, December 15
Rallo JR (2012) Los errores de la vieja economía. Una refutación de la teoría general del empleo, el interés y el dinero de John Maynard Keynes. Unión Editorial, Madrid
Reisman G (1999) Capitalism: a treatise on economics. Jameson Books, Ottawa, IL
Rezneck S (1950) Distress, relief, and discontent in the United States during the depression 1873-78. J Polit Econ 58(6):494–512
Rezneck S (1953) Unemployment, unrest, and relief in the United States during the depression of 1893-1897. J Polit Econ 61(4):324–345
Rezneck S (1956) Pattern of thought and action in an American depression, 1882-86. Am Hist Rev 61(2):284–307

Ricardo D [1810] (2004) The high price of Bullion. In: The works and correspondence of David Ricardo: Pamphlets and papers 1809-1811, vol 3, ed. Piero Sraffa with the collaboration of M.H. Dobb. Liberty Fund, Indianapolis, IN, pp 47–127

Ricardo D [1816] (2004) Proposals for an economical and secure currency. In: The works and correspondence of David Ricardo: Pamphlets and papers 1815-1823, vol 4, ed. Piero Sraffa with the collaboration of M.H. Dobb. Liberty Fund, Indianapolis, IN, pp 43–141

Ricardo D [1817] (1973) On the principles of political economy and taxation. Dent & Sons, Dutton

Ricardo D [1821] (2004) Ricardo to Wheatley. In: Sraffa P (ed) The works and correspondence of David Ricardo: letters July 1821-1823, vol 9. Liberty Fund, Indianapolis, IN, pp 71–74.

Rist C (1966) History of monetary and credit theory: from John Law to the present day. (trans: Degras J). Augustus M. Kelley, New York

Ritschl A (2002) International capital movements and the onset of the great depression: some international evidence. In: James H (ed) The interwar depression in an international context. Oldenbourg Verlag, Munich, pp 1–14

Ritter G (1997) Goldbugs and greenbacks: the antimonopoly tradition and the politics of finance in America. Cambridge University Press, New York

Rockoff H (1990) The "Wizard of the Oz" as a Monetary Allegory. J Polit Econ 98(4):739–760

Röpke W (1995) The economics of full employment. In: Henry H (ed) The critics of Keynesian economics, 2nd edn. The Foundation for Economic Education, New York, pp 362–385

Rothbard MN (1976) Deflation reconsidered. In: Corbin P, Sabrin M (eds) Geographical aspects of inflationary processes, vol I. Redgrave Publishing, Pleasantville, NY, pp 35–41

Rothbard MN (1990) What has government done to our money, 3rd edn. Ludwig von Mises Institute, Auburn, AL

Rothbard MN (1991) The case for a 100 percent gold dollar. Ludwig von Mises Institute, Auburn, AL

Rothbard MN (1995) Deflation, free or compulsory. In: Making economic sense. Ludwig von Mises Institute, Auburn, AL, pp 237–240

Rothbard MN (1998) The ethics of liberty, 2nd edn. New York University Press, New York

Rothbard MN (2000) America's great depression, 5th edn. Ludwig von Mises Institute, Auburn, AL

Rothbard MN (2001) Man, economy and state: a treatise on economic principles. Ludwig von Mises Institute, Auburn, AL (reprint)

Rothbard MN (2002) A history of money and banking in the United States: The colonial Era to World War II. Ludwig von Mises Institute, Auburn, AL

Rothbard MN (2003) An Austrian taxonomy of deflation: with applications to the U.S. Quart J Aust Econ 6(4):81–109

Rothbard MN (2006a) Economic thought before Adam Smith: an Austrian perspective of economic thought, vol I. Ludwig von Mises Institute, Auburn, AL

Rothbard MN (2006b) Classical economics. An Austrian perspective on the history of economic thought, vol II. Ludwig von Mises Institute, Auburn, AL

Rueff J (1947) The fallacies of Lord Keynes general theory. Quart J Econ 61(3):343–367

Salerno JT (2001) Does the concept of secular growth have a place in capital-based macroeconomics? Quart J Aust Econ 4(3):43–61

Salerno JT (2003) An Austrian taxonomy of deflation – with applications to the US. Q J Aust Econ 6(4):81–109

Sargent T, Wallace N (1976) Rational expectations and the theory of economic policy. J Monet Econ 2(2):169–183

Say J-B (1845) A treatise on political economy: of the production, distribution and consumption of wealth (transl. from the 4th French ed. by C.R. Princep). Grigg & Elliot, Philadelphia

Schacht H (1931) Das Ende der Reparationen. Gerhard Stalling, Oldenburg

Schumpeter J (1929) Grenzen der Lohnpolitik. Der Deutsche Volkswirt 3(26):847–851

Scrope PG [1833] (1969) Principles of political economy. Deduced from the natural laws of social welfare and applied to the present state of Britain. Augustus M. Kelley, New York (reprint)

Selgin G (1995) The "Productivity Norm" versus zero inflation in the history of economic thought. Hist Polit Econ 27(4):705–735

Selgin G (1997) Less than zero: the case for a falling price level in a growing economy. The Institute for Economic Affairs, London
Selgin G (1999) Hayek versus Keynes on how the price level ought to behave. Hist Polit Econ 31(4):699–722
Shannon FA (1945) The farmer's last Frontier: agriculture, 1860-1897. Harper & Row, New York
Shannon FA (1957) American farmers' movement. D. Van Nostrand Company, Princeton, NJ
Shields RE (1977) Economic growth with price deflation. Arno Press, New York
Shiratsuka S (2000) Is there a desirable rate of inflation? IMES discussion paper series 2000-E-32. Bank of Japan, Tokyo
Siegel JJ (1998) Stocks for the long run, 2nd rev. edn. McGraw-Hill, New York
Šíma J (2002) Deflation—an underlying feature of healthy economy. Working paper, 1/2002. Economic Faculty of Prague
Skidelsky R (2002) The Great Depression: Keynes's Perspective. In: Harold J (ed) The interwar depression in an international context. Oldenbourg Verlag, Munich, pp 99–112
Smith VC (1990) The rational of central banking and the free banking alternative. Liberty Press, Indianapolis, IN
Smith A [1776] (1976) An inquiry into the nature and causes of the wealth of nations. In: Campbell RH, Skinner AS (eds) The glasgow edition. Liberty Press, Indianapolis, IN
Somary F (1959) Erinnerungen aus meinem Leben. Manesse Verlag, Zürich
Stamp J (1932) Papers on gold and the price level. P.S. King & Son, London
Statistisches Bundesamt (1972) Bevölkerung und Wirtschaft 1872-1972. Kohlhammer, Stuttgart
Stiglitz JE (1993) Economics. W.W. Norton & Company, New York
Stock CMN (1996) Rural radicals: righteous rage in the American Grain. Cornell University Press, Ithaca, NY
Stolper G (1966) Deutsche Wirtschaft seit 1870. Continued by Karl Häuser and Knut Borchardt, 2nd rev. edn. J.C.B. Mohr (Paul Siebeck), Tübingen
Strigl R von (1934) Kapital und Produktion. Julius Springer, Vienna
Stucken R (1953) Deutsche Geld- und Kreditpolitik: 1914-1953, 2nd edn. J.C.B. Mohr (Paul Siebeck), Tübingen
Studenski P, Kroos HE (1963) Financial history of the United States, 2nd edn. McGraw-Hill, New York
Svensson LEO (2003) Escaping from a liquidity trap and deflation: the foolproof way and others. J Econ Perspect 17(4):145–166
Svensson LEO (2000) How should monetary policy be conducted in an era of price stability? NBER working paper 7516. Cambridge, MA
Taussig FW (1892) The silver situation in the United States. Publ Am Econ Assoc 7(1):7–118
Taylor JB (2001) Low inflation, deflation, and policies for future price stability. Monetary and economic studies (special edition). Institute for Monetary and Economic Studies, Bank of Japan
Thornton M (2003) Apoplithorismosphobia. Quart J Aust Econ 6(4):5–18
Thornton H [1802] (1978) An enquiry into the nature and effects of the paper credit of Great Britain. Augustus M. Kelley, New Jersey, NY (reprint)
Thorp WL (1926) Business annals. NBER, New York
Torrens R (1834/1970) On wages and combinations. Reprints of economic classics. A.M. Kelley, New York
Tullock G (1967) The welfare costs of tarifs, monopolies and theft. West Econ J 5(3):224–32
Unger I (1962) Business men and specie resumption. Polit Sci Quart 74(1):46–70
Unger I (1964) The Greenback Era, a social and political history of American finance, 1865-1879. Princeton University Press, Princeton, NJ
US Department of Commerce (1975) Historical statistics of the United States. Colonial times to 1970. Government Printing Office, Washington, DC
Viner J (1975) Studies in the theory of international trade. August M. Kelley, Clifton, NJ (reprint)
Wagemann E (ed) (1935) Konjunkturstatistisches Handbuch 1936. Institut für Konjunkturforschung. Hanseatische Verlagsanstalt Hamburg, Berlin

Wagenführ R (1933) Die Industriewirtschaft, Entwicklungstendenzen der deutschen und internationalen Industrieproduktion 1860 bis 1932. Vierteljahreshefte zur Konjunkturforschung, Special Issue 31, Berlin.

Walker FA (1883) Money. Henry Holt and Company, New York

Warren GF, Pearson FA (1933) Prices. Wiley, New York

Warren GF, Pearson FA (1983) Gold and prices. Garland, New York

Weinstein A (1970) Prelude to populism: origins of the silver issue, 1867-1878. Yale University Press, New Haven, CT

Wells DA (1891) Recent economic changes: and their effect on the production and distribution of wealth and the well-being of society. D. Appleton, New York

White L (2005) The federal reserve's influence on research in monetary economics. Econ J Watch 2(2):325–354

Wicksell K [1898] (1968) Geldzins und Güterpreise: Eine Studie über die den Tauschwert des Geldes bestimmenden Ursachen. Scientia Verlag, Aalen (Corrected reprint)

Yeager LB (1986) The significance of monetary disequilibrium. Cato J 6(2):369–399

Zumpe L (1980) Wirtschaft und Staat in Deutschland 1933 bis 1945. Topos Verlag, Vaduz

Author Index

P. Bagus, *In Defense of Deflation*, Financial and Monetary Policy Studies 41,
DOI 10.1007/978-3-319-13428-4

Subject Index

P. Bagus, *In Defense of Deflation*, Financial and Monetary Policy Studies 41,
DOI 10.1007/978-3-319-13428-4

N

O

P

R

MIX
Papier aus verantwortungsvollen Quellen
Paper from responsible sources
FSC® C105338

If you have any concerns about our products,
you can contact us on
ProductSafety@springernature.com

In case Publisher is established outside the EU,
the EU authorized representative is:
Springer Nature Customer Service Center GmbH
Europaplatz 3, 69115 Heidelberg, Germany

Printed by Libri Plureos GmbH
in Hamburg, Germany